Centerprise Publications
Coronation Cups & Jam Jars

'Coronation Cups & Jam Jars' is Ron Barnes' second book. His first,
'Licence to Live', was a personal autobiography based on his life in Hackney,
and East London generally. On the merit of his first book, he was awarded
an Arts Council Writers' Bursary of £500 which has enabled him to take
off some time from cab-driving to further his writing activity. Now at the
age of 43, he says he has discovered a second lease of life following the
publication of his first book. He has taken up painting and is already an
accomplished artist, painting scenes of East London working class life in
both oils and water-colours. He meticulously keeps a diary, recording
everyday incidents that together form a comprehensive picture of life in
the East End, and is an active member of the Hackney Writers' Workshop.
Having experienced a great deal of hardship and lack of opportunity in
much of his life, and aware of the continuing inequalities around him, he
is a committed socialist.

CORONATION CUPS
AND JAM JARS

RON BARNES

A portrait of an East End family through three generations

Centerprise

Copyright 1976 Ron Barnes
Published by Centerprise Publishing Project, 136 Kingsland High Street,
London E8
Printed in Great Britain by offset lithography by
Billing & Sons Ltd, Guildford, London and Worcester
Typeset by Rye Express
Design and cover photograph: Neil Martinson
We are grateful for financial assistance from Hackney Borough Council,
Greater London Arts Association and the Arts Council of Great Britain
ISBN 0 903738 27 9
Casebound 0 90378 26 0

Contents

Introduction

After finishing my first book, 'A Licence to Live', I certainly had no intention of writing another. However, two main reasons explain why I attempted this second book. First is the encouragement I received from many people who had said how much they enjoyed my first book. The second reason comes from the great satisfaction I derived from seeing my somewhat disorderly first manuscript made into a book. It was a thing I never thought possible. And like most ordinary working people, I thought that anything I wrote wouldn't be worth publishing.

True there have been a few books published that have been written by working class people, but in comparison with those writers who have come from more exclusive backgrounds, the number of working class writers who have had books published is minimal. If one is a prominent and respectable trade unionist, or well known in some other field, like the stage, or in crime, then it's not too difficult. But the ordinary working person who wouldn't even merit a second look will find it most difficult to get into print. And these are the people that Centerprise caters for in Hackney.

I have always been fascinated with the past of my older relatives, and so I decided to get what information I could get from them, and write about it. I must say I have not found this book easy, for I don't think I could call myself a born writer, not by any means. But once you have had one book published, and experienced the sense of achievement and satisfaction that it gives, it seems to give one the enthusiasm necessary to try another. I feel now that I could carry on writing about other things. Perhaps when I get some time to spare I will.

The book deals with the early life of my parents, the little street they lived in and the sort of environment and way of life they endured for the best part of their lives. I also deal with my own difficulties in finding and keeping a job. 'Licence to Live' was rather a sad book, in spite of its humorous episodes. I have tried, as much as one can, to make this book a happier one, a thing that does not come too easy when dealing with the lives of those who went through hardships in their time that would seem unbelievable today.

I would like to thank all those who helped me in getting together the details that you find in this book. I would also like to thank my wife and daughter who put up with my continual disappearance from our living room during my writing, and my bouts of oblivion when making notes at times. I would also like to say a special thank you to Ken Worpole for his particular encouragement, to Fanny Ravensdale for the time, effort and patience she so willingly gave to tidying up and re-typing this lot, and to the Arts Council of Great Britain for the award of £500 I received following the publication of my first book. This grant was a god-send which helped me enormously. It was due to this award that I had more time to think about what I was going to write and how to put it together. It freed me from many evenings of having to get my dinner down me, have a quick wash before getting to my typewriter. I sincerely hope the Arts Council continues to give awards to working people like myself, for I am sure their help will be genuinely appreciated by all working class writers.

I have deliberately delayed my mention of Centerprise till last. And what can I say about them? How can I express in words the gratitude I feel. I once expressed the feeling I had that my past years had been wasted, and that is how I felt, until it was pointed out to me that if I had not experienced the things I had, then I would never have written two books. Due to my contact with Centerprise, and the publication of my first book, I have made more friends than I have ever done in my life. I have been invited to schools and other such places. I have received a letter from America and one from Germany, and one or two others from people in this country. But there are other feelings I am unable to express. The feeling I get when I see my book in a shop window. For some reason it doesn't seem real. I have to keep convincing myself that, 'Yes, that is your book in that shop — you have written it'. It isn't easy to express one's feelings, when someone tells me they have seen my book in a shop miles away from Hackney. Perhaps I should write a number of chapters in gratitude to Centerprise. I'm afraid I can't but I am sure they will know how I feel if I just say a simple thank you.

I would like to conclude by saying this, a thing I have said before but which will do no harm to repeat. It doesn't take a certain kind of brain or high intellectual ability to write. It doesn't take some special gift of genius to write an autobiography, a story or a poem. And of that I am living proof. The writing is not too difficult. The difficult part is getting what you write published.

All the characters in this book are real people. I have only altered some of the names to avoid embarrassment to the people I have written about. The characters are there as I saw them, and I have tried to convey to the reader as far as I am able, what life was like for them, myself included, during those years that I have written about.

Ron Barnes
January 1976

1. 'Mary wait till he goes to bed and claw his...'

After my parents were married on April 29th 1933, they lived in Marion Place, off Hackney Road. From there they moved to Poyser Street, back to the place where both their parents lived and where they were brought up.

My mother's family didn't really approve of my parents' marriage because my Gran Gullis was what you might call a little better off than Gran Barnes. There was never any bad feeling between the two families, despite their different standards of living, but there was always a suppressed antagonism between my Gran Gullis and my father.

I remember my mother once telling me that my father came round to take her out one evening, wearing a suit that looked as though it had been slept in for a month. Gran looked at him, rather disturbed that he was going to take his daughter out dressed like that.

'Oh,' she said, 'that just reminds me, there's a suit of Sonnie's in the wardrobe. I think it might just fit you, Bill.'

Sonnie was one of Gran's boys. His real name was Edward, but I think Grandfather had always called him Sonnie and the name stuck.

'I'll go and get it,' said Gran. She was back in no time. 'Here, Bill, try it on.'

Dad did try it on and it fitted him a treat.

'Oh yes,' Mum and Gran agreed, 'it fits you just right, Bill.'

'It looks that nice, Bill. that you'd better keep it on now,' Gran urged. And so he did.

Gran would have to make some excuse to Sonnie when he came home. The best excuse would be that she had taken it round Uncle's. Uncle was no family relation, but he might just as well have been, considering the times he was visited by people down the street when they were hard up. For Uncle's, as everybody knew, was the pawnshop.

This slang term was used so that people who were better off had no idea who Uncle was. Going to the pawnshop was not a thing that one would want the world to know about. It didn't matter too much if someone down the street saw you going in with your pram or if you met a neighbour on entering because they were the same as you, poor. But to meet a more well-to-do friend or relative on your journey would be rather embarrassing. It would be no good trying to make up some excuse like 'Oh, hullo Fred. I'm just going round to the cleaners' with this lot.' For Fred would know immediately where you were off to, by the way the bundle was held with safety pins. All Uncle's bundles seemed to be wrapped in the same fashion.

So Gran would tell Sonnie that his suit was in Uncle's and that she would get it out as soon as she could. Sonnie knew that she had to go to Uncle's occasionally nowadays, for my grandfather had died at the early age of thirty-two, through being gassed in the first world war. He was discharged at the end of the war with a disability pension, which was why their family seemed better off than most. For when Grandfather was alive he worked at a cigarette firm, where he would have a good fiddle, as you might say. With his wages and pension, the family weren't too badly off. But of course when he died, my Gran was left with seven children to bring up, and the only answer to her problems was Uncle's in Cambridge Heath Road.

So Gran was sure that her excuse to Sonnie would satisfy him. The only thing now was that my father would have to make sure he avoided Sonnie whenever he was wearing the suit. If the cat was let out of the bag, there would be hell to pay. But of course it was bound to come to a tumble eventually. The cat was let out of the bag, hell was paid, but my father was allowed to keep the suit. For Dad had been so skilled at avoiding Sonnie that as the months drew on, the suit grew more shabby, and it was hardly worth taking it back now.

When my parents got married they did not have two halfpennies to rub together. As always, my Uncle George, Dad's best mate and brother-in-law by marriage to his sister, came to the rescue. George had the uncanny knack of always being able to acquire whatever was needed. Be it goods or cash, Uncle George was infallible, and no questions asked. But on this occasion it seems that George's luck was out. My father needed a decent suit for the wedding, and my mother a dress. The money for the beer would have to wait, the important thing was wedding clothes.

George had to do something. His reputation was at stake and if he let Bill down on such an occasion as this he would never live it down. After all, he was noted – no, notorious – for coming to the rescue at times like this. He was unable to steal or borrow the money that was needed. He had tried the former (well, that was only natural) and only as a last resort did he try borrowing. But without success. He spoke to Polly about it, my Dad's sister.

12

'I don't know what to do, Poll,' he said. 'I've tried everything I know this week but, well, I just can't make a touch at all. What can I do, Poll? What can I do?'

'Well, you're the expert, ain't yer?' Poll mocked. 'Why ask me?'

This hurt George considerably. He genuinely wanted to help my dad out, it's true, but also his unblemished reputation of acquisition was liable to take a bashing if he let his best friend down on an occasion like this.

I mean, this was not just a matter of getting hold of a couple of bob for old Mother Marshal. No, if he was unable to meet the demand of such a trifle as that well, he could have got away with it. It would be forgotten and no one would even know about it. But this, this was a large order. A big occasion. It was necessary — no, imperative — that he met the requirements such an occasion demanded. This was a wedding and all the street would know about it. If he let my father down now he would never be held in the same high esteem again.

It would be something always to drag up in conversation, in the pub or at one of the house parties. He could hear them now.

'Oh yes, George, but what about that time at Bill's wedding? You let him down all right didn't you?'

'Never would have thought it of you, George. Well, I mean, after you being so reliable and all. Still, we all have to come up against it at the finish, I suppose'.

Oh no, George just couldn't stand the humiliation of that. Something had to be done, and done quickly, if he was to keep his high standing among his friends and relatives.

Suddenly he had it. 'Poll, Poll,' he shouted. 'Here, quick. Give me an 'and ter git these cages orf the wall, quick.'

Uncle George loved canaries. He had cages of them all round his kitchen, whistling and chirping from dawn to dusk. The only way to get any peace would be to cover them over with a sheet.

'Poll, for Christ's sake hurry up, woman,' he shouted.

She came out of the bedroom. 'Can't you sodding wait a minute?' she moaned.

'Look,' said George. 'Take hold of these cages as I 'and them dahn to yer. Careful now, these are me prize cocks. Now place the cages on top of each other for the time being till I get down off the table and then I can sort them out and price them. I'll take 'em dahn the Lane in the morning and sell 'em. They'll bring in every bit of a fiver, they will.'

Polly looked at her spouse, wide-eyed and stunned. 'You gunna wot? Well Gawd bleeding hell, you gorn nuts, have yer?

You must er dun. Gorblimey you fink more er them bleeders then yer do of me. No I can't believe it. You all right, are yer?'

'Yes, I am,' answered George in a defiant, drawn-out voice. Poll looked at him suspiciously.

'What you got up your sleeve, eh?' she questioned.

'Gorblimey, woman, nothing,' George answered in his tenderest tone. 'I've got to get some money for your brother Bill, ain't I, or he won't have a fing to wear for his wedding. He can't get married in that suit he's got. Blimy he's had that on about six months. He can't go in that.'

Poll looked at him more tenderly now. 'You mean to say you're gunna part with all your best birds so Bill can get married?' she asked.

George swallowed. 'Well yes, yes,' he answered uneasily.

'You mean, you've spent all that time with those canaries and reared 'em and looked at 'em for hours on end, and now you're gunna get rid of 'em?'

'Well, that's all I can do, gal. I mean, I can't let Bill down, now can I?'

She sniffed, turned away from him, and wiped her nose. 'Be a good job, it will. Thank Gawd I won't have all that sodding bird's shit and seeds to clear up off me floor.'

'Yer, well, that's wot I say,' George answered, trying his best to put a tone of satisfaction into his voice.

Her back was towards him now and she busied herself at the sink. He looked at the back of her head, trying to detect some emotion in her, but there seemed to be none. But only seemed to be Poll knew what those birds meant to him. She felt so much for him. But it showed itself in a peculiar way, as it did with a lot of working class people — with harsh words, fault-finding and ridicule, as though it was not the right thing to show tender emotion. as though it was not the right thing to show too much tender emotion.

So the next morning George rose early and made his way down Slater Street to the animal lane, found himself a low wall to rest his cages, and within a couple of hours was back home with the predicted five pound.

'Blimey, we could do with that ourselves, I don't know about a wedding,' Poll said when George showed her the money. But then Bill and Hetty had to have a decent wedding. That was the important thing, they agreed. 'Bill will pay me back later, anyway,' hoped George. He gave my father the five pound which was never to be seen again, but George was hardly surprised at that.

14

So on the 29th April at St. Jude's Church, my parents were married in style and dignity. I have an old photo of them in my scrapbook, taken outside the church. To look at that, you would think that they and my uncle in the background were worth a fortune. My mother wore a hat that came down each side of her head, a white blouse and an ankle-length dress in rose. My father looked a toff in his pin-striped suit, sparkling black boots and an Anthony Eden hat. And my uncle at the back with an imposing black bowler resting on his ears, looking every bit like one of the landed gentry.

It was a Saturday afternoon. Mum and Dad and the guests walked back to Gran Gullis' place, Craven Buildings; an antiquated block of flats that stood between rows of crumbling terraced houses. They did not have far to walk. St. Jude's Church was in Old Bethnal Green Road and Poyser Street ran off it, so the walk took only a matter of minutes. Just as well, for I doubt if they could have afforded a wedding car or a horse-drawn wedding coach.

Guests came by the million to the church. In those days, large families were the fashion. My father's mother alone produced about sixteen. So with sixteen brothers and sisters in all, plus their friends and relations near and far, coming from both sides, one can well imagine the congregation. Enough, I should say, to fill the church to capacity.

Gran's place would never accommodate such an army. Mum and Dad had decided to have a quiet turn-out. This decision was made more from the lack of money than from choice. Anyway, when they saw the mass of relatives and friedns making for Gran's they began to get a bit worried. Gran had plenty of food ready, but the beer? This was what the guests were more interested in.

Mum and Dad made their way up the winding concrete stairs that had grown shiny and dangerously smooth with wear. Here and there was a great hole in the centre of the stair that no-one had bothered to fill in. They climbed four sets of twenty, with the rest of the family and friends. Gran always held onto the iron railing at the side of the wall, to make the task easier as she climbed the narrow stairs. The two opposite walls each side of her were only a yard apart, so you can well imagine how wide these stairways were. And when she reached the top she would always say the same thing: 'Hooo, those stairs kill me.'

The flat was crammed full to capacity. The piano was given a good hiding and seemed to be crying out in agony. Guests were spilling out onto the landing, which began to get more and more cramped as the snake-like procession continued from St. Jude's church right the way up to Gran's flat. Neighbours in the street began to appear and decided to join the multitude and pay their respects by downing a pint.

But Mum was worried. 'We ain't got no beer.'

Then something strange happened. Mum spotted one or two guests on the balcony, trying to make a slow and crushing escape from the doorway of the flat, each clutching a pint of beer which was being held well up in the air for safety.

Dad and Mum looked questioningly at each other, puzzled as to where the beer had come from. The one to find now was Gran. If you wanted any information about anything that went on in the family or the street, Gran was the one to consult. They crushed their way through the crowd, Mum looking a little less like a bride now. After gaining the living room there was Nan by the sideboard, which was stacked high with beer and glasses. She was holding a gin and tonic.

'Where's all the drink come from?' asked Mum.

'Hic,' said Gran. 'Bertie and Sonnie decided to buy all the drink for you as a, hic, wedding, hic, present.'

Bertie was another one of Mum's brothers. Mum was thrilled.

They were poor in those days, but how close they all were — friends, neighbours, brothers and sisters, the lot. All helping out the best they could manage. We are better off than they were, it's true, and I for one don't envy their life one bit. What I do envy them, though, is the warmth and friendliness that people had towards each other in those hard, crushing days of the thirties. A neighbourliness so rarely seen in this new jet-set era.

The quiet turn-out that Mum and Dad had decided on snow-balled and carried on all Saturday night, right through to Sunday evening. It must have cost my two uncles quite a bit of cash.

So on Sunday evening, apart from one or two guests who managed to keep going with a croaky version of 'Don't Throw the Lamp at Father, It's a Shame to Waste the Oil', everything had begun to quieten down and quite a number of people had departed. Mum and Dad left Gran's, amid good wishes and farewells — the never-give-up drunken chorus still in progress, determined to finish 'Mary, wait till he goes to bed and claw his. . .'

With that, Mum and Dad made for Marian Street, only about three minute's walk from Craven Buildings. But to see Nan, you'd have thought Mum was going to the ends of the earth as she sobbed and choked in her handkerchief.

Two young people now started a new life, with very little
money and even less experience, ignorant of what life had in store
for them. Just one couple, one of many on that day. Thousands
more had started in this same way in years past, and many more
to come would do the same. To wait and save for marriage would
be never to get married at all. So with literally nothing to start
with, they took this most serious and blind step into life, oblivious
of what the future would hold for them.

I wonder if they ever thought that twenty years after, they
would be facing each other in the divorce court.

As they came out of the block, Mum looked up and waved to
all those looking over the balcony. Suddenly she felt a blow in
the eye. It was an old shoe. Someone who had had too much to
drink had probably thrown it over the balcony. There were quite
a few who indulged in this practice in the block.

Well anyway, the funny part is that the next day Mum's eye
came up like it had been inflated with a pump, and as black and
blue as they come. You can imagine what people thought the
next day.

'Ho, he's started early then, ain't he, Hett?'

'Hooo, first night an' all. I've never in all my life ever heard of
such a thing.'

'You wanna put your foot down, Hett, right away. 'Cos if you
don't, Gawd knows what he'll do to yer when you've been
married a few years.'

The gossip lasted for weeks. What a sensation this was, a black
eye on your first night. Husbands and wives in the street were
always at it, especially Saturday night — shouts and screams of
abuse, articles flying out of a window, in between bouts of swear-
ings and threatenings. This was nothing. A passerby, on hearing a
schermozzle coming from one of the terraced houses, would
casually cross to the other side of the street to ensure safe passage
from any stray missiles that might come smashing through one of
the window panes. But to receive a shiner on your first night, well,
what a terrible thing to happen.

The tale of the famous black eye never really died out, and I
don't think my grandmother even today is fully convinced that it
was caused by a shoe being thrown over the balcony.

When Gran saw this colourful bump, she went mad. 'I'd better
not see him. Tell him to keep out of my way. I tell yer, Baker'll
murder him when he finds out, he will.'

Baker was an ex-Regular, a big, dominating man. He was now

about fifty and strong as an ox. After my Grandfather died he became a sort of Uncle to the family. Mum tried to convince him that Dad hadn't done it, but Gran had heard such a lot of gossip about the notorious black eye that she wasn't convinced.

'I know you're only trying to cover up for him, that's all. I told you what to expect from his like as soon as you started courting him, didn't I? That's all they know down that end, is bloody fighting. Wait till Baker sees it. He won't let it drop, I can tell you that.'

Mum was getting annoyed now. 'Now look here, Mum. If Baker touches Bill, I won't come round to you ever again. I'll take oath on that. Bill didn't touch me. It's all these bloody know-alls round here that have put it about. Now who are you going to believe, me or them?'

Gran didn't answer. She looked at Mum, not knowing what to believe now.

Mum reported back to Dad, telling him the whole story and not forgetting to mention the fact that he might be finding himself at the wrong end of Baker's fist. Now Dad was only a small man, standing about five feet tall in his socks if he stretched a bit. He was very lightly built, quick on his feet when boxing at the Repton Club in Hoxton, but his weight and strength nowhere matched that of Baker's. The fact that Dad had caught diphtheria at three years old – a disease that meant certain death for many youngsters in those days – did nothing to give him an advantage over Baker.

'I don't know if Baker will be after you or not,' said Mum. 'I've told Mum that if he starts anything I'll never go up there again.'

'Hmm,' Dad said, thoughtfully.

Dad didn't want to be no hero at the expense of his features. I don't blame him for that, for he was quite a good-looking man. He was blessed with jet-black hair. He had a high forehead, wide-set eyes, a broad, manly face, his chin wide and strong. His only fault was a rather large and dominant nose.

Dad's character was certainly written in his face. He had a sharp brain. He was shrewd, forceful, deliberate. Whatever he did, he did much slower than the average person, but what he did, he did properly. In his good moods he was fun. But get on the wrong side of him and he would never rest until he got revenge, even if it meant inconvenience and botheration to himself.

Weeks ran into months. Dad had now been up to Gran's a

number of times with Mum, since the scandal of the black eye. But I think Gran sort of tolerated Dad, rather than welcomed him. He had passed Baker in the street several times without incident, but he was always on the alert when Baker was around.

Dad knew that Baker would be too much for him. He needed a bodyguard, in case the sergeant launched a surprise attack. The obvious one for this post was George, otherwise known as Brownie. Brownie was made for this type of employment. In their teens, he had been Dad's best friend, the unelected, unappointed but assumed leader of the gang.

George Brown was a tall, slim boy. His thick hair was parted at the extreme left. A shock of coarse, brown hair continually hung over his right eye. He had deep-set eyes and a thin nose that tilted at the end. His hand would cover a full-size dinner plate, without a stretch. George looked as though he was built of steel. If he wasn't, then his hands certainly were, for he would push off the tops of the cast-iron railings that stood outside the flats with the palm of his great hand, the metal snapping like toffee under a hammer. So it is plain to see why George was Dad's choice of protector.

The confrontation was to come on a peaceful Sunday afternoon. The spot, a small archway at the end of Poyser Street. Brownie stayed glued to Dad now, whenever he could.

'If he does sort you aht, Bill, when I'm not there,' George told him, 'then we'll have one night together.' This was little consolation to Dad. He didn't want a bloody hiding, revenge or no revenge.

Dad and George had just come out of the Salmon and Bull pub. They were both tipsy, but not too drunk to know what they were doing. Somehow or other Dad had taken the lead, and George was some way behind. In this fashion they walked down Cambridge Heath Road, intending to turn left under the narrow archway that led to Poyser Street.

Dad, of course, was the first to turn off. The narrow street had only one footpath, on its right-hand side as Dad entered. The footpath only allowed for one pedestrian at a time. A person coming in the opposite direction would have to step into the road, or vice versa. But when Baker came from the other side of the arch, there was going to be no vice versa about it. Here the conflict showed itself.

The distance between the two rivals diminished by the second. Dad looked straight at Baker in defiance, in an effort to hide his fear. Baker's great feet came marching and echoing down the street. His studded boots struck the stone paving. There they were, on the brink of battle, like a David and Goliath. Closer and closer Baker came, as Dad strove determinedly with his fear. Plunk, plunk, plunk came Baker's boots and then . . . silence. Dad was now facing Baker's chest.

'Move, laddie,' came the order from Baker's fat throat.

This was it. Baker had offered the gauntlet.

'No, you move,' answered Dad defiantly. Baker began to go a beautiful shade of crimson.

'Laddie, I'll give you three to move.'

Dad's stomach was telling him to move, but his pride dictated otherwise. He stood there, tense for battle.

'Two, three.'

Baker's gnarled, hairy hands came down on Dad's shoulders and clutched, each grasping a handful of Dad's coat. Dad felt himself being lifted. The next thing he knew, he had hit the cobbled road with a bump. Now all fear had left him, to be replaced with a venomous hatred. All thoughts of George had left him completely.

Baker continued loftily down the street, his self-respect intact. Dad was now on his feet and he followed Baker rather unsteadily. Before Baker reached the end of the street, George appeared. He needed no prompting by Dad to grab Baker. As tipsy as George was, he knew that Dad and Baker were not down the little street that was known as the rendezvous for settling old scores and grievances for a tea party.

George stepped onto the pavement, blocking Baker's path. They looked hatefully at each other. George's long body seemed to ripple like a piece of string when shaken at one end, due to his intoxication.

'Move,' came the order again from Baker.

George's face took on a drunken grimace. 'Move?' George growled. He clenched his leg of pork fist. 'Wanna see that move, do yer? Do yer? It moves fast, Baker boy, even when I'm pissed it does. Oh, it's a real good 'un, this one.' George looked at it in admiration and Baker with apprehension. Baker recoiled slightly.

'Now, come on George. Be a good lad and let me pass.' George didn't like the authoritative way that Baker used the term 'lad'. He didn't mind being called 'lad' like other people used it. But when Baker said 'lad', it seemed to have a derogatory tone.

'Oh no . . . old man. You let me pass.'

George moved close up to Baker now and pressed against him, his thick forelock almost touching Baker's face. Dad was now

20

with the two, watching developments. The opponents grabbed each other and swayed like two ballroom dancers. They swayed like two ballroom dancers. They swayed and rocked together, leaning to one side then the other at the most dangerous angles, defying the force of gravity.

Of course it had to happen. Down they both went. They leaned over like an old galleon in a high wind. They met the ground with a wallop. Baker came off worst, for he was underneath George. Beneath the hammer and the anvil, as you might say, poor Baker, taking the full impact of the fall.

George was now sitting on top of his opponent. 'Come on, Bill. Don't just stand there, get his trousers off.'

Baker struggled even more furiously when he heard this. 'Get off, you bloody scum,' he shouted. 'Get off. I'll bloody kill you for this. Get off.' Baker's face had now taken on an even more ruddy appearance, redder than any traffic light signal.

'Shut up, you fat git,' George panted. 'Undo his braces, Bill. At the front.' Dad obeyed orders and away he went under Baker's jacket, searching for the crucial buttons. Baker rolled and kicked as Dad made contact, fumbling and pushing against buttons and braces.

'For Christ's sake, Bill, hurry up,' shouted George.

'I'm doing me best,' answered Dad, his tongue protruding fron the side of his mouth with concentration.

'Got it,' he said. Baker's front buttons were now undone.

'Right,' George ordered. 'Take hold of the bottoms of his trousers and pull. And hurry up.'

Dad jumped up from the ground and went into action, pulling and tugging for all he was worth. The trousers came suddenly away. Dad fell back and found himself on his rear end once again. Baker fought like a madman now, but George had the situation well under control.

'Right,' he shouted. 'Tie his feet up with his braces.'

Dad rubbed his backside and began to tie up the giant feet. George looked at Baker's red face. 'Now you know what to expect if yer starts again, don't yer?'

'You bastard,' panted Baker.

George quickly jumped up and ran down the archway into Poyser Street, Dad following behind. At the end of Poyser Street stood a lamp-post. George climbed it like a monkey and hung the victim's trousers at the top.

'Right,' said George. 'Home to my place.'

They ran down Poyser Street, knocking on every door to make

sure that Baker's streak through the streets would not go unnoticed. They both hid in a doorway, waiting for Baker to emerge trouserless from the archway. And there he was. Screams and laughter greeted him. The women were chattering to each other, none listening to what the other had to say. Children danced up and down with glee. An elderly man in shirt sleeves and braces looked calmly on, as he puffed at a clay pipe. His thumbs gripped his braces.

Baker came running down the street towards Craven Buildings, unaware of his trousers hanging on the lamp-post. Women screamed and ran inside as he approached. The initial shock was over. The laughter quietened down somewhat. A child shouted, 'There on the lamp-post, Mister.'

Baker looked round, saw the trousers and sprinted all the way back down the street again. He climbed frantically up the post, and this act caused a renewed and even more vigorous frenzy of convulsive laughter.

Baker was down now and his trousers were on. He went once again into his usual march, looking down his nose at his quite unwelcome audience. Dad and George exchanged smiles of satisfaction as they stood in the doorway. Then they made off to George's place in Russia Lane — one of the most notorious streets in Bethnal Green.

So now Mum and Dad lived in Marion Street. They were both at work. My mother was employed at the Kensitas cigarette firm which once stood at the corner of Old Street. My father worked for Carter Paterson, road hauliers. His father had served there for about fifty years and had received a gold watch on his retirement, a watch he was most proud of. Dad was the eldest and favourite son, so it was he who had the honour of having his father speak for him to the boss to get him the well-sought-arter post of van boy.

At that time, about 1920, it was all horse-drawn vehicles. My grandfather taught my Dad the ropes of harnessing and driving a horse and cart. This included knowing how to hump large, awkward and heavy parcels without getting a rupture. Grandfather explained to Dad how to get goods signed for. 'Never leave anything without a signature,' he told him.

'Now don't forget,' he emphasised. 'After they've signed your slip, always hold on for a few seconds to see if they tip. That's if they're a new customer. Now look, you're not expected to hump stuff from the factory onto your tailboard, understand? 'Cors if you break yer leg in the process you're not insured by the

22

firm. But if you break your leg while you're on the tailboard, then you are insured.

'Now this is where it's to your advantage. When you first pick up the goods from a firm, you hump the stuff out. Now then, if they tips yer then, you hump out whenever you call. But if they don't part up, then you stay glued to yer tailboard. It's no good taking the chance of an accident if they ain't gonna give yer a tip. You usually get about threepence, but you'll get to know all the tippers and non-tippers as you go on.

'Always give yer horse the nosebag if you're gonna be some time at a firm or if you're gonna have a cuppa in the coffee shop, uvverwise you'll find him gorn when yer git aht. If 'e is gorn, the first place to look for 'im is back at the yard, 'cors he hates work as much as we do and sometimes he might fancy an early day.'

Grandfather would start at about seven in the morning. He would be up at six. The first thing he would do is go out into the yard to the cold water tap, turn it full on and thrust his head under it. He would do this summer or winter. He was a very fit man indeed. He was over seventy when he died and had never seen a doctor, or the inside of a hospital, nor taken a tablet or a drop of medicine in all his life. He did about twelve hours' work a day, reaching home at about seven or half past in the evening. He never lost a day's work in his life. Fifty years of toil, day in, day out. It is unbelievable just what the human body can stand, let alone the mind.

Grandfather earned very poor wages at that time. There were eleven children. Two had died, otherwise it would have been thirteen. He would give Gran his wage packet, after deducting a few pence for his baccy and beer. By Wednesday, Gran would be broke, but Grandfather's tips from Monday and Tuesday would get the family out of trouble.

Clothes were bought down the Lane in Cheshire Street, off Vallance Road. There were no summer holidays then and no luxuries. These were the times when the pawn shop in Cambridge Heath Road was a last resort in an effort to get money. A rather degrading business, but not as degrading as going to the Board of Guardians or the Workhouse. This is just a rough outline of what it was like when my father was a boy of about fourteen, around 1924.

My father stuck the job. By now, the firm had motorised vehicles and Dad now worked in the yard. His job was to shunt the five-ton lorries onto the bank for loading. Dad was proud of this job, for there weren't many people who could handle a motor vehicle in those days. To be a bus driver was prestige indeed.

Mum had always worked in the tobacco trade. Like my father, Mum's father had spoken for her and she started at Kensitas as a trainee machine operator.

I remember being taken to the factory once. I must have been about six years old. It was an experience unpleasant enough to have stuck in my mind all my life. I think my mother had been off work for some reason or other and she went to the firm on the Friday afternoon to get what pay she had to come. I shall never forget the sickening, offensive smell of that factory. It smelt nothing like tobacco to me. It was a smell that attacked the nostrils instantly. Once the nose was penetrated, it would then seep down to the throat, almost choking you to death. If you survived this, then the poison would attack the stomach. I felt as though I had eaten something vile.

The girls looked neat and clean as they stood at their monster machines, dressed in their white aprons and hats. Even at that young age I wondered how these young, attractive girls could keep so jolly with this stench and nerve-shattering machine noise around them all day. Those machines turned out thousands of cigarettes a minute, while the girls worked continually, packing them into trays as they came off the machine.

'Hello, Hett,' they shouted above the racket. 'All right now, are yer?'

I, of course, was completely spoiled that afternoon.

'Ho, he's a smasher. He's gonna be a real lady killer when he gets older, I bet.'

A luscious blonde young lady of about twenty-odd picked me up. It seems funny perhaps, but I was most attracted to her, for she really was beautiful. I can see her golden hair now, tucked under her white hat, her lively — and, yes, lovely — sparkling, bright blue eyes looking at me with admiration, her bright red lips parting to reveal snow-white teeth as she smiled at me.

I was very shy as I was held there in her arms. Much as I was attracted to her lovely face, I had to hold my head down to hide the blushes that her compliments had brought on.

Then all the other young girls flocked around me. The blonde bombshell put me down. I would have much preferred to have remained in her tender arms. This was surely my first ever love affair, at about six years old and she at twenty-four. It could never have worked out. But why worry. I had the pick of all the girls in the factory for they all seemed to fall in love with me at first sight.

I tried to put on a smile, despite my poisoned stomach. I think the smile looked genuine enough to hide my distress, for no-one seemed to notice any change of colour in me. Perhaps this was because I was always a very pale child anyway. The dinner bell sounded and out they all rushed to the cafe across the road. Once inside, a giant dinner was placed in front of me. This made me feel even worse. They all sat chatting and smoking after they had eaten.

'What's the matter, boy? Why don't you eat your dinner, then?' they asked.

'I don't feel hungry,' I answered, guiltily.

The hooter discourteously disturbed their rest and the rush was on once again, but not as fierce as the rush that the first hooter had given birth to.

'There you are, son.' An array of hands came towards me and each one held out a sixpence. This was the best part of this outing.

On the bus, I was sick. The smell of the factory and now the bus ride was just too much.

'Why didn't you tell me you felt sick before?' my mother scolded.

'I don't know,' I cried. 'That smell in that factory, Mum. It's rotten, it is.'

'That's because you're not used to it. I forgot about that. Working in it day after day, you don't notice it.'

I certainly noticed it and I have never forgotten it since. The next time Mum went to the factory I would be staying at home, sixpences or no sixpences.

Well, now I have explained about my parents' work.

They had ordered some furniture, on which they paid two-and-six a week. Their rent was about five bob a week. This was quite an outlay in those times, but Mum and Dad both had jobs. They had nothing to worry about, or so they thought. They had no experience as yet of just what domestic disasters life had in store for people, so they were in happy ignorance.

The months went on and, as was to be expected, Mum became pregnant. She would not be working for many more months now, but they would still get by on Dad's money. She was about six months carrying when it happened.

Dad was on night work, shunting the lorries onto the bank. At the front of the vehicle, a handle protruded from the engine. This had to be turned to start the motor. Dad had to wind the handle. All the lorries were lined up side by side, facing a wall. The lorry he wanted was in the centre of the line.

He went to the front of the lorry and with both hands turned the thick, brass handle with all his might. This could be a rather dangerous operation, for sometimes after the handle was let go, it would suddenly spin back at the operator in an anti-clockwise direction. A lorry handle could break a man's hand like a matchstick and this was not uncommon in those times of engine handles.

Dad turned the handle a few times, waiting for the engine to start up. Then a most terrifying thing happened. The lorry began to creep forward. Closer and closer it came, driving Dad back to the wall. He had little time to think. Although the lorry was only just about moving, it seemed to be coming much faster, due to the small space between the lorry and the wall. There was no escape. Dad was frozen. There was only about a foot left now. Suddenly, like a flash of light, he went into action. Just as the bumper of the lorry embedded itself into the wall, in a split second Dad had jumped onto the bonnet. But he did not get off scot free. He had got his legs wedged between the bonnet and the wall. If he had not jumped, it is almost certain that he would have lost his legs. But he escaped with bruises.

Dad was unable to go to work now. So Mum had to stay at work until he was fit again. After a few weeks his legs healed up, but other symptoms took over — depression and hostility. He seemed to become completely uninterested in work and life in general.

The weeks went on, and eventually Dad lost his job at Carter Paterson's. I don't know if they got compensation then, but I know that Dad didn't get a bean. As far as the leg injuries were concerned, well, they had healed up. But how do you prove that mental illness is caused through your job, or injury at work?

In any case, it was not clear just what had brought on this withdrawal. Some of the family said that it was because of his deprived childhood, others that it was the great responsibility of getting married. Some said he only got married to prove to my Gran Gullis that his family was as good as theirs, so adding just one more antagonism to the already strained relationship between Gran Gullis and my father.

His sisters had told how he would shut himself in the boxroom for hours. I tried investigating this a little further and discovered from his closest sister that he shut himself away like this so that he could read his books in peace. This was understandable, seeing there were about eight little ones running about the house. So what was it that brought Dad's sickness on, his childhood, his marriage or the accident, is a question that I feel will never be answered.

Well, I was soon to make my appearance into the world. I decided to do so at a most inconvenient time, a characteristic that seems to have stuck with me all my life. George Brown, Dad's mate, courted and eventually married my father's sister Polly when Dad started courting Mum. The four of them would go out together, and did so right up until about 1950 when my aunt and uncle moved to Beacontree.

So there the four sat in the cinema in Bethnal Green Road, munching at peanuts and popcorn. Suddenly there came a cry from Mum: 'Me water's broke, Poll, me water's broke.'

Poll jumped to her feet. 'Aw me Gawd, George, her water's broke. Quick, we'll have to get her up the London.'

George, not the least disturbed, slowly arose, plunging his cast-iron fingers into his crumpling popcorn packet, his eyes welded to the screen, chewing away as he slid down the row of seats, looking back over his shoulder at the screen to see as much of the film as time would allow before leaving. Poll walked in front of George and behind my mother. My Dad was at the front.

They made their way up the aisle as quickly as possible. All, that is, except George. He had lost some distance between the rest of the party, due to his much aroused interest in the film. Aunt Poll looked round and saw him. He was dawdling along a few yards behind, his popcorn bag held well up to his mouth. His hand dived in. Suddenly, the whole bagful seemed to explode in his astonished face with a bang in the left ear. Aunt Poll had brought over one of her left-hand specials, with utmost force and accuracy.

'Come on, you half-daft git. Move your f. . . . ing self. She's nearly having it.'

This wallop had put new life into George and away he went without complaint, holding a red and throbbing left ear.

My mother had told me what a terrible time she had at my birth. 'Everything seemed to be in a rush,' she told me. 'They literally pulled you out. And the pain, well.' I think this was perhaps why my mother had no more children for eleven years. After that time I was to be presented with a sister, of whom I was extremely proud.

So now Dad was out of work, Mum was out and now there was a baby. The hire purchase man began to suffer. In return, he made my parents suffer, with letters at first, then verbal warnings and finally the bailiff. Now the young couple were left with no bed, no table, no chairs.

Is it any wonder that they were unable to make their marriage work after twenty years of trying? Neither of them had ever courted before. They were, as they say, childhood sweethearts. But as soon as they got married they grew further apart instead of becoming closer, and who can wonder at it? A husband out of work, a new baby and now no furniture.

No wonder my father's condition grew worse. What else could be expected? They tell us money isn't everything, money isn't happiness. That's all very well when you've got it. But tell me this. Is it better to be sick, lonely and rich or sick, lonely and poor? If you suffer, let us say, from rheumatism is it better to have to endure the climate of London or Spain? The answer, of course, is obvious and the ways and means of getting there need no elaboration.

2 Grandparents

Well, now Gran Gullis informed Mum that there was a flat going in Craven Buildings, Poyser Street, on her landing. Craven Buildings was no Buckingham Palace but the flats did have indoor toilets and seemed to be cleaner looking inside. This was much better than Marian Street, with its crumbling walls and the water tap in the yard. At Craven Buildings Mum had her own kitchen, which was separate from the living room. At Marian Street the kitchen and living room were one. Mum was glad to get out of Marian Street. She told Dad about the flat in Craven Buildings but he seemed to have no interest one way or the other. He was becoming more and more withdrawn now.

So into Craven Buildings they went. What did they do about furniture? Well, as usual, Gran Gullis came to the rescue, as she did right through my mother's married life. She always put on an act of austerity and hardness, but underneath was a loving, compassionate heart. I can remember the Christmases that she bought me new clothes, fitting me out from top to bottom, paying for my new rig-out on weekly instalments to the Whickam's tallyman. A widow herself, having no-one to depend on, she would get herself into this debt for the sake of her family. But I will tell you more about Gran later.

Mum and Dad moved into Craven Buildings on the Saturday. A costermonger's wheelbarrow was all the transport necessary to convey their few possessions to their new habitat. The barrow would be hired out at threepence a day. The moving job didn't take an hour, but the threepence still had to be paid, whether the customer had the barrow for ten minutes or all day. Anyway, threepence was not a bad price to pay for a moving job.

No sooner had Mum brought up the last bundle than Gran was at the door, dressed in her best coat which almost touched her ankles. Round her neck hung an expensive looking fox fur. She wore a deep purple straw hat, decorated with a large, white flower. Her face was lightly powdered and her lips lightly touched with lipstick.

Mum looked at Gran with surprise. She only dressed so grandly on high days and holidays, christenings, marriages and funerals. Gran, of course, did dress rather well on these occasions, compared with the other locals. As I have explained, my grandfather was fairly well off compared to a lot of others down the street, due to his army pension. Gran drew a widow's pension after Grandad died and I think the 'Buffaloes' helped her in some small way.

My grandfather, you see, having a little money to spare, set himself up as the local money lender. As the wife of such a person, Gran had to keep up appearances.

Well anyway, Gran was all ready. 'Come on,' she said in her usual authoritative tone. 'Get your coat on. We're going down Bethnal Green to get some furniture'

Mum was stunned. 'Furniture?' she exclaimed. 'What do you mean, furniture? I've not got a pot and I won't get HP anywhere, now that they've taken my other lot back.'

'Don't worry,' answered Gran. 'Just leave it to me. Come on.'

Mum went back in and put on her coat, and away she went with Gran down the Bethnal Green Road. They came to the largest shop in the market. In the window stood a medium oak bedroom suite.

'Do you want that?' Gran asked.

'It's lovely,' said Mum.

'Right, we'll have that,' Gran replied. 'Now, you'll want a dining room suite.'

'But Mum. . . . . '

'Shut up,' Gran put in quickly. 'Now,' she went on, 'curtains. Yes, we'll get them and a couple of mats as well. Right, come on. In we go.'

Gran held her head high, stretching herself up to her dignified four foot six inches, her dress making her look much wealthier than she really was.

The young, well-dressed salesman came towards them as they entered the shop.

'Good afternoon, Madam. Can I help you?'

Gran explained to him what she wanted. He then quickly disappeared and returned with a more senior looking gentleman.

'Well, Madam,' he said as he approached, with a false smile.

The junior had probably told him about all the gear that Gran intended to buy. I suppose it wasn't every day that he had the good fortune of an order like this. He stood there, displaying the walrus moustache that perched on his smiling upper lip.

'If you are paying cash, Madam, we can deliver today,' he informed Gran.

'No, I want HP,' said Gran.

He went to a drawer and produced some giant-sized forms.

Nan knew all about filling in forms. She made it her business to know. With no husband and five children, you just couldn't go into anything or sign anything without thinking. Gran had to read and re-read. But with HP and talleymen she knew her onions. Mum just looked on in amazement as Gran put her own name and address on the form.

'Sometime next week,' said the manager as the business was concluded. Gran thanked Smiler and away they both went. As soon as they were outside the shop, Mum started.

'Now what you done?' she questioned. 'They think it's your furniture. If I'm unable to keep the payments up, it's you they'll be after. And when they come to take it away it won't be in your house. It'll be next door in mine.'

Gran was unable to conceal an amused smile as they walked home. 'It's nothing to laugh at,' Mum grumbled. 'Suppose I can't pay it?'

'Oh, stop worrying,' Gran told her. 'Let's worry about that when it happens. Come on, you ought to be pleased that you've got another lot of furniture coming home. Let's go to the Dundee for a stout to celebrate the occasion.' The Dundee Arms stood immediately adjacent to the archway that led into Poyser Street.

They entered the pub. In the corner sat Mum's mother-in-law, Gran Barnes. Gran Barnes had quite a different appearance to Gran Gullis. Although they were about the same height, Gran Barnes was much more fully proportioned. She had beautiful silver, wavy hair. She was always full of life, ready for a laugh and a joke. She had always been poor and looked upon Gran Gullis as one of the upper classes. Of course, Gran Gullis was nothing of the sort.

Gran Barnes was of rather different background to Gran Gullis. Gran Barnes was born in the Workhouse, which at that time many women entered just to have a baby. Others entered because they had no other means of subsistence. Gran Gullis was born in Ely Place, High Holborn. A rather respectable area, where her father served as a clerk just across the road at Staples Inn. He had taken this post up after finishing his time in the Regulars. The two Grans seemed to get on quite well during the few occasions that they were in each other's company.

So the three sat there, drinking and talking. Gran Barnes was told about the HP deal. This made her think that Gran Gullis was even more well off than she did previously.

There were no bedroom or dining room suites in Gran Barnes' house. It was hard enough bringing up the kids, let alone such extravagances as this. Who could blame her for having a drink now and then? Like many other women in the area, there was nothing else to keep her going from day to day. What was there to look forward to from one day to the next but the feeding and looking after a load of kids, shopping, clearing up, washing up, making beds and wondering if you had enough money for the day's grub? No wonder men and women in those days went on the beer. At least it was one way of numbing the senses. It helped to escape from it all for a short while and made it possible to face it all again for another week or so.

Gran Barnes was said to be a most beautiful looking woman in her young days. I can only remember her from when she was about fifty. I did not see a lot of her, for one reason or another, but the limited number of times I did see her left a great impression on me. This was due to her very strong and happy-go-lucky character. Her language could be shocking, and she would use it at any time, anywhere, without discrimination, to prince or pauper. This was her natural way of expression.

She really was a smasher. She was only about four foot six tall, and a little package of dynamite. She was the sort of person who smiled immediately, as soon as you met her. It was not an ordinary smile, it was a smile that seemed to make you feel like going into a laugh, if you know what I mean. A smile that seemed to be saying, 'Why worry? Sod it all.' That sort of smile. She was always out for a lark or a joke.

The first I can remember of her was when she lived in Poyser Street. Number one, right on the corner of Old Bethnal Green Road. Now I can't think why, but at that time I was terrified of her. I'm not sure why, but I think the reason was that when Gran was put out or pissed, she had a gate on her like a barrage of heavy artillery.

I was passing number one to go to Dixon's sweet shop one afternoon when my ears caught the full blast of Gran's penetrating voice, giving out for one and all to hear. All the defamatory acts of my grandfather, past and present, real and imaginary misdemeanours, many of which my grandfather was unable to recall.

I think it was this experience that made me a little wary of Gran Barnes at first. She knew that I was a bit scared, and would try to get me up to her place. Eventually, she succeeded. If she saw me coming down the road, she would hide behind her curtain and wait until I was just level with her window. Then she would suddenly poke her head out at me as I went by and she would blast out, 'Hold him, somebody. Hold that little bleeder, hold him.' I was terrified and would run like hell. This was just how she was.

Of a Sunday, I had to pluck up courage to go up there to see my granfather. He would give me my Sunday penny, a brand new one. True enough, it was in mint condition. How he was able to find such brand new pennies, Sunday after Sunday, I don't know. Perhaps he saved them, though I doubt it, for any money in the house at that time would be quickly consumed.

Gran would be sitting in her high-backed, wooden armchair, keeping an eye on the dinner. She cooked it on the kitchener, which combined a kitchen fire and an oven. They said that these kitcheners cooked much better than a gas oven. But they had their drawbacks when making stews.

Gran would put the pot of stew on the top of the kitchener. Now above the pot of stew was the chimney. If the chimney needed sweeping, then bits of soot would drop into the stew and Gran would have to scoop it out with a spoon.

'Ugh, Gran,' I said once, when I spotted her fishing out the soot. 'Is Grandad going to eat that?'

'Well, course he is,' she replied. 'He don't know, does he?'

My poor grandfather's inside must have had more soot in it than Gran's chimney. But it never seemed to have harmed him. He was as fit as a fiddle.

To get back to my Sunday morning penny. My desire for the penny overcame my fear of Gran, and so there I was. She would look at me as she clutched her cup of bitter. 'Come here, you little bleeder.'

I would walk timidly forward, as she put on her most unfriendly look.

'Don't torment him,' Grandad would say. 'Frighten the life out of him, yer do.'

I would stop just out of Gran's reach.

'Come on, come on' she would say.

I came on. She would grab me with her free hand and press me against her enormous belly. I could smell the starchy freshness of her flowered apron.

'Oh ho, he's a good little bleeder, though. Ain't yer?'

She'd almost squeeze me to death and then finish off by giving me a resounding smack of a kiss, flavoured with bitter.

'I know why you're frightened of me,' she'd say. 'It's those Gullises. Don't think we're good enough. That's why.'

In Poyser Street Gran had gas light. Many's the time I've been up there and seen just one gas flame shooting out of the pipe because they had no money to buy a gas mantle. You put the mantle on and this would cause a white glow. Some nights there would be a row because Gran had been in the pub during the course of her shopping, got pissed and hadn't put the dinner on. This was one of the main reasons my grandparents used to fight.

Saturday and Sunday were the worst. Saturday was Bethnal Green Market and then the White Hart. Sunday was Club Row Market and the White Hart. Gran's Sunday visits to Club Row were for second-hand clothing off the stalls, for the kids. The ones who were a bit particular and wanted to make sure that a dress or pullover fitted properly would go with Gran. The not too fussy put on what was brought in. Gran could get a bagful of gear for two bob.

It was at the weekends that Gran was most likely to go missing. It might be a Sunday, say. My Grandfather would be round the pub. Now my aunt Flo was about fourteen or so then. She would see the time getting on, and no dinner on yet. She knew if Grandad came home a bit drunk to no dinner, a battle would ensure when Gran got home.

So Flo would go hunting for Gran in all the local pubs. If she couldn't find her, she knew she was bound to be in the White Hart. She'd take Gran's bag and home she'd rush and get the lot in the oven, ready for Grandad. Week in, week out, the peace was kept. But it was not always assured, for if Gran could not be found then it was all-out war.

Gran could lay her tongue to all the finest phrases, and Grandad was no novice either. Anyway, they'd go like two old champions. Gran did not go in for the punching technique. Her line of attack was to grab at you, tearing your coat or jacket to pieces.

My young Uncle ran out of the house many times his shirt in shreds, as though he had been got at by a lion. He probably deserved it for being saucy or for nicking a penny out of her purse.

Once Gran's children left school, they had to work. Gran would have no nonsense about this. Work was quite hard to find during the twenties, but she did not seem to appreciate this fact. I suppose she must have thought to herself, 'Well, I've struggled to bring them up. Now it's time they put some money into the home.' Who could blame her for his attitude, after rearing something like fourteen kids?

All the girls managed to get work and bring something in. Even so, they were not allowed out of an evening until they had done some housework. But my poor Uncle Ted was unlucky. He was unable to find a job anywhere, but Gran wasn't having any of that. On the Friday night, he again had no money and so, at about sixteen, he was thrown out.

He lived rough for a considerable time, sleeping many a night on the Vicky embankment and waiting for the Silver Lady soup van. They showed up at about three in the morning. He tried a number of times to get back home again, even if it was only for a bed. But Gran wasn't going to encourage his laziness. What happened was this. My Aunt Flo would wait until Gran went to bed, then she'd go to the back door and let Ted in. The first time she did this, Ted was caught by Gran.

This is how it happened. In the Washes (which is short for wash-house) stood a pram. The Washes was a sort of scullery with a concrete floor. A stone boiler stood in the corner. This is where all the washing of clothes was carried out. Flo had let Ted in so he could have a night's kip. The problem was, where to kip safely? He saw the pram at the side of the boiler and in he got. He was that tired, and, uncomfortable as it was, he went straight off to sleep.

Once again, Fate was against him. It had to happen that Gran woke up during the night and felt the need to relieve herself. She had to go through the Washes and into the Yard to do so. Well, she was bound to see Ted snoozing away, literally sleeping like a baby.

After Dad got married, he hardly went to see his mother. I think it was because it saddened him to see how she had taken to drink. I can remember my mother saying to him, 'Bill, don't you think you ought to go round and see your mother?'

'All right, I'll go in and see her on the way back from the Lane, Sunday morning.'

Sometimes he would go, sometimes not. I know that when Gran herself thought it was time to see her eldest son, she would call round. If Mum saw her coming up the street she would call to Dad, who would probably be sitting in the armchair having a doze (especially if it were Sunday).

'Yer Mum's coming up the road, Bill. I hope she ain't pissed.'

Anyway, they'd wait for the knock and in Gran would wobble. She always called like this if she thought too much time had lapsed since Dad's last visit. It was true, without a shadow of a doubt, that she liked to see him now and again. But there was also another motive behind her visit. Whenever Dad went to visit her he always gave her a dollar. So when she felt that Dad's rather infrequent contributions were getting yet more infrequent, she would make it her business to call. But seriously, I think she had rather a soft spot for him, being the eldest son. I think she called mainly to see him.

I can remember one Christmas Eve when she made one of these round-the-family collections. Being Christmas Eve, she was, of course, well Brahms and Liszt. She sat in the armchair, then it started.

'You ain't been near nor by, you ain't. Gor blimey, just up the road. What, you frightened to wear yer boot leather aht, are yer? And if I hadn't come rahnd, bet I wouldn't er seen yer all over Christmas, would I?'

Well, Gran's complaint was justified in a way. For it was true, Dad had neglected her somewhat since his marriage.

'I suppose it's her,' Gran started, 'keeping yer away.'

This was quite untrue. Mum had been on to Dad time and time again to go round and see his mother. Of course, Mum got annoyed over this.

'You don't know what you're talking about,' she snapped. 'Don't come round here accusing me of keeping him away from you, because I've told him time and again to go round to you. And another thing, don't raise your voice and show me up in these flats.'

Gran was up ready for action, though due to her age and size, it wasn't very swift action. Mum turned away from her to examine the Christmas pudding on the gas which was bubbling away as though it were being choked. Mum did this to try and subdue her bubbling anger. She turned the gas down a little under the pudding. Gran was still carrying on.

'Thinks she's too good for us, she does. That's her trouble. Always been the same, that lot. Never alter 'em, you won't.'

That was it. Mum could take no more. 'Bill, get her out of here.'

Before Dad could get to his feet, Gran and Mum were locked in combat. He tried to part the two of them. They were giving each other a sort of bear hug. Neither of them seemed to be suffering very much from such treatment. The three adults were all shouting at once now and I, at about five years old, was bawling my eyes out.

'You come up here upsetting the place. That's all you're fit for, upsetting people,' Mum shouted.

Then Gran cut through. 'Oooh, you saucy young cow, you. I'll kill yer, I will.'

'For Christ's sake. Turn it all in, will you?' Dad panted, as he struggled to part the two.

We all played our part in the uproar, Gran and Mum screaming and shouting hostilities, Dad bawling at them and me screaming blue murder. Then all of a sudden, there was a deafening explosion.

We knew it wasn't a bomb because the air raid siren hadn't sounded. We all stood looking at each other in bewildered silence. The ceiling was covered in Christmas pudding and currants. The walls were also covered. The gas stove was in a right mess.

Then we all burst into laughter, for we too had caught the blast. Gran's hair was smothered in it. On her nose sat a black raisin. Each of us was plastered with the stuff. I giggled, then Mum, then Gran caught it and passed it on to Dad. Then we all burst into great roars of laughter and it turned out a happy Christmas after all.

What caused the pudding to explode into a million pieces? Heaven knows. Mum certainly must have laced it with something good. Dynamite, no doubt.

My Gran Gullis always acted hard and military, perhaps because she came from a military family. But underneath, she was as tender as a kitten and would have given her last away to make sure that someone's kids had a meal.

The Collins had four kids and lived in Craven Buildings. First their mother was taken into hospital with a serious illness and then their father. The rest of the family, the uncles and aunts, didn't want to know about looking after four kids. So in spite of the fact that she had already been in hospital many times, my Gran volunteered to have them. Otherwise, it would have meant the workhouse or the orphanage for the Collins. Apparently she didn't receive a penny from anywhere to keep them. She already had two daughters (my mother was married) and Fred Baker, who used to come up for his grub. Fred wasn't married and had become a close friend of the family after meeting my grandfather at the Buffaloes.

So now Gran really had her work cut out. She made out she was hard, but how many people would have taken on that responsibility? Then came the news from the Bethnal Green Hospital about the kids' parents. The mother had died and there was little hope for the father. Gran could see now what she had let herself in for. It was she who had the unenviable job of telling these poor kids about their mother. This must have been a terrible strain on an already sick woman. But Gran was tough, or that was the impression she gave. When she sat in the kitchen armchair that night and the Colliers were put to bed, she looked dead beat. My Uncle Bert said to her, 'Have you told them, Mum?'

'Well, of course I've told them,' she answered sharply.

'You don't look too good, Mum,' Bert told her. 'Why don't you get into bed and I'll bring you in a nice cup of cocoa?'

'Into bed, what are you talking about? There's nothing wrong with me, not yet there isn't. Life is hard and you've got to face up to it, not go running off to bed like a bloody coward. I'm used to death, anyway. I've seen enough of it in my time, don't you worry.'

I wonder if she was thinking about my grandfather when she said that, for you could not help noticing the catch in her throat as she spoke. She lost him at the age of thirty-five, and was left with five young children to bring up. Yet Gran would never show her real feelings. She would shrug off any show of tenderness as sloppy. But I'm sure she must have lain on her bed alone many a night and cried herself to sleep.

By the end of the week, the Colliers' father was dead. This left Gran having to decide whether she was going to keep the children or not. The family advised her against it and so did the kid's relatives. 'You'll never be able to keep it up,' they told her. 'You need looking after yourself.' But Gran had made up her mind long before the others had forseen the present circumstances. Her answer was: I'll be in my box before those kids are taken to any orphanage.'

The strain on Gran did not quite put her in her box, but it did eventually put her in hospital. Once again, she became seriously ill with her stomach. The Colliers' relatives became worried — not so much about the kids, but in case they were going to be humped up with them. But they didn't worry for long. While Gran was in hospital, the relatives took the kids to an orphanage.

It was crucial that Gran should not be told about this until she was out of hospital. When my mother went to see her, the Colliers were the first ones she asked about. My uncles and aunts would say, 'Oh, they're all right, Mum.' Then they would feel guilty, for Gran had always told them, right from kids, 'Never lie to your parents.' But if they had told her the truth, it would have been too much for her.

On the day she came out of hospital, she kept on asking if the kids had been fed and washed, and if their bedclothes had been changed. Mum, my aunt and two uncles had to keep on changing

38

the subject until they reached home. Then the hard truth had to come out. Gran went in, after resting a few minutes on the landing to get her breath back following the long haul up four flights of stairs. She made her usual prophecy: 'Them stairs'll kill me, they will.'

Then she called: 'Ronnie, Teddy, where are you? Come on, I'm home. Billy, Freddie. Where, where. . . ? She looked round at my mother, her being the eldest.

'Hetty,' she asked suspiciously. 'Where are they? Where are they?'

My mother began to look nervous now. 'Well, Mum. You see, er, the kids', er, relations, er, er, have, er . . . '

'I know,' Gran shouted. 'I know. Why didn't you tell me before? I could have stopped it. Why didn't you tell me?'

Gran was shaking now. My two uncles took hold of her, to sit her in the armchair. She shook them off and sat in the chair without their aid. It took all her effort not to cry in front of her children. She just sat there, as upright and as stiff-lipped as a grenadier outside Buckingham Palace. She looked into space. Then she said, quietly, 'God. Why does life always sort us out?' She slowly shook her head and asked again: 'Why?'

They all stood in the room in silence, a little sad and a little more relaxed, now that Gran had been given the hard truth. This was only one part of what my Gran had gone through. Perhaps it explains why she had so much feeling for others in distress.

My Gran Gullis was brought up in a strict, austere, Victorian atmosphere. She appeared to me a completely different sort of woman to Gran Barnes. Gran Gullis was thin and put on a somewhat cold and reserved attitude. Gran Barnes was maternally fat and accessible. Gran Gullis sounded all her Hs, Ss, Ts, the lot. Gran Barnes dropped them all. Gran Gullis used to see that I was well fed and clothed during the rough periods. It was she who looked after me at six weeks old, when my mother had to go out to work. Even when I was five or so, she was still looking after me.

I loved Gran Gullis, naturally, but I think I must have inherited some of my father's Cockney nature, for although I spent much more time with her than Gran Barnes, I seemed to feel more a part of the Barnes side than the Gullises. I do not feel bias or favouritism to either side, but for some reason or other I seem to feel more a Barnes than a Gullis.

When I was in Gran Gullis' presence I felt more restricted. I had to speak correctly. I had to look neat and tidy. To have one

39

of my socks hanging down round my ankle was an absolute disgrace to the family. My forelock must never be allowed to droop over my eye. My hair must be combed back neatly at all times, and kept short. I must not lean over my plate while eating. This was Gran Gullis: a little strict, correct and orderly, fussy and apt to be a perfectionist. Yet underneath all this correctness lay a heart of gold. She had been very strictly brought up herself, in a deeply religious, Catholic, military family. As a child, she was not allowed to play in the street, or play with toys of any kind. She just had to sit in a chair and behave herself until it was time for bed. I can see why she was left with her armoured exterior.

If I was caught in the act, like the time I was about to throw a kitten over the landing, she would look at me and squint her eyes. With her hands on her hips, she would say, 'You've got the makings of a villain in you, you little devil. Just the same as your father, you're going to turn out. Mark my words.'

I would put on my most sorrowful face and try my hardest to look as pained and rejected as possible. I had to think of something really horrifying, like being impaled on the pointed railings that ran along the ground floor of the flats. These morbid fantasies helped me restrain an almost uncontrollable grin (another Barnes trait of never taking anything seriously). It was more than I dared do to let Gran see me laughing, especially after I had been caught red-handed.

Gran never used her hands on me. She was much too reserved for that. It was the strict tone of her voice, and her attitude, that really kept me in check. If she was right about me being like my father, then I'm sure she must have had her work cut out.

For some reason, Gran Gullis once wanted to try a hopping holiday. Grandfather wouldn't hear of it. 'We don't have to go on that sort of holiday,' he said. 'We want a decent holiday.' Somehow, Gran managed to get him to agree to her having a holiday on her own, with the kids. Perhaps he had to work that week or something. Anyway, Gran tells him she's going on a proper holiday, and all the time she's planning to go hopping. So away she went. She was there two days when Grandfather came down and had her and the kids out and home like a shot. Someone down the street had opened their north and south about it.

Hopping was the poor man's holiday. It was farm work, really, but people liked to look on it as a holiday. All the families would gather their things together before going. Cups, blankets, clothes, a few groceries. It would all be ready for Saturday morning. They would wait at the corner for the van, or horse and cart, to take them to London Bridge station. Some of the women loaded their stuff onto a pram. Those who missed the van, for one reason or another, would walk to the station.Away they went, down the road, their prams overloaded with bundles. Some of the prams were hardly able to take the strain, with their squeaky springs and wobbly wheels. They went along, laughing and chatting, wearing their customary aprons if the weather was fine. Behind them came a multitude of kids, just as excited as their mothers.

When they finally arrived at the farm, they would find themselves one of the huts which the farmer had so kindly provided. There was no furniture whatsoever inside these huts. The occupant would gather a number of stout twigs. On top, he would lay some straw, also provided by the farmer. This lot was laid at the far end of the hut and used as a bed for the whole family. The farmer also made a number of old fruit boxes available. These served as furniture.

Water had to be carried by the young men from a tap, sometimes as much as half a mile away. They would fill up their pots and pans in the evening, ready for the next day. The toilet facilities varied, but not much. The lavatory was a trench, about twenty foot long. Over the trench were a number of huts, each one with a board inside which was used as a seat. Every so often, quicklime was thrown into the trench. Some huts, although built in the same immaculate style, had bins instead of trenches.

Some of the living huts had one small window. Some had none at all. There was no door, just a gap.

In the evenings, the hop pickers would all sit round the camp fire telling jokes and stories, while baking potatoes on a stick. They would sing their Cockney songs into the mild and misty country air.

This was the holiday for the poor of East London. A working holiday in the poorest conditions. I don't think my elder relatives would dispute this.

I don't think many people go hopping now. They mostly go abroad. Some don't have a holiday at all.

I cannot remember anything of my Grandfather Gullis. I only know what I have been told about him. It seems he was quite a colourful character. His job allowed the family to have a somewhat higher standard of living than most other families. The flat dwellers were a mixed bunch, ranging from the well-off (by their standards) to the downright poor. If the Gullises had lived in the terraced houses, they would most certainly have been eligible for the posh end.

My grandfather was the smartest man in the street. In the summer, he would go to work immaculately dressed in his silver grey suit and straw hat. He would come home almost as fresh as he went out. He carried a black walking stick, decorated with a three-inch engraved silver band at the handle. His black, ankle-length boots shone like a guardsman's. He was a handsome young man, with thick black hair parted on the side. His hair shone brilliantly as his boots, due to the hair oil he used.

The rough-end dwellers would never waste money on things like hair oil. The young teenage boys would get round this problem by raiding mum's food cupboard. They would find the margarine, plunge the index finger into it and apply the charged finger to their hair. They would then dampen their hair under the tap in the yard. By doing this, the marge and water would hold their locks in place even better than expensive hair oils. The only thing was, it used to make their hair stink like a polecat after a couple of days.

Another disadvantage was that they could not all afford to go to the barber's shop in Cambridge Heath Road. So they all became each other's barber. They were far from skilled at this job, and the results were at times horrifying, to say the least. You always made sure to steer clear of a beginner at the communal hair-cutting sessions. Even so, a good cut was never guaranteed, even by the old hands. A bare, white patch would be seen at the back of a jet-black head of hair, as though it had been torn out, rather than cut off. Boys' fringes would be all shapes: jagged, triangular, sloping. Or perhaps, due to desperation, completely absent.

'Blimey,' they would say to each other, mockingly, 'what they cut that with, a knife and fork? Or did they put a basin on your head and cut round it?'

None of this worried them unduly. They were all the same. They used the public bar and not the saloon, where the book-makers, stallholders, money-lenders and such-like congregated. They had nowhere much to go, anyway. If they were not in the pub, they would be at home. In the summer they might sit outside their houses, talking. The only times they smartened up was for weddings, christenings and funerals. Even when they were smartened up, the poverty still showed through in the sort of frowning expression that never left their faces. It was like a feature handed down from one generation to another.

Their poverty was also apparent in the second-hand clothes they wore, which they got down Cheshire Street and Club Row.

42

Their coarse speech and manner were other features which made them easily identifiable in a crowd. The better-off would also visit Club Row occasionally for a bargain in the clothing line. They, of course, were much more discreet about it than those who lived down the rough end of the street.

I feel a little sad, as I think back to Poyser Street, that this sort of segregation, however mild, existed in such a potentially communal people.

Well, to get back to Grandfather Gullis. As well as his jet-black hair and boots, he sported a magnificent jet-black walrus moustache. He came from a large Cockney family, but somehow seemed to be isolated from them. For some unknown and peculiar reason, he never inherited the Cockney accent and brisk, bouncy attitude of the people. Another thing he was free from was the need to gesticulate with his hands and body in order to put over some point or meaning.

Richard, my grandfather, was much more reserved than any of his family, who were descended from French/Irish stock. It was this reserve that made him the black sheep of his clan. This description may give the impression that Grandfather was a quiet, introverted sort of man, but this was definitely not so. What he had inherited from his Cockney parents was their humour and quick-wittedness, their love of music and entertainment. Grandfather was a man of impulse. He was a devoted Buffalo, and held office in that order for many years.

My Grandmother never knew when she was going to be taken for a drink. Grandfather would come rushing in from work, full of life.

'Come on, gal,' he'd say. 'We're going down the Dundee tonight. Never mind the dinner, you're having a night out.'

The fact that they had been drinking all over the weekend made not the slightest difference to him. He kept his hat and coat on, while Gran obediently left her saucepans and prepared herself for the night out. After waiting about twenty minutes, Grandfather would start to get restless. This was him all over. He'd go into the box room and gather his drum kit together.

'Hett, where's me drum sticks?' he would shout impatiently. 'I'm sure I put them in here, Sunday night.'

'Oh, I don't know,' Gran would shout back. 'You should take your time more, then you'd remember what you done with your things.'

Grandfather would mumble something back, while Gran went on curling up her waist-length blonde hair, holding a dozen hair clips between her lips.

'Can't find them, gal,' Grandfather would try again. But Gran just ignored him, and put all her attention into getting ready at top speed, to satisfy my grandfather.

'Where the hell are the damn things? I'm sure I put them here Sunday night.'

Gran looked at him as he entered the kitchen, twisting the end of his moustache. 'Sunday night?' she said, with a smirking smile. 'You wasn't fit to remember anything, Sunday night.'

'I wasn't that drunk,' Grandfather answered, in a rather hurt tone. 'That's what I like about you. Always got to exaggerate, you have. Always, always.'

He looks at his watch. 'Now come on, gal. Are you ready or not? I'll put me overcoat on tonight.' He puts it on and disappears into the bedroom. Nan follows him. She is ready now, except for her coat. As Grandad puts on his coat, it sticks out at one side. In his pocket are the elusive drumsticks.

'Got 'em,' he laughs. Away they go, down the narrow steps of the flats, his bass drum booming as it touches the walls, his cymbals clashing and echoing through the landings. Off they go, down the street and under the arch, to the Dundee. A percussive departure.

Once in the Dundee, Gran would have her gin, and Grandfather his pint of brown. There was no fancy carpeting on the floor then. Instead, there was sawdust. Of course, that was only in the public bar, where the customers were just that little bit more careless when holding their beer glasses, and where one or two of the drinkers were given to spitting on the floor. My grandparents were too posh for the public bar. They went in the saloon, where much cleaner conditions prevailed.

Once Grandfather was boozed, he would set up his drums and accompany the piano player, singing at the top of his voice till closing time. He would sing songs like 'It's a Great Big Shame', 'Soldiers of the Queen' and 'We All Came in the World with Nothing'. His whole body would tremble with the effort of hitting the top notes. The reason for this was that he used to start off in too high a key. Rather than stop and start afresh, he would risk a double hernia. His head seemed to stand on his high collar, as though detached from his body, as his face and neck swelled almost to bursting point.

Then he would become silent, lay down his drumsticks, and stand up most solemnly. The mood had changed. Grandfather was now ready to give out with his tear-jerkers: songs like 'I'll

44

Take You Home Again, Cathleen', 'It's Only a Beautiful Picture in a Beautiful Golden Frame' and his real speciality which he could always depend on for a good cry, 'What is a Mummy?' This went:

'What is a Mummy, Daddy?
Everyone's got one but me.
Is she the lady that lives next door,
Who does the cooking and sweeps up the floor?
I have no Mummy to put me to bed
Or tell me to go out and play.
Daddy, I'll be such a very good boy
If you'll bring me a Mummy some day.'

His jet walrus moustache would tremble with emotion, while the gin-sodden females pulled out the hankies to dry their eyes. They loved my grandfather. He was very popular with everyone, especially the women, because of his good looks and artistic ability. Of course, this was a source of great satisfaction to my grandfather and a source of great unease to my gran.

These times I am talking about must go back to somewhere like the 1900s. Back to the time of music hall stars like Vesta Tilley, who dressed up as a man, comedians like Gus Elan and turns like Kate Karney. They all appeared at the London Music Hall in Shoreditch High Street, the Collins Music Hall by Islington Green, the Hackney Empire in Mare Street and all the other music halls in the East End.

In these halls, the gallery was for the better-off, at threepence and sixpence a seat. The more hard-up would go on the jam shelf. These were the seats way up, almost touching the ceiling. The performers looked like insects. But the accoustics were good and the performers had strong, clear voices (there were no microphones then) and they could be heard better high up than down in the expensive seats. So what those on the jam shelf lost on the roundabouts, they gained on the swings.

On leaving the theatre, a couple might go into the fish shop and ask for Eightp'ny and Ha'porth. This meant a piece of fish costing eightpence and a portion of chips to the value of one halfpenny.

In those days a loaf of bread cost a penny-halfpenny. If it was under-weight, you would be given a piece of cake to make up. Some mothers would take their joint of meat in a dish round to the local baker's, where it would be cooked for them while they went and had a pint. This was mostly on Sundays, the only day a roast was cooked. The pubs were open all day. When trade was brisk, the publican could not take the customers' money quick enough, so he would just scoop it onto the floor on his side of the bar and pick up the coins at the end of the day.

Those were the days when standing up to give a song was somewhat of a risk. If your audience disapproved, a rotten tomato or a bad egg would surely come hurtling towards you before the end of your performance.

Although Grandfather was always a placid, peace-loving man, one thing that used to bring his lower nature to the fore was when the caretaker of the flats used to come up in the early hours and tell him that his party would have to stop. Grandad always made the same reply: 'You can come in and have a drink, or go down by the stairs or over the landing.' The caretaker preferred to leave, and always chose the normal exit route.

At one period my grandparents moved away from the flats to Clapton, at that time a better-class neighbourhood. The rent was much more than Craven Buildings, but the house was ideal. They had it all to themselves, which was more room than they needed. It was clean and airy, with a beautiful large garden at the back, for the children. There were rose bushes and even an apple tree. This place was really something after the grubby old street they had just come from, with its stinking, noisy railway almost on top of them. This was just the thing for a family. A real nice house in a real nice street.

It lacked just one thing. Neighbourliness. It took some weeks to discover this. The women didn't sit out of doors when the weather was nice in this street. Oh dear, no. Nan missed her little chats with the women when she was on her way to the market of a morning. The journey there and back had always consisted of a series of short stops, as she exchanged interesting words of news, plus the latest local scandals. She missed her chats with the neighbours as she stood looking over the balcony, watching the trains go by. Poyser Street was a dump. The buildings were decrepit; the whole street gave you a feeling of gloom. But the people gave you the feeling of belonging, a sense of security and friendship, despite the fights and arguments which cropped up from time to time.

So, in spite of all the affluence and respectability of Clapton, Gran was back in her old flat in Poyser Street within six weeks.

In those days, only the fraillest children were entitled to have a spoonful of malt at school. Their mothers paid a penny a day for this. Those were the days when you could send round to the grocer's for a ha'penny worth of jam, which would be plopped onto a piece of greaseproof paper. Children who could not afford glass marbles used cleaned-up cherry stones. Most of the stones were acquired by picking them up in the street. It wasn't often that children then were able to taste the luxury of cherries.

It was during these hard times, when she was in her early thirties, that my Gran Gullis became widowed and left with seven young children to fend for. She was allowed three shillings a week for each child by the then Board of Guardians, who, from what I have been told, were not quite as virtuous as the name implies. If you were really in trouble with money, the Guardians' remedy was the Workhouse. This was the place that every working-class person dreaded. The place where my mother was recommended to go when she was pregnant and my father was sick. I am thankful that it never came to that, due to Gran's strong loathing of the place. She decided to help Mum out, despite her own problems. I am lucky indeed, not to have been born in such a universally despised house.

'I had to bring them up on three bob a week,' Gran told me. 'When Edie had to go to the convalescent, I had to pay it to the Board of Guardians. If I didn't pay on the dot, they'd be round after me. This woman called once, after I hadn't paid. A tweed suit, she had on. Her hair greying and parted in the middle, pulled into a bun at the back of her head. A real stinker, she was. "It costs us eleven shillings a week to keep your daughter in convalescence, you know," she said. "Well, does it now?" I says. "Then why is it you only allow me three bob a week for her when she's at home, then?" '

Gran used to talk about Grandfather as I sat at her hygienic tea-table, scoffing her apple tart or experiencing the succulence of her strawberry jam, spread liberally on soft, white, fresh bread.

'How come Grandad had two brothers named George, Gran?' I asked.

'Well,' she said, leaving her kitchener and sitting down at the table. She smoothed out her apron, as though this was going to take all her concentration. 'Your great-grannie was a lovely old soul, do anyone a good turn whenever she could. Real Cockney she was, too. She had only one shortcoming, drink. So she already had a boy named George, you see. Now, when it came to christening the next baby, no-one had a clue what to call him. It was just something that hadn't been discussed yet. I suppose they thought they'd leave it to your great-gran to decide.

'Well, on the way round to the church, Great-Gran is struck with an instantaneous thirst as she passes the Wheatsheaf. So, of course, in she goes, while the kids wait outside holding the baby. Well, by the time she gets round the church, she is not altogether clear just what is going on. The old vicar has the baby in his arms and is leaning over the font. He turns his eyes up to Great-Gran, peering at her through steel-rimmed spectacles. "Mother, what do you name this child?" asks the vicar (in that voice they use).

' "George," Great-Gran answered deliberately, although not altogether audibly. The whole family looked at her in astonishment. No-one was brave enough to confront Great-Gran on her decision or remind her that she already had a son named George, for fear of showing the family up in front of the vicar.

'Your great-grandad, summoning all his heroic courage to put forward the argument of the inconvenience of having two sons named George, moved over towards Great-Gran. "Er, hm, love," he risked. "We've already got a George . . . love," Great-Gran raised her voice a little at this and Great-Grandad went scurrying back to his original position like a frightened little pup, and who could blame him? Great-Gran stood there, one hand folded over the other, resting on her belly. Without moving her hands, she raised an index finger to the vicar, who stood waiting patiently, fascinated by such indecision. "Go on, Vic," she said. "George." And that's how it happened. Now go on, eat your tart.'

Despite the hard times Gran Gullis went through, she has always been a sincere Tory. Nothing has ever moved her from her Conservative beliefs. She explained her ideas to me like this: 'You have to conserve your money, like when you save up. I have always believed in saving something for a rainy day and I've always put something aside, no matter how hard up I've been. It's helped me out time and again. That's what the Conservatives stand for, conserving money, and it's a good thing. They wouldn't have stood for those Communist blokes in my time, I can tell you, wanting to overthrow our Government and all that. That's why the country is in the state it's in. It's those Communists that's behind it all, that's why.'

Gran was always proud of the fact that she once saw Queen Victoria go by in her horse-drawn coach, as she passed through Holborn. Gran used to live there as a child, in Ely Place. 'She was a dear old soul, was Queen Victoria.'

This was Gran Gullis. Middle class, in comparison with those who lived down the rough end of Poyser Street. A small, frail woman, but with a will or iron which prompted her to keep going. Outwardly strict and tough, she was inwardly a tender, sensitive person. An individualist who expected favours from no-one and who never asked for anything, she never owed rent and always paid her callers regularly. 'That's how I want it. You've always got your pride then,' she would say.

My grandparents on my father's side were a different proposition altogether. With Gran Barnes, it was an 'anything goes' atmosphere. Although I was not in day-to-day contact with her, as I was with Gran Gullis, there was something about Gran Barnes that seemed to attract me. She had no politics or passionate beliefs like Gran Gullis. She was never serious-minded enough for that. She seemed to me as though she never had a care in the world, although she must have done. She radiated a sort of love and joviality, the like of which I have never seen in any other person of her age, since she died. To be with her was to feel safe, as if everything in the whole world was just perfect, and there was nothing to worry about, nothing to fear. To be with Gran was just one big laugh. What a great character she was.

Of course, it was only as I grew older that I was able to appreciate her personality. It took some time for my childish fear of her calling after me to wear off.

Like many of the others down the rough end, she bought her foodstuffs from day to day. She could never understand why my mother did most of her shopping at the weekend, to see her over Sunday. Gran just bought what she needed each day from the Bethnal Green Market. Of a Sunday, she would shop down Brick Lane on the stalls. Mind you, there were always plenty of shops open on Sundays in that area, for the simple reason that it was mostly Jews who lived round Brick Lane, and their Sabbath is on a Saturday. This suited the Gentile population of Bethnal Green just fine. They could always run over the Jew's and get some more sugar or milk, if they happened to run out during the day.

Nearly all the families had the same sleeping arrangements. They usually had three rooms: kitchen and two bedrooms. The parents slept in one room and the children, of both sexes and varying ages, all slept together in the other. This was no hardship, for they knew nothing else, and were ignorant of the effects this sort of arrangement might produce.

Hospitals were best kept away from. It was not unknown for children not to be taken to hospital, even after a fall. A cut eye or a broken nose would be left to heal by itself, leaving the child with a peculiarity like a permanent bump on the forehead or a finger that could not be straightened. Bandy-legged children were not uncommon then. The mothers used to say, 'It comes from making them stand on their legs too early.' Perhaps this was one cause. Perhaps another was the lack of nourishing food.

I asked Gran Gullis how she came to meet my grandfather. 'Well, he used to work in the stables opposite my house. He used to take the horses out in the street to clean them. Me living opposite, well he used to look over at me. One day he plucked up his courage and came over to me and asked to take me out one night. And that's how I got to know him.' What a romantic setting, I thought. A stable in a slum.

3. Holly Bush Gardens

Well, I seem to have strayed from my main subject somewhat, that of Mum and Dad. They lived in Poyser Street for about four years or so, then they moved once again. This time to Holly Bush Gardens. This is the first place I can remember clearly. Don't let the name fool you. There wasn't a garden to be seen down the street. The roadway itself was little more than eight foot wide. On one side of the street were little sweat shop factories, horse stables and archways which were used as garages and owned by private transport firms.

I lived in a crumbling block of privately owned flats. It was only a very small block, housing about ten families. At the side of the flats stood terraced houses. We faced the dirty-looking factories, stables and garages. The layout was very similar to Poyser Street.

Holly Bush Gardens. What a name, as though the bloke who christened it was taking the piss out of us for living there. Holly Bush Dumping Ground would have described the place better. And this, Mum said, was a bit more refined than Poyser Street.

There were two landings in our flats. The stairs and banisters were made of wood. They used to creak in protest as you went up and down. Riddled with woodworm, I shouldn't wonder.

Our flat consisted of three small rooms. The kitchen, where we sat and Mum cooked. The front room, or best room, was used only when we had visitors. The furniture in this room was part of the HP stuff that Gran had signed for. It looked quite nice in there until Dad decided to hang wooden egg cases converted into bird cages on the walls. For Dad had now caught the same ailment as Uncle George — bird breeding.

The best part about the flat was that it was small and didn't cost a lot to keep warm. Mum had no gas stove but she did have a kitchener. This was a fire, oven and hotplates combined. They always said that they were much better than a gas oven. True or not, who knows. It might be just another old wives' tale. Who didn't like change after years of using a kitchener?

I slept with my parents. I could have slept in the best room, but with Mum's upbringing it was essential to have a best room to take our visitors. This was one of the first conflicts that I can remember between my parents. Mum wanted it just so, with everything in its right place. Dad wasn't too particular. The egg boxes hanging on the front room wall were no eyesore to him.

My mother was always in a rush of a morning. At Poyser Street Dad had been out of work, due to his nervous breakdown. As soon as I was six weeks old, Mum started work. She had to. They could not have lived, otherwise. She would get up, have a wash, wrap me in a blanket and take me next door for Gran Gullis to look after me.

Dad was out of work for a good while. He would stand on the corner all day with George Brown and all the other out-of-works. When Mum came home from work at six o'clock, Dad would still be out. He would not reach home till ten o'clock in the evening, some nights. But he nearly always seemed to get a little money. He would go out hoisting or screwing with Uncle George. Sometimes he'd be lucky, sometimes not.

Anyway, Dad seemed to have little interest in anything. The trouble was, he had been to his doctor who had sent him to hospital. Dad did not carry on with the treatment. I don't think he ever fully recovered from his breakdown. Even his sisters say that he was not an easy man to understand. It may have been this that always made me feel that there was a barrier between us, although he was always good to me.

Then, Dad struck lucky. He had got in with one of the local herbs. He put him in line for a job as a bookie's runner, for a maker by the name of Eddie Solomans. Dad's pitch was on his old territory, Poyser Street. He took his bets standing just inside Craven Buildings. So now at Holly Bush Gardens we were well-off again for a while.

My Dad used to stand in Poyser Street of a morning about twelve o'clock, taking bets. This was the arrangement. The big fish, who never came up in court and never had a blemish against him was Solly (short for Solomons). No one knew anything about him, what he looked like or where he lived, except, of course, Dad and his brother Ted. Solly was just a name. He was like a sort of ghost. Only his boys knew him on sight, and none of them would ever let on who the bloke was they'd been talking to. Solly was the gaffer, not only of the bookmaking game, but every other racket that went on. His boys didn't piss about with hoisting and pilfering just to keep their kids in food and clothing, like my Uncle George and my father and their mates did. He never lifted a finger. He left that to his boys.

My dad never qualified for promotion into the ranks of the elite, like being an info man, or a creeper, or wheeler, or something like that. He, like many of his mates, was only eligible for running a betting pitch. It wasn't easy to get in with the big boys. If you did, you commanded (and got) great respect from all, for at least a square mile of Bethnal Green. To get in, you bettered yourself, so to speak. The lob was higher, it's true, but the risk was greater. So a lot of the runners were content to live the peaceful life of taking bets. That is, it was peaceful until you got your collar felt. If that happened too often, the fine would increase and, of course, Solly's capital would decrease. So you had to be shrewd not to get caught by the Plain'uns too often. Otherwise, Solly would have to pension you off and get a new runner who had a clean slate, as far as the Law knew.

My father was as shrewd as they come. I think the most they ever done him was twice, in all the time he worked the pitch. His shrewdness was like a natural gift. The Law used to come down the street, at times dressed as workmen, or something like that. Dad seemed to know straight away. Old Jim Barber was a pensioner who stood in the road as look-out. He might not give a window cleaner coming down the road a second thought. But Dad would be onto him right away, even if he was taking a bet off someone. He seemed to know just who was about, from one end of the street to the other.

He used to say, 'Jim, I don't know what I pay you for. I smelt him a mile off.'

Yet Jim had done this sort of work for many years.

The Law were getting a bit sick of this and they were determined to have Dad. On one occasion, they did. The street was clear, not a Bogey in sight. Dad had two or three blokes waiting to put on a bet. He was working as fast as he could, 'cause it don't pay to have punters hanging round you in any numbers. You can't keep a proper look-out. A small van turned into Poyser Street from under the arch. It made its way slowly down on the nearside, the side where Dad was working. He didn't give it a second thought. He'd never had this' one worked on him before. As the van passed the pitch, out jumped a uniformed copper and grabbed him. Got him red-handed, with bets and money.

When they got him down the station, they charged him and treated him nice and friendly. They put him in a room on his own for a time. Now he really had the hump. A Plain 'un walked in with a friendly smile on his face. Right away, Dad knew the Bogey had something up his sleeve. He sat down beside Dad.

'Well, what are you going to do then, Bill?' the Bogey asked. Dad was more suspicious now. 'They don't use your first name for nothing,' he thought.

'What do you mean, what am I going to do?'

'Well, you know you're in for a good fine, don't you? And we've left you alone all the time you've been working that pitch.'

Dad knew that was a load of old cobblers. He knew it was only Jim Barber's skill and his own that had kept him safe. The Law hadn't had any choice but to leave them alone. The Plain'un pulled out a packet of cigarettes and offered one to Dad. Dad took one, his eyes on the Bogey at the same time. The Bogey gave him a light. They sat in silence for a few seconds. Then the Bogey said, with a deeply concerned tone in his voice, 'Well, look, Bill. You haven't been up at all yet, have you? After all this time and not a blemish to your name. It'll be about twenty-five quid, you know.'

Dad wasn't unduly concerned about that. What he didn't want was a run of fines, otherwise he'd be out of work. Tilly would pay the fines all right, but there was a limit to what he would stand.

'Well, look, Bill. I can get you off this one. But I've got to know who you're working for. That's all we want. Tell me that, then we can forget the whole matter. I mean, you don't want to be had up, do you? I mean, just for the sake of not telling us that, do you?' The Bogey was still using his sympathetic tone.

Dad answered deliberately and emphatically, 'No, sorry. Can't do that.'

He would rather go before the Beak than do that, for a number of reasons. One fine wouldn't strain his relationship with Tilly too much. If he told the police who he was working for, it would strain the relationship to exasperation point. Dad didn't fancy lying under the arch one night with a black eye. Also, if the police got onto Tilly, it could put Dad out of work as well.

So there were two good reasons, out of many others, why Dad wasn't going to turn grass. He kept mum, reported to Tilly about being nicked, paid his fine and continued his job of work. He kept extra alert now, in case the Law became more zealous in their duty of dragging in the street bookies.

But Dad was as shrewd as they come. To be one step ahead of the Plain'uns, he decided to employ the services of his younger brother Ted, who was out of work, as usual. Ted's wages would be something like ten bob a week, for a couple of hours a day. This was Dad's latest plan.

Now, if a Bogey jumped on you while you were on the pitch, he had to be sure that you actually had betting slips in your pocket. On your person, as they say. So Ted's job was to hang about with Dad and when Dad had taken about half a dozen slips, he handed them to Ted. Ted would then run like a greyhound down the street and make for Solly's place with the slips. Dad kept the money for the bets on him, for he could only trust himself with the stuff. Then he would pay Solly at the end of the day.

Dad also had a thick canvas bag, with a clock on it. Once the bag was shut at two o'clock, it could not be opened again. This was so that you couldn't work a crafty one in after the two o'clock race, backing the winner after it had been run. But Dad's ingenuity was not to be defeated in this matter.

First, let me tell you a little more about Ted's job. They used to call the pitchman a bookie's runner. He was not a bookie's runner as such. It was those who did the running from the pitchman to the bookie himself who were called runners.

Ted really could run. The faster you ran, the smaller the odds of being seen by a Bogey. The bookmaker's place would not be very far from his pitches. Ted was well fitted out for the job. He always wore a pair of canvas plimsolls. This was not solely for the purposes of making a quick get-away, but also because plimsolls were cheap and durable. On one occasion, a Bogey must have been waiting for him at the end of Poyser Street. That Bogey chased him right down Old Bethnal Green Road but Ted was up the street like a Mick the Miller in his prime. That copper had no chance.

Now the canvas bag which the bookmaker had provided Dad with was foolproof. It was well-known by the pitchmen that the bag could not be fiddled. Solly had emphasised this fact when Dad started work for him.

'It's never been known, Bill,' Solly informed him, his fat chops shaking in agreement as he spoke. 'There's no way of getting a dodgy one in there, so I wouldn't advise trying it.'

But Dad was never one to take people's word on anything, especially where money was concerned. So he thought he would try out just how skillful he was at putting in a dodgy bet. He thought about it for days. He examined the bag and the clock inside and out. He tried to puzzle out a way of stopping the clock until his already-won bet had been popped in.

Then, after several weeks, it clicked. Just like that. It was useless tampering with the clock. The way to do it was simplicity itself. He waited to hear who had won a certain race. Then he wrote out his bet, putting the winner down. He'd have about five or ten bob on it. The slip would be very small, only about one-

55

and-a-half by two inches, and on the thinnest paper. He would then get a matchstick and shave it down a little. Then he would roll the betting slip into a cylinder round the matchstick, till it was nice and firm. He'd take the corner of the canvas bag and gradually work the matchstick through the closely stitched seam. When the slip was almost through, he would withdraw the matchstick.

After learning this trick, Dad started to do even better. He would slip one in every week, until Tilly began showing signs of discontent about it.

'Every week this one, Bill. Ten bob to win. To win, mind. Every week this little bleeder comes up. Can't make it out, Bill. Do you know who the bloke is?'

'No, no idea, guv. Too many punters to remember the bloke.'

Solly sat at his desk, his fat, bulging belly pressing up against it. He looks at Dad, his big fat chops hanging and his eyes squinting. There is silence, the silence that comes after watching the stunning performance of an illusionist Solly knows that Dad's up to something, and Dad knows that Solly knows he is. But nothing can be proven.

After these few words with Solly, Dad decided to leave a longer period between his dodgy slips. He controlled his natural love of wealth and popped one in every month or three weeks. This seemed to calm Solly's nerves to some extent. Still, he knew who that monthly slip belonged to . When he opened the bag, he'd say, 'There it is again. That little bleeder again. I wondered when he was due again.'

Dad always tried to look as serious as he could on these distressing occasions of Solly's , he knew what he was up to, but could not for the life of him find out how this piece of work was done. It was a trick that would have left the members of the Magic Circle bewildered.

Now to explain the flat further. At Holly Bush Gardens my mother would sit me on the kitchen table of a morning, quickly wash my arms, legs and face, plonk me down on a chair and give me my breakfast, if she had time. She would then tear round to Poyser Street and dump me onto Gran. If I was a bit early for school, I would have a slice of toast and a cup of tea. The school was just in Old Bethnal Green Road – St. Jude's Infants.

We had no sink in the flat. If you wanted a wash, you either went out on the landing and used the communal sink there, which amounted to washing in public really, or you got a kettle, filled it up and put it on the hot plate at the side of the fire.

56

There was one toilet on the landing, which you shared with the neighbour opposite. This arrangement of sharing was a continuous source of conflict. One woman would accuse the other of not taking her turn at washing it out. Also, it did not do to have an attack of diarrhoea. If you were unfortunate enough to contract such an ailment, you could bet your bottom dollar someone next door would be in the toilet.

My father would get wild over this. He would wait and wait, getting more impatient all the time. Suddenly he would say, loud enough for the bloke inside to hear, 'I reckon he's bleeding well died in there.'

The bugs nested comfortably in the wall as by right, having been in occupation many a year. Only we didn't call them bugs if we were on a bus, or if we were not sure if other people within hearing distance had them or not. Of course, almost everyone in these old houses had them. But in front of teachers and people like that, who we thought were posh, we would be quite ashamed to mention the word 'bug'.

To get round this, our Cockney slang was brought into operation. If you were sitting behind a boy in class you might detect one of these fellows crawling down his back. You see, these bugs had the nasty habit of getting under your coat collar for warmth and breeding purposes. If you spotted one, as I have said, you said to the boy in front, 'Oi, Jimmy. Mahogany Baxter.' Jimmy would know immediately that a bug was taking its constitutional along his back. I suppose the word 'mahogany' was used because the bugs were deep red in colour. 'Baxter' was, I suppose, because they seemed to favour people's backs rather than any other parts of the anatomy.

They were also known as Hearth Rugs, or Steam Tugs to the well-initiated. Or the Red Army, though this term would only be used if the house was really overrun with them. In that case, a sulphur candle would be purchased at the oil shop in Bethnal Green Road. It would be left in the infested room all night, while the whole family slept in another room.

By the next morning, the sulphur would have done its work. Not a bug to be seen. It would not be long, though, before Mrs. Jones next door started to complain of a Red Army attack. The bugs, you see, had been driven from one household to another by the sulphur. So what it amounted to was that the more sulphuring you could carry out, the longer your place stayed bug-free. Miss it for a week and the rotters were back again. What a terribly unsettled life it must have been for those Mahoganies.

You would frequently come across a lone bug on the bed or wall. Some people, of whom I was one, could not resist the urge to take hold of the intruder and smash him between the thumbnails, or between the wall and thumbnail. This became an immediate instinct to many, adults and children alike.

The only thing that ruined this pleasurable and intriguing activity for some youngsters was the vile smell that the bugs gave off when they were smashed in this way. Not only that, you would have to make sure Mum wasn't about before carrying out the execution. The deep red blood that spurted from the victim would stain the wall. This would be sufficient evidence for Mum to know that a lone Mahogany had been slaughtered by the thumbnail.

'Who's been smashing bugs on the wall?' she would moan as she ran the damp cloth over it. 'The times I've told yer, use a match and burn the bleeders to death. Not your bleeding thumbnail. Look at the mess on this wall.'

A real buggy house would have them in the armchairs, in the bed and the curtains too. If bugs were found in the bed, it would be stripped and paraffin would be applied to the whole of the frame and springs. Everything would be all right again for a while, but really these poor wives were fighting a losing battle.

They became so used to the bugs in some houses that to have two or three sitting on your shoulder would cause no undue concern. You would just casually pick them off and throw them in the fire. Then you would hear a crisp pop. If the family had visitors at the weekend and felt in a jovial mood, they would bet on two or three bugs making their way slowly up the wall. At the end of the race the runners would be put to death.

Mice were another nuisance. In those days no-one had a fridge to protect their food. The mice would eat their way through the wooden cupboards and devour whole, or in part, whatever was there. Time and again, my mother has thrown away food that had been got at by mice, a thing she could ill afford to do. Those who were really desperate would cut off the part of cheese or bread that hadn't been eaten by the mice and use it. They may or may not have realised that the mice could have been walking over that part of the food, even if they hadn't actually eaten it. It was a terrible strain on the nerves, too, if you were afraid of mice. To have one jump out of an armchair you were about to sit in. Or if you were about to draw the curtains and a mouse was hanging on for dear life on the inside.

Other quite frequent visitors were fleas. A nurse would visit the school religiously every week and would run her steel comb none too tenderly through your hair. If fleas were found, you would immediately be ordered to the cleansing station. Possibly your home might be visited, culminating in your bedding also going to be fumigated. But this sort of thing was not frequent, and it was a disgraceful thing to have your bedding carted out. So as you may have gathered, I have become somewhat of an authority on vermin.

I was still quite young when we moved to Holly Bush Gardens, but I seemed to miss Poyser Street somehow. I couldn't remember much of it really, but I somehow seemed to feel safe there. I suppose that was because it was only a tiny street. Everybody knew everybody else, and their business. It seemed like one big family. Not always happy, it's true, but reliable.

At Holly Bush Gardens I was bored stiff. I would spend most of my time pinching the nose of a small, six-month-old baby who sat in a pram outside the flats. That is, until the father caught me red-handed and delivered a resounding wallop to my left ear.

We were fairly well-off now, for Dad was working the pitch in Poyser Street then. I can remember at that time I had a summer suit bought me, as well as a navy blue one. The latter resembled an air-force uniform, for some reason or other. Perhaps that was the fashion for children then. I don't know. But the thing was that these suits, shirts, socks were bought brand-new, in a shop, not on a stall down Cheshire Street.

Oh yes, at that time we was well-off. Dad's pocket was full of bees and honey, as you might say if you were in the pub. For everyone knows how suspicious the law is if they see a bloke with plenty of cash. You use words that the Law don't understand. But even then, the Law would pick up these slang terms and decode them.

I had a new, three-wheeler bicycle bought for me, and a cowboy suit. We were certainly in the money then. But the war was to alter that. If Dad had been able to keep working the pitch, we might have been quite well-off today. But, as they say, all good things come to an end. The only thing is, the bad times seem to exceed the good times, don't they? Well, we were in the good times. No second-hand clobber for me. Posh I was, not like most of the other kids. Do you know, their mothers used to buy their clothes second-hand, down Club Row?

Now Club Row was, and still is, very cheap. But the mums would make it even cheaper. They would buy a suit or a pair of trousers a size or two too large, so that as sonny boy grew, the clobber wouldn't have to be renewed. The more he grew, the better it fitted. I can remember boys down Poyser Street. They'd be running after a ball, or away from a house where they had been playing Knocking Down Ginger. They'd get half-way up the road and down would come their trousers. What a laugh that would be. They'd just pull them up, as though it were an every-day occurence.

Another way of extra economy by the mums was to go in for a little hoisting. They would do this to save money. Or perhaps the stallholder wanted too high a price for the garment. Or perhaps little Johnny's jacket had worn out before he had had time to outgrow it and Mum wasn't going to lay out another tanner or so for a further one. Not already, anyway.

So this was the drill. She would sort out a stall with plenty of people around it. She would work her way to the front. Her largest shopping bag would be hanging from her left arm, but by one handle only, so that it lay open towards the stall. She would scan the stall and sort out what she was interested in. She would make up her mind what she fancied. Now her full attention would be on the stallholder. His attention would only have to be drawn away and his head turned for the minutest part of a second, and part of his merchandise would quickly disappear into the large mouth of a shopping bag.

Sometimes two women would work together at this game. One to draw the stallholder's attention and to keep him rabbitting, the other to do the hoist. The stallholder would need eyes all round his head, like a band, to catch the quick and skillful hand of a well-seasoned hoister.

Although in Holly Bush Gardens we had never had it so good, I still seemed to be bored stiff. I even got fed up with the drum set my father bought me. It was eventually ruined after my boozer of an uncle had put a broom through the bass drum. This was one night at one of the house parties that my father used to give.

These parties were for no special reason, other than to get well pissed and enjoy the good fortune that we now had. They'd all congregate in our small flat at about half-past seven on a Saturday night. It was that packed, it was worse than being on the Tube in the rush hour. Most of the visitors stood up. They had no choice. They'd all be elbow to elbow, knocking back cups of tea and jawing about the dogs or about work.

One thing they all liked to talk about was boxing. This must have been because the East End produces a lot of good fighters. The more up-to-date John Stracey of Bethnal Green springs to mind here. Joe Louis was the greatest champion ever, by their reckoning. I can just remember him, a great mountain of a man. They were more colour prejudiced in those days than now, but although Joe was black this was nothing to them. His great skill and fighting record made him that much whiter to them.

You would never see a coloured person in the streets then at all. The only dark-skinned person you would see then was the Indian Toffee Man. You would look upon him as some sort of mystic or curio. He wasn't part of your world then. He was sort of outlandish to us. In your childish mind you imagined him going all the way back to India to stock up with more strands of toffee.

Many of the old people were very superstitious when I was a lad. I think it may have been the influence of the Catholic Church, though many say it was from the Romany stock within the community.

A superstitious grandmother would never change her furniture round on a Friday, for fear of bad luck. It was safe to change it on a Sunday, but heaven knows what would befall her if she turned her bed tick over on the Sabbath. You were never to accept hand-me-downs from a pregnant woman. Her condition would certainly be handed down to. If you put the kettle on, you had to make the tea as well, else bad luck would stalk you for a month after. Unless, that is, a dark-skinned man happened to be the first person to knock on your door the next morning. If you touched a sailor's collar it would also break the bad luck.

Superstition came into street-betting as well. When people went to make a bet, they took a lucky charm with them, like a rabbit's foot. If someone they knew had taken a good win the day before, they would seek him out and rub themselves up against him, hoping that some of the luck would rub off onto themselves.

There are those who just laugh at all this, yet a good many people still sincerely believe it all.

Anyway, in our flat at Holly Bush Gardens they congregated, kids screaming and crying all over the place, the woman downstairs almost demolishing her ceiling with a broom handle, banging up to tell us to keep the noise down. If she thought it was noisy at half-past seven, the Gawd knows what went through her mind at eleven o'clock, when they all came back pissed. They would sing at the top of their shocking voices as they came staggering down the road, leaning on each other for support. The chorus would continue up the wooden stairs and into our flat. It would go on until about two in the morning and, noisy as we were, no-one would ever call the Law.

This was always the unwritten code of the true, genuine working-class Londoners then, and I think it still prevails in some degree today. Even if someone had nicked something from you and you knew the bloke who done it, the Law would never be brought in. If the bloke was caught, you might give him a telling-off, or a seeing-to, and that would be the end of it. But never the Law.

Yes, my father was in the big time then. He used to smoke Kensitas cigarettes, one of the dearest there was. What's more, he'd buy twenty at a time, not ten or five, like most people bought. Or even one. They used to sell them in ones then. My Dad was popular with everyone then, even with the Gullises. If they were in the pub it would be Bill (my father) who would pay. He would spend like mad on everyone he met in the boozer. He was the tops now, not like earlier on when he had nothing. Even Fred Baker came to love him after innumerable pints of free beer. But the war came and Dad's popularity gradually faded with his wealth.

Let me tell you a few more of my experiences while I lived in Holly Street Gardens. There was never much to do round there. I always seemed to have to play on my own. It seemed as though I was the only kid in the street, and even my sadistic pastime with the baby in the pram was now finished. I didn't want another bash in the ear.

One Saturday afternoon, when my Mum was doing a bit of cleaning, I came across an electric fire. It had a long cord on it. I had recently seen a film about deep-sea divers and it fascinated me to think what it was like under the ocean. So now I was going to be a diver. The long wire would be my airline. I wound and wound and wound it round my neck, ready to gradually let it out as I descended deeper into the sea. But I began to feel very unhappy as I felt the pressure of the cord round my throat. I could not call out, hard as I tried. My face now seemed to be swelling up with the presssure. I must have been red as a beetroot.

Then, as luck would have it, my mother came out into the passage for something or other and saw how uncomfortable I was with an electric fire wrapped round my neck. She went crazy.

'Oh, my Gawd. Oh, blimey. Come here.'

She unravelled the cord as quick as she could, got it off, and then sat there looking at me till the usual pasty look came back to my face.

'Oh blimey, you look better now,' she said. 'What ever was you doing, tying that round your neck? Don't you ever do that again. I don't know why you don't go out and play like other kids. You've got a brand new bike and all to go out on.'

Mum was right. I had a cowboy suit with two beautiful silver guns, a smashing bike, a pair of roller skates, the lot. Yet I would have given them all up for an old, home-made, wooden scooter, a piece of wood as a gun and a bit of material for a pirate's hat, if only I could have been with the kids in Poyser Street.

Some Sundays, my father would come back from Club Row with a chicken. Alive and kicking, but not for long. I used to hate the ritual of killing it. Yet at the same time, the way Dad broke its neck fascinated me.

'Why don't you buy dead ones, Dad?' I would ask.

'No,' he would say. 'They're fresher when you does 'em in yourself.'

He would take the poor thing out of his shopping bag, where it had probably been cooped up all morning. Its wings would be flapping about in terror, as though it knew what it was in for. Dad would tie its legs together and hand it upside down on a nail that protruded from our kitchen door. The nail was there solely for the purpose of killing chickens.

Dad would take the bird's neck and give it a sharp twist and pull. All the flapping and struggling was over. I often wondered how my father could do it, but in those days nearly everyone killed their own poultry, and I suppose my Grandfather handed the practice down to my Dad. I always thought of my father as a kind man, who wouldn't hurt any living creature. He used to love animals.

Seeing that I thought so highly of my father, I could have accepted this slaughtering without question and, in my young mind, thought that there was nothing wrong in it. But I just could not accept it then and I find it very hard to accept it now. Of course, we have all got to eat, but the thought of killing any living thing still does not seem right to me, somehow. But then, a lot of things in life do not seem right, and in fact are not right. Unfortunately, we have to live with them.

4. Coronation Cups

Well, it must have been about 1938-39. I was at the ripe old age of five, and I still longed to live in Poyser Street again. The only time I saw that street now was when my parents went round to Gran Gullis. They did this religiously every Sunday afternoon, for tea. Sadly, there don't seem many families who do this now, but the ones who have kept this old custom up, despite modern living, are very fortunate indeed.

Families don't gather together today like they used to. Either they've moved out to a remote suburb, or they've worked their guts out all week to pay the HP man, and have got no life in them to socialise. Some of them have had a go at buying their own houses and think they are middle-class now.

Anyway, we used to go round Gran Gullis' of a Sunday for tea. It was never Gran Barnes' place. She had enough to do to feed her lot, let alone us as well. These Sunday teas were real middle-class turnouts. Gran had a dining table with flaps that could pull out, which made more room for us. There was always a good crowd round Gran's of a Sunday afternoon. I knew I was good for a few bob then.

The table-cloth would be blindingly white. Everything Gran possessed was absolutely clean and pure. Even the wooden seat in her toilet was scrubbed white and clean enough to eat off. 'Cleanliness is next to godliness,' she would say.

Although Gran was scrupulously clean, tidy and correct, you weren't afraid to move in her house. If you wanted to smoke, then you smoked. If I wanted to eat a bag of crumbly crisps, then I ate them. But one thing she would not tolerate was picking your nose at the table, or anywhere else for that matter.

'Ugh, you dirty little tyke, stop that,' she'd say, if she happened to catch me. 'You'll have your eyes fall out.'

This was one thing I didn't like about Gran. Sometimes, as I sat in one of her armchairs by the fire, after having stuffed myself with winkles, cockles, tea and some of Gran's famous apple tart, I would derive some small comfort from my nose-picking activities. Then suddenly, Gran would bring her hand across my prodding finger, almost bending my nose double.

'Now, stop that,' she would say.

Everything on the table was perfectly set out, as though it had all been done with a ruler and T-square. The glass salad bowl sparkled. The whiteness of the plates blended in with the white table-cloth. The smell of cockles and cakes was smashing. It was one big confusion, all trying to sort out where we were going to sit. These teas were regular, every Sunday, yet on every occasion we had the same old thing.

'Well, you sit there, Mary. Bill and George can get up in the corner. Well, no, wait a minute. If we can move the piano up a bit, then George can sit next to Mum, and Fred can . Or would it be better if . . .'

That's how it used to be every Sunday. No organisation whatsoever. All this went on in a room no more than about ten foot by eight.

My Gran's house was real posh. She even had a middle-class aspidistra, a sort of big plant in a pot. She wasn't really well-off. It was was just that her place was reasonably furnished and well-kept. She spoke in a more genteel sort of manner than my Gran Barnes, who was much more boisterous by nature. I suppose this was one of the reasons why I classed Gran Gullis as posh and Gran Barnes as what we call rough and ready. But small and lady-like as Gran Gullis was, she was a spitfire when she was put out.

Even at this early age, I was aware of the difference in the two families, one living at the posh end, the other at the rough end. It seemed as though I had to class myself with one or the other of them. This confused me terribly because I loved both families the same. Although they greeted each other and drank together in the pub, there were still the two different cultures (I suppose you could call it that) which seemed to separate the two.

The two families' speech was also different. Gran Gullis would say 'pardon', Gran Barnes would say 'wot'. The Gullises would say 'Where have you been?', but for the Barneses it would be, 'Wer yu bin?'. To the Barneses, you were pissed. To the Gullises, you had had too much to drink, or you were drunk. To the Gullises, it was your bottom, to the Barneses, your arse. My mother's words and pronunciation remained different to my father's, even after years of marriage, though she picked up bits of my father's dialect. That left me between the two.

I would come back from Gran Barnes' place with an accent like 'rahnd the corner' or 'dahn the road' and other Cockney variations that would be impossible to spell. Gran Gullis would say, 'Ronnie, it isn't "an ahus", it's "a house".' All things like that.

If she gave me a piece of bread and jam, she would say to me,

'Now, what do you say?' and, dutifully, I would say, 'Thank you, Gran.' Round Gran Barnes' the offering wasn't so luxurious. Round there, it was bread and dripping. Although you were deprived of jam, the deficiency was made up in the three-inch thickness of the slice Gran would hand to me.

' 'Ere y'are, you little bleeder. Get that across yer guts.'

When I went to school, I noticed how posh those old teachers spoke. They seemed about a thousand years old to me. Long tweed skirts, flat suede shoes, wire glasses, cameo brooches. Nothing of youth about any of them. They looked and spoke even posher than Gran Gullis. I was really different from them. They dressed better than us and, as I was led to believe by Gran Gullis and my mother, they *were* better than us.

Of course, now I am more experienced in life and have put aside all that some people would have us believe. I can see now that this is all a lot of cobblers. The only thing that separates class is those who exploit and those who are the exploited. Whether they say 'bottom' or 'arse', the two extremes of wealth and poverty are the real obscenities.

Anyway, the strength and character of the Cockney dialect had to win. I couldn't speak posh for the life of me. If I did try it, you could tell a mile off that it was all put on. Not only that, I'd have a right piss taken out of me,

Neither Gran Barnes nor my father ever attempted to teach me to speak like them. They couldn't have cared less. Can you imagine it if they had done? 'No, Ron. Not "ovha there", "ovuh there". Not "pardon", "wot".' It took my Gran Grullis almost a lifetime to make me sound the 't' in butter. At forty years old, I still leave it aht. But a little later on, I will tell you something about my two grandparents' upbringing. Just now, I would like to keep the subject to Poyser Street.

Opposite the terraced houses and flats ran an overhead railway. My Aunt Maud also lived in the flats, on the top floor. How she stuck it up there, I can't imagine. Every ten or fifteen minutes, a train would come rattling by. It was a devastating affair. The crockery on the table would do a jingling dance. Everything in the house seemed to rattle like mad. My uncle would be sound asleep in the armchair, having the guts shook out of him, oblivious to it all.

'He sleeps like the dead,' my aunt used to say. 'That's all he does. Comes home, has his grub, in the armchair and off he goes. Every sodding night. He livens up of a Saturday night, though. Ready for the Dundee Arms.'

If you were up my aunt's place when one of these monsters came roaring past, you put your cup of tea down quickly if you didn't want it all over you. All conversation would stop in midstream, until peace prevailed again for the next ten or fifteen minutes. God knows how they slept through that all night.

Perhaps that's why my uncle was always asleep when he came home from work. He was a master tailor. They tell me they got good pay in those days, but had to work their balls off for it. If that was the case, I could see no evidence of wealth in my aunt's home, though I suppose they weren't exactly starving. But if master tailors were that well paid at that time, what were they doing living in a dump like Craven Buildings?

Their son, Johnny Crawford (not to be confused with my Dad's young brother Johnny Barnes) influenced me in a lot of ways. I think he must have been about four or five years older than me. One thing I liked about him was that he didn't torment the guts out of me, like some of the other bigger boys down Poyser Street did. It was John who taught me the firewood business. He was a born capitalist. The things he used to get up to, to make some bees and honey.

It was usually of a Saturday, when we had plenty of time. He would take me all round Bethnal Green, looking for old timber. We used to search old houses, take a few loose floorboards or chop up an old door that had fallen off its hinges. To start with, we might jump over a wall into a timber yard and nick a few planks. We had a wooden cart that John had made and we put the lot in there. By the time we got back to Poyser Street, we had ample stock to supply the demand, and not a penny outlay in capital.

John was expert at making wood carts and scooters with steel ball-bearing wheels, which we got out of the rubbish bin standing outside a garage. We'd take turns at pushing each other up and down Poyser Street in a go-cart, another one of John's products. The ball-bearings would drive the old girls mad as we blasted past their houses. Once we had a narrow escape from a bucket of water, thrown by a distraught housewife whose old man was on night work.

Anyway, once back in Poyser Street we would take our raw materials and start chopping the wood into small sticks. John had a smashing chopper. It had a shiny polished handle and the head was painted black, all except for the sharp end. It was a beauty. I had my own tool also for the work, one that I had found somewhere or other, but it was nothing like John's. He knew I liked his, so after we had got a good bit done he would let me use it. It was smashing to hold the wood steady with one hand and then, crunch, it'd go straight through. Not like my one. As blunt as arseholes, that was.

Right, so we had all the wood chopped up and piled in the barrow. By now, all the rest of the kids in the street were round us. They'd been asking us to let them help, all the time we'd been chopping up. They knew there was money about, didn't they?

'Well,' said John ('cause he was the governor, the major shareholder, like). 'We'll take you and you.' The two happy faces came foward, the others stood looking disappointed. 'And you lot? Piss off.'

They walked away, threatening to give us the same treatment when they started up in business. So away the four of us went, down Poyser Street. John gave the orders.

'Right, you two. Go up the flats. And you, Ron, start on the houses. And don't forget, it's a Joey a bucket.'

We had plenty of custom. The only snag was, we only had one bucket between three salesmen. This slowed us down quite a bit. But by about three o'clock, we were completely out of stock and had a pocket full of money. Loads of Joeys, a good few bike spanners and even a tosheroon. So we had a share-out.

John kept count of the buckets we sold and knew just how much we had to come. There was no flies on him and he wouldn't stand for no welching. 'Get your money right away,' he'd tell us. 'None of that "next week" lark.' John knew that next week would never come.

After we had all received our profits, we would first make for Dixon's sweet shop which stood right on the corner of Poyser Street and Old Bethnal Green Road. There we would buy these bleeding great gobstoppers. You had to have a mouth like the Blackwall Tunnel to get them in, and a good wallop on the back to get them out again. We'd buy yards and yards of Spanish, which looked like a load of boot laces. There were tubes of sherbet, with a piece of Spanish tubing to suck it up. There were lucky dips for about a halfpenny, with a little novelty inside, toffee apples, ice blocks and many other mouthwatering sweets. There weren't any ice lollies on a stick then. It was just a tube, coloured orange or red.

After gorging our guts round Dixon's, we would make for Bovey's in Cambridge Heath Road. This was an Italian shop, where we would continue our feast with cold lemon drinks, ice cream, oranges, apples and perhaps a bag of peanuts to settle our stomachs. If I was to eat that lot now, I would be sick for a fortnight.

We couldn't go to the extravagance of buying sound fruit, but old Bovey used to let us have specked apples and oranges. They're the ones that are a little bad on one side. He used to cut the bad part away and give you what was left. It used to cost about a farthing, or a halfpenny. You don't see the farthing any more now, but we used to know it as a dadler.

Old Bovey could only speak broken English, though he had been in Bethnal Green for years. Well, you can't wonder at it. What chance did the poor sod have of learning to talk proper among us lot of East Enders? We couldn't speak what some call standard English ourselves, even. But our way of talking is more English than the way that lot talk, as though they've just undergone major surgery on their throats.

Anyway, Old Bovey may not have been able to talk proper English but he had all the swear words off to a T. Course, when we got a bit boisterous in the shop and he knew all our money had gone, he used to chuck us out, using all the English and Italian swear words he knew. Old Bovey had only one eye-ball, but it still wasn't easy to nick an apple or a bag of nuts off him. He was always alert when he had kids in there, and that one penetrating eye would be on you as soon as he saw your hand come up to the counter. It seemed as though that one eye had the power of two. Gawd knows how observant he would have been if he had the other eye to go with it. He had an alertness about him that would have done a top Plain 'un proud.

On the way to Bovey's shop we would have a lark with old Coker, who was right next door to the Italian. He had one eye and all, but what with the dust all over his Boat Race and his heavy eye-lids, he didn't seem to have any eyes at all, just two dark slits. He was a Jewish cabinet maker. He must have been about five hundred years old, a sort of Bethnal Green antique. He never looked clean. Wood dust in his matted hair, dust ground into his shirt, an apron as stiff as a board with glue and dirt.

We'd go in there and watch him working. A real craftsman, he was. He would make a whole suite, right from the planks, and you should have seen him carve wood. He was fantastic. We were more friendly with Coker than Bovey, though. We were that close that we found out from Coker how he lost his peeper.

'Vell, I vos carving der vood von afternoon. I suppose I must have cut into a knot. A piece flew up into mine eye and, brrm, dat vos it.. Finish. It was very awkward at der first, to work like diss, but I soon get used.'

He was a good old stick, was Coker, but of course we used to play him up at times. As we went by, we would bawl in at him, just for a lark you know, 'Coker, Coker, Tapioca.'

Sometimes we would torment the guts out of him, while we stood in his shop. Things like hiding his pencil. He'd hunt high and low for it, turning over all the shavings that lay under his feet. Judging by the amount of dust and shavings on the floor, I don't think he ever used a broom in his life. After we thought he had suffered enough, we'd put the pencil back on his bench. But of course, he knew we'd done it.

There was only one way of getting rid of us. This was Coker's last resort. 'Course, if he was busy he would say, 'Now come on, boys. You've got to go now and let me get on. I don't want to be here till 1 am again tonight.' They really worked in those little shops then. But we used to hang on and hang on. So at the finish Coker would use his weapon, the weapon that gave him the full advantage. He'd get as close as he could to you, and take out his glass peeper. It'd fair turn you over.

'Ugh,' we'd say. 'Put it back, Coker, for Christ's sake.'

He'd chase you all round the shop with it. You knew, once he'd started that lark, that he would keep it up till you pissed off. Having one eye seemed to be some sort of advantage to him, as far as us lot were concerned. The thing was, though, me being only small, I was tempted to see if I could get me own pork pie out. Then Johnny told me that Coker's eye wasn't a real one and that he couldn't see anything out of it.

'Then what's he have it for, if it can't see nothing?' I said.

'Oh, shit.' John answered, and went on to Bovey's.

That was the trouble with me, my mother used to say. I asked too many questions. She was right. Well, I mean, look at the glass eye. I had to know everything about it. It puzzled me considerably. I kept wondering why he put it in the empty socket, if it didn't make the least bit of difference. If John had put up with me a bit longer, instead of pissing off like he did, I would have tried to find out from him what it was made of, how they made them, and where you could buy them. But all of these questions questions went unanswered.

I remember once my dad answering my questions about money. He had the patience of a saint with me. It all started when I asked him why we have to use money. This one had him beat for a minute.

'Well, you've got to use it, that's all. It's . . . it's the stuff they value everything by. That's why.'

'But why don't they let you just go into the shop, Dad, and have what you want? Why do you have to use money?'

'Well, look.' Dad tried once again to satisfy me. 'This is how it all come about. Years and years ago, they used to change one thing for another. Right?' I nodded.

'If I had, say, a boat and didn't have any meat, and you had just been hunting and had caught a rabbit or something, and you wanted to use my boat; then you'd give me your meat and I would lend you the boat. That's how it all started. But they found it wasn't a very convenient way of going on. So what they done was, they collected certain stones and used them in lieu of the goods. That's how you come to use money today.'

'Yes, but Dad,' I said, 'that ain't fair. 'Cause I might find more stones than you do. Then I can get more gear like that, can't I?'

'Well,' Dad answered, getting a little exhausted now. 'Yes, that's true enough. But there's nothing you can do about that.'

I persisted. 'Yes but Dad, supposing. . . .'

'Oh, that boy,' my mother broke in. 'If he don't stop asking questions, I'll go bleeding crazy. Now give it a rest. You want to know the ins and outs of a nag's arse, you do.'

My mother was right. But when you are a child you never seem to get to the root of anything, somehow.

Anyway, after visiting Coker and Bovey's, the last call, for our final blow-out would be the pie and mash shop in Bethnal Green Road. We'd go in and have a pie and mash each, covered in liquor, and smother the lot in salt and vinegar. It was grand.

Now we might have a couple of coppers left, so with that we could buy a fag each, to relax with. A lot of shops used to refuse kids. But the Italian cafe (which is still standing in Bethnal Green Road, near the Salmon and Ball) knew me because I used to get my father's fags in there. They knew I only lived over the road. So we had just enough for a fag each, and in I used to go.

'Four fags, please.'

'But you usually have twenty Kensitas,' he would say.

Then I'd say, 'Yes, but my Dad's had a bad week on the book this week,' meaning his bookmaking pitch, 'and he can't afford it this week.' It worked every time.

Well, now I was about six and old enough to solve my own problem of having no kids to play with where we lived. So I used to take a ball of chalk round to Poyser Street. My mother done her nut when she first found out where I was going, but after she got used to the idea she didn't take a lot of notice. Perhaps she

72

didn't like me playing down there, with that rough lot. But I loved it. Anyway, my dad was there of an evening on his pitch, paying out and taking bets for the late racing.

At this stage, I began to visit Gran Barnes a bit more often, of my own accord. I liked her all right, but I was still a little timid of her, after the way she used to bawl after me.

Again on these visits, young as I was, I could see the difference between Gran Gullis' place and Gran Barnes'. Gran Barnes was every bit as clean and pure as Gran Gullis, but there was a difference. The two Grans always looked as though they had just been sent back from the laundry, they were that particular.

As you went into Gran Barnes' place, you would notice that she had newspaper for a table cloth. Gran Gullis had a pure white linen one. But under Gran Barnes' newspaper, the wooden boards of the table top were scrubbed every bit as white as Gran Gullis' toilet seat. Gran Barnes never had a cup that was truly serviceable. They all had the handle missing, a crack down them or a lump chipped out. The kids sometimes had to make do with a jam jar for their tea, if there were too many adults in the house.

Grandad Barnes had his own special cup. It was a real beauty. As soon as he had finished his tea, it would promptly be washed up and put on the highest shelf of the food cupboard, out of harm's way. Sometimes, if I kept on enough, he used to let me hold it and examine it more closely. All the time I had it in my possession, neither Gran nor Gramps could relax. When the strain became too much for them, it was taken away and put well out of harm's way.

It wasn't a cup, really. It was mug, a coronation mug of Edward the Seventh. Of course, I didn't know anything of that. It was the shininess and the colours on it that fascinated me, I suppose. On it was the face of a bearded old man, and when I first saw the cup I asked, 'Who's that old bloke then, Gramps? Is it your Dad?'

Grandfather Barnes was always a quiet man and didn't have a lot to say. He just grinned down at me and said, 'Wish it bloody was.'

Many of the jugs which were kept specially for getting beer were very attractive. Most were made of porcelain. I remember one in particular which was a bottle-green at the base, merging gradually into a brighter green, until at the top it became a very pale green. The base, the top and the elegantly curved handle were decorated with gold leaf. A beautiful piece of work indeed.

There were also more modest efforts made of plaster, painted with white enamel. Even more modest was the cheap, metal type of mug, also white enamelled, which had innumerable chips all over it.

Gran Barnes never had any mats, as far as I can remember. There had been one in front of the kitchener, with a great hole in it. It's reign didn't last long, after Grandad nearly broke his neck on it when he caught the toe of his boot under the hole. But the bare boards were always scrubbed and kept spotless.

Gran had a gas oven by now. The only trouble was, you couldn't turn it on without a pair of pliers. The switches had broken for some reason or another. The bedroom was furnished with a bed, and that was it. Of a night, the passage was in complete darkness. The Washes and the toilet were downstairs. If the kids wanted to tom tit after dark, they used to hold themselves right to the next morning before going. It wasn't only the dark. They had to go right out into the yard to get to it.

My father used to tell me what he used to do of a night, when he came home and the passage was pitch black. 'Used to leave a newspaper under a mat inside the passage. When I came home I got out me matches, lit the newspaper, and then made one flaming dash up the stairs. It seemed as though I'd never get there. Not only that, there was a rumour that the place was haunted. We used to hear noises at the top of the house,' Dad said. 'But the authorities said it was the movement of the place. It got so bad, though, that we could definitely hear footsteps walking up and down the floor up there. When we all went to have a look, there would be nothing.

'Well, we complained again. They had one of these blokes in who knows all about this sort of thing. What they done was, they sprinkled powder all over the place, and left a table up there with cups and saucers on it. We all sat up all night listening, and the bloke heard the footsteps for himself. When he goes in there the next morning there ain't a footmark to be seen. And lo and behold, all the bleeding cups and saucers are on the floor.

'It was in the papers about it, an' all. Anyway, they couldn't get rid of them, whoever they was. We still carried on living there for a long time afterwards. That's why we all had the wind up. When we did finally move, they sealed the place right up. So there must have been something dodgy going on there.'

Dad also told me how he slept. 'Well, at first me and my brother Ted used to sleep together. Our mattress had had enough, it was only fit for the rubbish. So we had a few planks running across the bed and we slept on them. I must have been about

74

eleven or twelve then. It was nothing to hear old Ted go bump in the night, right on the Rory O'More. The boards would gradually move apart and, course, old Ted used to fall right through them. Me being the eldest, I used to take the side where there were the two wide boards. But Ted had to put up with about three or four narrower ones to lay on. Course, they used to slide apart every time he moved, poor sod.

'If he ever upset me, he knew what he was in for. I used to tie his shirt and trousers in a thousand knots of a morning and make him late for school. You should have seen him. He'd be crying his mincers out and at the same time shouting with rage, tears streaming down his face. I used to give him a life, I did.

'But Ted was a crafty bleeder with money. If I had any, I always shared with him. But not him with me. If he got brassy, he used to hide it. I always found it, though, and then he got none of it. One night he hid it where I wouldn't be able to hoist it, so he thought. The crafty git, he tied it in the tail of his shirt, what he slept in. Course, we never used to wear pyjamas. We always slept in our shirts. But I caught the crafty sod, didn't I? He didn't suss anything. I goes out into the kitchen, after making sure he's gone well to Bo Beep. I gets the scissors and gets back into bed. To my advantage, he's turned his arse on me. Right, out come the old cutters, and with a quick snip his money and the tail of his Dicky Dirt were gone. He gave out a few choice sentences the next morning, I can tell you.

'If we couldn't get up in the morning, your grandfather soon livened us up by pouring a kettle of cold water over our feet. He seemed to love cold water of a morning. He'd douse his whole head in it.

'At one time, I had me own bedroom. I used an old tea chest for me wardrobe. Working clothes, Sunday best suit, everything was in there. That's if the old woman hadn't put them in Uncle's. I think my suit spent more time in Uncle's than in the tea chest.'

I used to love it down Poyser Street, especially when I was with my cousin John. He taught me a lot, he did, though he must have been a bit sadistic. I think a lot of kids down there were a bit like that. We found a kitten on our landing once. We took it in his house, and for some reason he dares me to put it in the lavatory pan and pull the chain on it. Perhaps he'd seen some of the old dears do that when their cat had had kittens and they didn't want the bother of them. Perhaps he didn't have the guts to try it himself, and got me to carry out the experiment for him. Anyway, I put the kitten in the pan and it was trying to claw its way up the slippery surface. It was now soaking wet.

'Go on,' John said. 'Pull the chain now.'

I stretched up. I could hardly reach it, but eventually I had my index finger through the loop. I was just about to pull the chain when his mother came up behind us. She had just come in from shopping. She saw right away what we were up to. She took each of us by the hair and banged our heads together, as though she was trying to crack two coconuts. I have never seen such an array of different coloured lights. It was a bit like the lighting they have in discotheques these days. By the time she'd finished, I felt as though I had gone ten rounds with Joe Louis.

'You wicked pair of little bleeders. Let me catch you doing that just once more and I'll give you the hiding of your lives.' Little did Aunt Maud know that she had already done just that. We both sat crying our mincers out. I resolved never to be led on so easily again by anyone, not even my big cousin John, who was my hero then.

5. Jam Jars

Poyser Street was a smashing place, and so were the people who lived down there. It consisted of small, terraced houses, with the flats in between. It was a narrow, cobbled street. Opposite the houses were garages and small factories, under the archways. Poyser Street was a cul de sac. There was an archway on the left, which I have already mentioned, leading into Cambridge Heath Road. If you went out under the arch and turned right, you would find the Dundee Arms on your right. A little further on was the local pawn shop.

It was most convenient, having the two in close proximity like this. After leaving the pawn shop you could, if you wished, pop into the Dundee for a quick one. That is you could, provided the pawnbroker hadn't cut the value of your old man's suit too much, after frequent loans on it. The old man never wore this suit, except at weddings and funerals. The old woman wouldn't let him, if she could help it.

What I did love about Poyser Street was the different tradesmen that used to come round. The one I loved and remember most was the roundabout man. He'd come in through the archway and make his way down Poyser Street at a very slow pace, crying out, Ha'penny or a jam ja, ha. Ha'penny or a jam ja ha.' I don't suppose there are many people today who would have a clue what this cry meant if they heard it in the street. Well, if you haven't guessed the meaning yourself yet, I will tell you. The roundabout man's cry meant that you could give him a halfpenny or a jam jar for a ride on his roundabout. If your jam jar was a clean one, you would be entitled to two rides. As soon as he entered the street, all the kids would cry out, in a far from orderly fashion, 'Mum, Mum, Mum.' Each shout for Mum became louder, the longer she delayed in coming to the street door or looking over her balcony.

'Mum, can I have a halfpenny for the roundabout?'

'No, I ain't got no halfpennies. It's bleeding Wednesday.'

'Well, ain't yet got a jam jar then, Mum?'

'Oh, wait a minute and I'll see if I can find one.'

'Well, hurry up then, Mum, or I'll have a big queue to get behind.'

Mum would come out again, the jam jar in one hand, her

broom in another and a scarf tied round her head.

'Cor, fanks, Mum. You couldn't just wash it out for us, could yer?'

Mum had already been stopped from doing her housework to find a jar, and now it wasn't clean enough. She would raise the broom handle, tighten her lips, thrust her chin out at the boy and put all her displeasure into two small words. 'Shove off.' Of course, this language caused no lasting displeasure to the boy. He was used to his mother talking to him in this way.

Now he was on his way down to the roundabout. The boys would come running up to the man. Some of their jars would be only partially clean. An argument would then ensue between the boy and the man as to whether the jar warranted one ride or two.

The happiness soon turned to grief for some boys. One might come running up and, in his excitement as he went past, knock his jar on the lamp-post that stood outside Craven Buildings. Or he might slip, and smash the jar to pieces. Some got away without being cut, some were not so lucky. The kid would sit where he had fallen and break his heart, not so much from the shock of falling but from the disappointment of missing a ride. Perhaps this was his first taste of reality, his first lesson in how life can be so good and pleasurable and then suddenly turn round on you like a monster. The monster was never far away from Poyser Street. Yet the high spirits and joviality of the people made you feel that nothing in the whole world could harm or upset you while you were among them.

The roundabout man would make his final stop at the end of the street to give his last ride. He must have done quite well at his trade, but whatever he made, he certainly must have earned it. Turning the roundabout, which was fixed onto a horse-drawn cart, was no easy job. The roundabout itself must have been about twenty feet or so across. It turned on great iron cogs. By the time the roundabout man reached the end of the street, he was sweating balls of dripping.

Another man who always fascinated me, and who gave all the boys a certain amount of pleasure, was the lamplighter. The street lighting was gas then, and the lamplighter was usually an elderly man. He carried a long pole, with a hook at the end. He would open the glass of the lamp, put the hook inside, pull a lever, and the lamp would light up.

I have already mentioned the lamp-post that stood outside Craven Buildings. This was the lamp that always gave trouble. The lamplighter would come down the road from Old Bethnal Green

78

Road. He would light the first one OK, then the second. By this time, the boys would have spotted him coming down the road. Whoever saw him first would cry out to the other boys scattered round the street, or playing on the landings of the flats, 'Lampo, lampo.' This would bring all the boys together. They would then gather round the lamplighter. Then they'd follow him right to the other end, where he lit his last lamp and disappeared under the arch.

Before that, of course, he just had to have a bit of aggravation. Although these different traders were known down the street, they didn't actually live there, so they could hardly expect to be considered one of us. Well, how was the old lamplighter made to suffer before he left us, then? Any boy standing on the first floor landing of the flats could easily reach the lamp's glass door. The lamplighter would light it. This was his last but one in the street. He would be slowly making his way to the last lamp. Then, when he was half-way between the two, the boy on the landing would switch the lamp outside the flats off.

'Look, Lampie,' the boys would shout. 'It's gone out.'

The old man would turn, with a puzzled look on his face. Hands on hips, he would slide his fingers under his cloth cap and scratch his head in bewilderment. This lamp played him up every time, and he just could not understand the cause. Back he would come again and light up once more. He would get halfway down the street again, when out would pop the boy's hand once more and out the light would go.

'It's out again, Lampie,' they'd shout.

Well, after two or three trips he would give up. Looking up at that lamp, still scratching his head, 'Have to report this one again, I suppose,' he'd say, as he wrinkled his brow and walked away. Poor old man. What we used to do to him.

The pawnbroker was another victim of the street. He certainly endured an enormous amount of suffering. Women would have curtains, clothing, sheets and blankets off him, and some of them were rather unreliable payers. Did I say some? I should have said most. The women would order the sheets, or whatever, from the tally man on the Saturday and the goods would be round Uncle's on the Monday morning. You would always see a queue outside Uncle's, Monday mornings.

Why they called it Uncle's, I don't know. He was nothing of the sort. 'Uncle' was just a code word and in no way described the true character of the man. The pawnbroker made a living out of other people's property. His shop had a peculiar, musty smell about it.

I can remember my mother visiting the pawnship at one time. It was partitioned off from the second-hand goods sales department. This was an ordinary shop. In the window stood goods belonging to people who couldn't afford to get them out. They would pawn their most treasured possessions when things got really desperate. It might be their father's watch which he had left them when he died, the one he got for doing forty years' service with one firm. It might be the wedding ring that their mother had worn all her life, now handed down to a daughter to pass on to her children. I heard a couple discussing whether to pawn a wedding ring once.

'All right,' one said. 'I'll do it. But for Christ's sake don't let the family know, or they'll kill me.'

A wife might even pawn her own wedding ring. She'd replace it with a brass one, and then be sure to keep her left hand out of sight as much as possible until the original was back on her finger. Some were not so lucky. Some never recovered their wedding rings and other possessions. The good fortune that they convinced themselves was just round the corner never seemed to turn into their street. Here, in Uncle's shop window, was the story of the poverty of many. They stood there like the pawnbroker's trophies, showing that he had at last won the game of goods being taken one week, out the next; until the owner began to leave it a couple of weeks before coming back. Then three weeks, then four and so on, until, in absolute defeat, he came back no more.

After three months, the goods were displayed in the window. I've seen people looking in that window. Old and young alike, not a penny in their pockets to buy anything, but still they looked, standing there a long while, motionless. Just looking. Perhaps the old widow was looking at the gold watch that the firm had given her husband when he retired, which he had been so proud of. An old man might be gazing at a brand new pair of boots. He had bought them cheap down Club Row and intended keeping them for a rainy day. But it had rained a little harder than he thought, and now the boots were out of his possession for ever. The young girl, without a doubt, was looking at her wedding ring, which, after all, she had only worn for the last six months.

I stood in the pawnshop with my mother and waited for one or two people in front of us to be seen to. The man behind the counter had the thinnest face I had ever seen. Close-set eyes, steel-rimmed spectacles, his thin nose pecking its way into the bundles that were handed up to him. The counter was always high at

80

these places. It would come up to an adult's chin. I think this was for a very simple reason. When people are boracic they can become desperate and violent, so I think this high counter was to protect the man and his goods. He would look at the women's stuff with a sort of contemptuous expression on his face.

'Can only give you 1/6d this week, gal,' he'd say. 'It's been in a good dozen times now, you know, and it's looking a bit ribby.'

The woman would try to point out all its virtues to the pawnbroker. It might be a suit that she had been successful in persuading her husband not to wear too often. She might have given it a good pressing the night before, to make it look better than it was. It was not for wearing purposes, of course, but for Uncle's stock. But you couldn't fool that old vulture. He knew exactly how many times an article had been pawned. Every item was recorded when it came in and when it went out.

'Can't you let me have two bob, just for this week?' the woman would plead with him. She knew it was hopeless asking, but she still had some faith in the pawnbroker's good nature. She and everybody else always treated him with respect and agreed with all he said, as though this would make a difference to what Uncle offered them for their goods.

A more relaxed attitude seemed to be taken when dealing with the tally man. I don't think he was reckoned to be of the same standing as the pawnbroker. He was treated almost as though he was one of them. You will see later why I say 'almost', and not 'the same'. Why he seemed different from the pawnbroker to them is a mystery. The tally man was after what money they had, just as much as Uncle was. I suppose the main reason why he was treated almost as though he lived in the street was that the women's natural friendliness just had to come out. Any weekly callers would be asked in for a cup of tea. It wasn't any wonder that the callers used to knock at the door and ask to use the toilet during their rounds.

My Gran used to have them all in. First the milkman, then the coalman, then the baker, insurance man, tally man, Christmas club man, window cleaner, and God knows how many more.

Is it any wonder that I loved Poyser Street so much? That place has never left my memory, even though it is so long since I lived there. There was poverty there all right. There was violence too. There was sickness and distress. There was hatred and malice. There were bugs, fleas, dirt and dampness. But the people who lived there overcame them all with their natural love and communal instinct. I don't think such closeness and sense of duty to your neighbour will ever be seen in London again. What a pity that is.

My mother has often told me about how she got 1/6d deposit on a pram for me. 'Your father was out of work then,' she would say. 'So what I done, I pawned his Daisies. I got exactly 1/6d on them. I went straight round to the pram shop and put the 1/6d as a deposit on a pram. By the next week, you had the pram and I was walking up and down the street, showing it off. It wasn't a second-hand one, either. Brand new, it was. There wasn't many could afford new prams then. When your father got his Labour money at the end of the week, he gave me the 1/6d to get his boots out of Uncle's.

'They were hard times for us then. There were times when I didn't even have a penny for the gas and I had to boil your milk up over the fire. Not with coal, though. Couldn't afford coal. Your father might bring in some wood from on the furniture factories and we'd burn that.

'How about your Grannie Barnes, though? We got married on the Saturday. Course, your father bought a new suit to get married in, out of what George Brown gave him. Gor blimey, the suit was hardly off your father's back when round comes his mother. "Bill," she says. "Do you think you could lend me your suit to take round Uncle's? Only I ain't got a penny for a bit of dinner. I'll have it out again by the week-end."

'Your father's face dropped like a kite. "Well, all right, then," he said unhappily. "Don't forget to have it out again Friday, will you?" Your Gran's face lit up. Not so as you'd notice, though, because she always had a jolly expression on her face. She was quite excited by now. "Where is it, Bill? Let's have it right away, then. I've got to get round Uncle's and then up Bethnal Green Road to do me shopping."

'Your Dad took it off the back of the door, where it was hanging on a wooden hanger. He handed it over to her. "Look after it then, Mum, won't you?"

' "Of course I will," she replied. She took tne suit with one hand and patted Dad's cheek with the other. "I always said you was the best of all me kids, and so you are. Ta ta, Het. Ta ta, Bill. Bring it back Friday night, I will. Ta ta." Away she wobbled, content and happy that Wednesday's financial troubles were over, anyway. And tomorrow? Well, we would have to wait and see.'

The women used to dodge the tally man week after week, if they owed him money. When he knocked, the whole family would have to sit and not make a sound. in case he heard them. If he thought you were in and you wouldn't answer the door, he would shout through, 'Come on, I know you're in there. I'm not bloody silly, you know. Come on out and pay your debt.'

My Aunt Polly was an expert at getting loads of gear off him, even if she already owed a packet. He could never catch her in the street when she hadn't paid, either. It seemed as though the Good Lord had given her the two most envied gifts in the street: first persuasion and then evasion. No matter how much she owed the tally man, she would always get away with not paying, and wheedling more goods out of him, into the bargain.

One of her lines went like this: 'Well, look, Cyril.' (She always made a point of addressing the man by his first name.) 'My George ain't had a very good week of totting. But next week he's going to make a packet. He's got to clear out a whole factory, and then we'll be loaded. You know what I'm going to do then, Cyril? I'm not going to pay you off for one week. Nor two, nor even three. You know what I'm going to do? You won't believe this. I'm going to pay you right up, and on top of it I'm going to give you half a sheet for yourself. How's that?'

The tally man hasn't come up against this one yet. The prospect of an extra ten bob in his pocket next week takes the pain out of having nothing from Aunt Polly this week. So he agrees. Once again, Aunt Polly's art of persuasion had helped her out of trouble.

My aunt didn't have only one tally man, she had several. This was because the first one would be owed so much that it was sometimes beyond even Aunt Polly's inspiration to wangle a much-needed pair of sheets out of him until she had got her bill down a bit. So what she did was wait for a new victim to come a calling with his wares. When he had been made to suffer like his earlier victim, he would eventually be adamant that he was not parting with any more goods. So Auntie would wait for yet another caller. This was how she managed to accumulate such an army of tally men, and also how she managed to acquire the necessary goods for her home. It was all done by what was known as welching.

But not everyone is alike. My aunt was fortunate. She didn't care a sod for anyone, she'd say. Or anything, I might add. If one of the tally men banged on the door and bawled through the letter-box, 'Come on, pay up. I know you're there,' Polly would be sitting there in silence with her family. Her face would be scarlet as though she was going to burst with laughter any minute. It was a great source of entertainment for her to hear the cries of the suffering tally man. He would rant and rave about how much he had to pay in to his boss each week and how much his commission would suffer from my aunt's wickedness. Polly always controlled herself until he had gone. Then she would let rip with abandon. She had won yet another round in her battle of wits.

Some women were more sensitive than my aunt, and afraid of the tally man. They wouldn't dare face him if they had no money. He would be banging at the door of some of these poor creatures. They would be sitting in their kitchen, their hands clutching at their apron in anxiety and shame, while the tally man shouted for all to hear, 'Come on. You know you owe me two quid, don't you? You ain't paid for three weeks, you know.'

If the woman had a sturdy husband, all this would sometimes be brought to an abrupt end with two well-timed and accurate movements. The husband makes for the door, which is trembling under the heavy-handed and heavy-voiced efforts of the tally man. The door is opened with one swift movement and a large fist makes an even swifter exit, quelling in a fraction of a second the ravings and hammerings of the unfortunate caller.

One of the tally man's tricks was to just walk away from the door and then hide somwhere in the flats. He would wait there for hours on end, until the woman had to go out for something or other. Then he'd pounce. Aunt Poll didn't give a damn. She still went out, no matter what she owed. She could always talk her way out of it. Of course, once you started owing the tally man money he was not only deprived of his payment, but of his cup of tea and chat as well. The other women used to say of Aunt Polly, 'Well, I don't know how she gets away with it.'

Another way the tally man was made to suffer was if a family was moving. This worked especially well with a new caller. The tenant who was moving out would have as much as she could get the caller to part with, say a couple of carpets, two pair of sheets, one or two pairs of shoes. She would give something like half-a-crown in down payment. When the tally man called the next week, the flat would be empty or occupied by a new tenant. This trick used to come off quite a few times.

I used to love going round the fish shop in Cambridge Heath Road and getting a penn'orth of chips. They didn't have bags then, the chips were put straight into the newspaper. When I got my chips, I would try to drown them in vinegar, until the proprietor would come round the counter, snatch the bottle from my hand and shoot me an agressive look.

'Look,' he'd say. 'Next time I'll sell you a bottle of vinegar and give you the chips. OK?'

Of course, my young mind had not a clue what he was inferring. But when I realised how he used to watch me when I went in for chips, especially when it came to the vinegar, I began to see what he was so agitated about.

Newspaper had other uses, as well as being good for reading and wrapping chips in. If you got a nice bundle of papers, the fish shop man would be glad of them. He might give you a halfpenny, or even a penny for a really good bundle. After it had been read, a newspaper would become a table cloth. Or it might find itself being torn up in little squares and hung up in the carsey. You could make paper hats out of it and then paint them different colours. Some kids would roll the paper up into a ball and bind it with twine. This would make a good cricket ball to go with your milkbottle wicket and stick bat. Not only that, with a paper ball the risk of smashing someone's window was lessened.

The consequences for breaking windows differed somewhat, according to whether it was a posh end window or a rough end one. At the rough end, you would receive a wallop if you were caught, of course, plus some abusive language. At the posh end, they would inform your parents if they knew who you were.

Then there was the salt and vinegar man. He would come into the street with his horse-drawn cart. On this, he carried great blocks of salt, which he cut down into smaller blocks, ready for sale. There was also a large barrel on the cart, holding a fair quantity of vinegar. The women would come over with their bottles for him to fill up. If a customer didn't have her own bottle, he would sell her one. The vinegar they sold then really was vinegar, not like the diluted stuff they sell today. Just one small drop on the tip of your tongue, and its tangy acidity would hang on for quite some time.

We used to follow the cart down the road. While the trader wasn't looking, we would stick our fingers under the tap of the barrel. There was always a small drop of vinegar hanging there. Then we would apply the vinegar-charged finger tip to our tongues. It was smashing. Eyes screwed up, tongues hanging out, faces as red as beetroots (due to our intake of minute drips of vinegar), we followed the cart to the other end of the street. By this time, we had had all the vinegar our palates could take.

Another street trader was the whitening man. He had great chunks of brilliantly white powdery stone. The women at the posh end would use this whitening with water to make a semi-circle of white, just in front of their doorstep. The whitening could also be used on the grey-coloured stone before the kitchen fire.

It would be no exaggeration to say that these women were absolutely spotless, in their homes and in themselves. Of course, at the posh end it was entirely different from the rough end, where the women were not all that particular. Except, that is, for the few like my Gran Barnes. Her floorboards and table top were scrubbed as white as the whitening on the doorsteps of those down the posh end.

'Whitening on your doorstep,' Gran Barnes would say, mockingly. 'It's a wonder they don't whiten their coal cellar.'

I've seen many a caller get a right telling-off from the posh end women, if they opened the door to catch him making the fatal mistake of actually standing on their doorstep while using the knocker. Did he get a mouthful.

Another favourite was the ice cream man. He used to come round with a box tricycle. There were never any motor vans, like now. No refrigerators, either. The trike was specially built to keep the ice cream hard for quite a long time. Its compartment was insulated, like a vacuum flask. Between the walls was a substance called cardice. This was like ice, only instead of being transparent it was pure white. It would stay hard and cold for about three or four times as long as ordinary ice.

The kids went mostly for the ice lollies, the grown-ups for ice cream. They were not really ice lollies like you get today. Walls used to make a stick of ice, triangular in shape and about six inches long.

When the salesman came into the street, he used to call: 'Penny a lump to make you jump. Ha'penny half to make you laugh.' I say call, but he really used to sing it out. Translated, his cry meant that for a penny you could get a whole ice stick, and for a halfpenny you could get half of that stick.

The local small-time ice cream firm, started up by Benny and Sammy Rood who lived in the locality, were always in fierce competition with the giant firm Walls. Benny and Sammy's ice blocks were not a patch on Walls'. They were much bigger, it's true. They looked good, with their different colours – orange, lemon, lime, cherry and many others. But they were completely and utterly flavourless. There was no more excitement in sucking an orange block than sucking a block of frozen water. Walls' were smaller, but their flavour was enormous.

Roods tried desperately to fight back. Their Cockney tenacity and flair for making money were to save them by the skin of their teeth. It has been said that Roods were the first firm to make the choc ice. All ice cream firms had difficulty making the chocolate hold on to the ice cream. After getting it on there at all, that is. Benny and Sammy discovered the secret, and it was this that saved them. They were the only firm down the street who sold the choc ice. As they were a novelty, these sold like hot cakes, to the adults. At threepence each, they were much too expensive for the kids to buy.

Very, very occasionally, an adult would buy a fruit bowl. This was full of ice cream and fruit and cost the fantastic price of sixpence. The way they used to look at my father when he bought one as he stood at his pitch. He used to buy one every time the ice cream man came round. He loved it, and could well afford to indulge his appetite then, on the money he was making.

Well, this was Poyser Street. One of the many grubby, grey, dank, narrow streets that existed in the East End and, I am sorry to say, still do exist. Despite all the drawbacks of being brought up in this kind of place, you can still find a soft spot for it, amid all the feelings of resentment and hatred you may have fostered over the years.

These streets have a character all of their own. These little Victorian terraced houses still echo with the sounds of those ancestors who made matchboxes, spun or wove, working sixteen hours a day. The less industrious earned their keep by more illicit means, such as lobbing, hoisting, creeping or working the mace, plus many other underhand practices which it would take far too long to go into. Poyser Street was just one street of many.

6. Dad, George and Dr. Jelley

The following account deals with the years between 1916 and around 1930. In 1916, Dad was about six and his father was fighting in France. He was four when his father left, and eight when he came home. Perhaps this acounted for the distant relationship that existed between them. Dad's father seemed to prefer his daughters to his three sons. My father took after him. He always took to girls, but he would never take the slightest notice of boys.

As a child, Dad was a great source of worry to Gran Barnes, due to the fact that he was always out for a laugh at someone else's expense. His main enjoyment was sitting at the window, holding an egg which he had nicked from his mother's basin, and for which she had paid one and six a dozen. He would wait for someone to go by looking rather well dressed. Perhaps someone from the posh end, who was foolish enough to make their way through the rough end to get to Hackney Road or Mare Street. For a Posh-ender to walk through the rough end, especially if he was dressed up, was to court disaster. He would be pelted with all manner of unsavoury missiles. Horse dung was a main source of ammunition, as there was an unlimited supply from the stables opposite the terraced houses. Of course, Dad had a hand in this sort of thing too.

Another of his pastimes was playing with matchsticks in the gutter where water had gathered after a spell of rain. He soon stopped this, after a horse and cart ran over his hand and broke a finger. People were for ever knocking at his mother's door:

'Your Billy's pushed my kid in a puddle.'

'Your Billy's dropped an iron bar on my kid's foot.'

He was trouble, trouble, trouble. Yet he was Gran's favourite out of all her children. As soon as she'd told him off, he would be on her knee again, being made a fuss of.

When my father was about sixteen, around 1926, two brothers, Charlie and Archie Sexton, lived down Poyser Street. They had come from a boxing family, and both became famous fighters. One (I think it was Archie) held a world title.

Dad used to tell me how he would go round the Sextons' house and how their Dad used to train them in the back yard. 'The old man used to try to get me to train with them,' Dad told me. 'Well, I didn't mind that at all, 'cause the Sextons were real class in the boxing world and I thought it would do me a bit of good. But my mind was quickly changed after their old man planted one on my chops. He never made any attempt to pull his punches, and freely admitted the fact. He used to say, "If you get the full impact, it'll teach you to keep out of the way, won't it? As well as being able to put up with a hiding." So I decided that the training he had to offer was not for me. I just went and watched the two brothers take the punishment, while I stood comfortably by the wall.

'It was funny, though, one time when the old man stepped back to avoid a blow from Archie. His old woman had left a broom standing up against the wall. 'Course, there wasn't much room in those back yards to move about. Anyway, the old man stepped back to avoid this punch, and his heel came down on the head of the broom. Well, 'course, the broom handle shot up and struck his napper with a sickening crack. You should have heard him: "What a place to leave a sodding broom." He picked it up and threw it across the yard. Archie was trying desperately not to laugh at his old man, because he knew he would give him a right seeing to if he saw his amusement.'

The Sextons' father trained them hard. I suppose this is why they got on so well in the boxing game. But of course, the whole family were devoted to the noble art.

Dad left school at fourteen. He was on night work, which nearly ruined his courtship with my mother. He would go to bed in the morning, and then oversleep and let Mum down. But when she made it clear that she would stand no more, he decided to pay one of his sisters twopence a week to wake him up at six o'clock. By this means, his courtship was able to continue.

Dad was the eldest boy, and expected to be waited on at home by his younger siblings. When he woke up in the evenings, one of them would have to run round the coffee shop for him, to get him some tea, or something to eat, or perhaps a packet of fags. There was no choice. The brother or sister he picked had to go, and no arguing. Why did his mother allow him to hold such a high position? There were a number of reasons, the main one being that he was in employment and contributed to the family income.

If the old man had had a bad day on tips from his job as a driver and was unable to give Gran any money for grub, Dad always helped her out. If Gran had to go out and Dad saw that the place was untidy, he would clear up for her. Dad's father was not a man to amuse kids in his young days, perhaps through being too exhausted after a day's work. So Dad took over here, also. He would make his young brothers and sisters a swing in the back yard to amuse them. He would draw different objects, and they would have to guess what they were. He would show them card games, tell stories, buy sweets. There was always something for the kids to do while he was about. He had terrific patience with children.

Dad was also a very sharp-brained boy. The school offered him the chance to go on to higher education, to become a teacher. But Gran had it hard enough already, bringing up all her children. She needed him to go out to work now, to lighten the load a little.

The load wasn't lightened for long, for at twenty-one, Dad was married. Gran cried as though he had died, though he only went to live just up the road. Her Billy was gone, never to come home again. This was how she looked at it. The kids missed him, too There was no one to entertain them now. 'It was nice not having to stand by the wall while he got ready every night, so as to keep out of his way,' said one of them. 'But the whole place seemed dead once he was gone. He was strict, just like a school teacher, but he amused us for hours and taught us a lot of things to do.

'He used to tie a penny on a piece of string and lower it down to the pavement. We would sit at the window and wait for old Mother Marshall to come back from the Wheatsheaf with her jug of beer. She wore an apron made of canvas, with a shawl round her shoulders. Her hair was tied into a bun at the back of her head. On top, rested a cloth cap with a vicious-looking hat pin stuck through it. Just as she passed our house, Bill would pull the cotton and then let it go. Mother Marshall would stop instantly, thinking she'd dropped some money. She'd walk back and have a good butchers all along the pavement, look in her purse and go down her pockets before she carried on. We'd be in fits.

'When we got fed up with that, we'd tie a piece of cotton across the street and watch people's hats being knocked off as they walked past. We'd end up on the kitchen floor, screaming with joy. No wonder we missed old Bill when he got married.'

Dad's mother tried to console herself with the thought that her Billy would come round to see her during the week and at weekends, which he did do.

He had been out of work now for a considerable period, after coming out of hospital. The shock of almost being crushed by a lorry had affected him very badly, but now he was much better than he had been.

He was working the book for Tilly and making money. Gran Barnes could see by his clothes that he was getting posh. Wearing a bowler hat and leather gloves. I think Gran resented this, somehow. She like the idea of him getting on, all right. 'But you don't have to walk about in bowler hats and all that, do you?' What she did not realise was, that to feel part of my mother's family this was how he had to dress when he went out drinking with them. them. Gran Barnes would sit at her window some Saturday nights and see Dad coming along the street, after a night out with his in-laws. They would be singing, but keeping their voices low enough for respectability. Her eyes would moisten. 'He'll go drinking with them, all right,' she would get out. 'But he wouldn't come out and drink with us, would he?' She would then get up and slam down the window.

George Brown was Dad's best friend, and was later to become his brother-in-law, by marrying Dad's eldest sister. George was one of twenty-two brothers and sisters. They lived in Peacock Street, off Cambridge Heath Road, just past the pawnshop. Peacock Street was even narrower than Poyser Street; a cul de sac, with no pavement. This was most convenient for George's father, for they lived at the very end of the street and he was able to keep chickens in a run he had made. He could also keep his home-made wooden cart outside the house. He used this to carry out his business as a chimney sweep.

George's father was only a small man. Looking at George himself, you wondered how such a small man as Mr. Brown senior could have produced such a tough, strapping son. 'I was five years old when I started work,' George told me. 'I helped the old man do his chimneys. By the time I was seven, I was an expert at it.'

But by the time George was in his teens, he had left the family business. He became an all-round machinist in the wood game, an age-old industry in and around Bethnal Green. This was the trade in which he was to lose a thumb while working a spindle. These spindles were notorious in the wood game for slicing off fingers. The worker's whole attention had to be on the job in hand. If the wood was held too close to the spindle, it could gauge a piece out of the timber and send a splinter flying into the arm or eye of the worker, or a bystander. Or the spindle could just grab the whole piece of wood, taking the operator's hand with it. If the wood was held too far away from the spindle, then the groove made would not be deep enough. As you can see, using this machine took a great deal of skill and care. Yet with all the experience the men had, it was not uncommon for a wood machinist to have one or two fingers missing. My father used to say, 'You can always tell a wood machinist. Just look at his hands.'

Due to his strength and daring, George was the self-appointed leader of the Poyser Street gang. The same street that I was to play in as a child. To join the gang, you had to prove yourself worthy by having a fight with one of the boys, under the arch. George would choose which boy. Or you might have to stand on the canal bridge at Cambridge Heath Road, and jump in. Having gone through some ordeal like this, and having faced it in the approved way, you were then initiated into the gang. Disobedience, or a contrary attitude, would mean instant dismissal. The gang's main pastime was making themselves a general nuisance and tea leafing.

Saturday night was thieving night for some of the boys. The shops in Bethnal Green Road were the victims every time. The market would be open as late as midnight. Some families would find their cupboards a bit sparse on Saturdays, and it was the boys of the family who were to correct this deficiency. Most of the parents, glad of the victuals found in the cupboards the next morning, were not much inclined to examine too closely where and how they had been acquired and who had put them there.

Mum might say on Sunday morning, 'What you been up to, Jimmy?'

'Nothing, Mum. Honest. I been up to nothing at all.'

'Well, if you have been up to something, you won't half cop it if they catch you, you know.'

Jimmy's eyes would move up to his forehead. 'But I ain't done nuffink, Mum. You don't believe me, do you?'

Mum would never answer, except by taking the joint of meat out of the paper and stuffing it into the kitchener oven. By the time everyone had finished their Sunday roast, the matter would be completely forgotten.

How did these boys work the hoist? A group would meet on the corner and section themselves off into groups. The leader would say, 'Right. You, you and you, Cullen's grocery shop. You, Dobson's butchers. You lot, Griffiths' greengrocers.' They would make their way to Bethnal Green Road, and there they would part.

Dobson's was a walk-over for a young hoister. Old man Dobson himself would be outside the shop, auctioning the meat that he had been unable to sell during the day. It was the less well-off who would be bidding now. Old Dobson would have a pile of meat on his right, and the crowd would make a semi-circle round him. He would hold up a nice joint above his head.

"Ere y'are, then,' he'd cry. 'One and six. One and bloody six. Who wants it?'

Little did he know that there were three boys in the crowd who wanted it and intended having it, but not in the accepted fashion that Dobson was used to and preferred. Dobson's face was red and fat, and bore some resemblance to the pig's head hanging in the window behind him. He wore a straw hat and a blue and white striped apron, the strings of which were stretched to the limit round his abundant paunch.

The boys had to be patient and wait for exactly the right second for attack. They had to make themselves as unobstrusive as possible in the crowd. Firmly but gently, they worked themselves to the front till they were on the left side of the semi-circle, as close to the meat as possible. Dobson's son stood by the pile, on guard. But when a sale was made, or the dwindling pile got smaller, the boy would have to go to the back of the shop to replenish the meaty mound.

This was when Dobson's stock was seriously open to attack. But easy as the hoist was, they had to be sure that people's minds were on the salesman at the time, to lessen the risk of detection. They had to make sure that Dobson was holding up a joint to his audience and holding their attention. When conditions met the boys' requirements, they were in and out like a flash and away up the road. This was how the hoist was worked, though it might vary from shop to shop, depending on the layout of the place and so on.

After getting what they had come for, they would make for their regular rendezvous under the arch. There, they would share out their loot as fairly as they could and then depart for home.

It wasn't always as easy as that. If a hoister was discovered by a Plain'un, the only thing for it was to run like hell. The place for refuge was Poyser Street. You had to run at top speed and make the distance between you and the Plain'un as long as possible.

This gave you a chance to turn into the arch and out of sight of the Bogey. You could then run into any of the terraced houses at the rough end, where you'd be safe. After getting into Poyser Street, the policeman wouldn't have a clue where the thief was. But if he just happened to see you pull the string that worked the door latch and go in, he'd be after you. Only by the time he got there, you would have jumped over the back yard wall into the next door yard. If questioned, nobody would know anything about the boy.

'No, mate,' they'd say. 'Ain't no-one come through here.'

Another thing a boy might do, if a copper was hot on his tail, was to push open one of the doors of the terraced houses as he ran past and throw the meat, or whatever it was he had, down the passage. Then if he got caught, he wouldn't have the goods on him. If the Bogey let him off, he would go back to the house where he had left the meat. Then home he'd go.

Some hard-up families would be their own gas man, as they used to say and break into their own gas meters. Some boys even robbed their own parents' meters. This was not an every-day occurence, but by no means a rare one. The art of avoiding detection was to cut across the locking arm with a fine hacksaw, and put the lock back in the same position as it had been in before you emptied the meter. That way, the foul deed would not be discovered till months later, when the gas collector called.

I remember one mother who had her son sent to an approved school for setting himself up as the gas collector. She might have been able to take that without saying anything, but he had previously nicked all her bedclothes and taken them in to Uncle's. He then lost all the money at cards. The woman was quite understandably at the end of her tether.

The poorer children used to wear clogs for school. They had to take them off as they went in, and the clogs were then lined up along the classroom wall. This was because letting children walk round with those great studded things on their feet would have meant that everyone's nerves were torn to shreds by the end of the day. They were only allowed to put the clogs on during break and when it was time to go home. Some kids wore no shoes at all. George was one of them. His mates once dared him to walk to school in thick snow with nothing on his feet. George, never one to turn down a dare, obliged without any sign of discomfort. Like his feet, he was as hard as nails.

George and Dad told me a story once, about when they done a creep at a factory. It was a chocolate factory, and all the boys went home with boxes of the finest chocolates. A box of chocolates was something of a rarity in the houses of the East End then. Dad knew he was in for a possible hiding if his mother saw them, and the same applied to George. So dad hid his dozen boxes in the kitchen boiler, not realising that this mother would be boiling up the next day. In went the water she had brought in from the yard in a bucket, and on went the gas. You can imagine the result. Gran knew that someone had been up to no good, but who? It was hard to tell, with so many children.

George had hidden his lot inside the piano. They were discovered a few weeks later, at a Saturday night party. George described the events:

'Aunt Ethel was going to play the piano. I knew that she always dismantled as much of the instrument as possible, before she struck up. "Don't dismantle the piano, Aunt," I said. She looked at me suspiciously. She knew something was up, and, 'course, I had to tell her. I told the truth, but it was just too much for her to believe. "Oh, go on out of it," she said, and carried on taking the front of the piano out. You should have seen her eyeballs. My Dad went up in the air at first, but then he decided it was a bit late in the day to do anything about it. The party carried on with the added luxury of chocolates.'

The gang were walking along Bethnal Green Road one Saturday afternoon. They happened to stop just outside a pub. No particular reason. It was during the summer and the pub door was open. A barrow stood on the kerb directly outside the pub door, loaded with boxes of kippers. The boys had not given the barrow a second thought. They didn't feel like nicking anything on this particular Saturday. Suddenly, a dirty-looking, fat man, dressed in a grubby, black suit with what had once been white stripes, came hurriedly to the door. He wore a battered Anthony Eden hat and a greasy-looking waistcoat. He looked as though he hadn't shaved for a fortnight.

'Gorn aht of it, you thieving little sods. Piss orf, gorn.'

The boys met this bit of abuse with one resounding and unified raspberry. The scruff made to run at them, hoping to make them run off. They did nothing of the kind, but just stood there, defiantly. Scruff could see that there were too many of them to do battle with. He decided to go inside and finish his drink, while keeping a close watch on the boys. They stood tight outside the door, blocking the scruff's view of the barrow. George went behind the boys, lifted a box of kippers from the barrow and threw it to the ground, causing it to break open. Each boy grabbed what he could and ran for it. Out charged the scruff, like a pensioned-off stallion, waving his fist at the boys and shouting such abuse as to put one in doubt whether their mother was married or not.

It must have been around 1928 when Sir Oswald Mosley's party was in full swing. The Jews were the ones to hate then. Most East Enders knew them as 'four by twos' or 'kangeroos'. The slang words for Yid were 'tea pot lid', or 'backward skid', or

'Billy the Kid'. The last name was only applied to the very orthodox Jews, the officer of the synagogue, who wore (as they do today) a large, black, wide-brimmed hat which looked a bit like a cowboy hat. My father watched these Billy the Kid films in his time, and I was to get my excitement from exactly the same Billy the Kid when I was young. Only mine was a more up-to-date version.

One of my uncles became a Blackshirt when he was about eighteen. He used to feel right proud of himself, marching with the Party down Bethnal Green Road, dressed in his black jackboots and black shirt. I have never heard him say anything about Jewish people in all the time I have known him, and he never tried to convert anyone else. Really, I think he was only in the Blackshirts for the sake of the uniform. I don't think he was ever truly devoted to the Party.

The cry then was the same as it is today, only then it was the Jews and today it is the blacks, Greeks and Indians. I can instantly bring to mind all the old cliches, which I have heard so often. 'They come over here and buy up all the houses,' and 'they go right to the top of the housing list'. Another one is: 'they're bone idle. Won't do a stroke of work. They come here and work for cheap labour and put us out of work.' I could go on for hours, putting down all the contradictions I have heard about all the immigrant people that this country has received. Old phrases, which are not capable of holding one ounce of water.

There was one advantage for my uncle in being a Blackshirt. For at least two nights a week, he looked as if he had just come from the laundry. The rest of the week, he looked as if he had just fallen off the dustcart.

Uncle George, Dad and the gang got most of their kicks out of causing inconvenience, and at times even suffering, to whoever was unfortunate enough to be nearby at the time. Their favourite victims were the unfortunate four by twos in the area. They had no particular hatred for the Jews. But what made them the main source of enjoyment, was that they seemed to get much more excited when tormented than the local inhabitants. It may have been that the locals had had so much of the boys' pranks in the past that they had grown almost immune to it all. Consequently, the locals, though they naturally got fed up with having their bicycle tyres let down or having a stack of apples outside their shop knocked down, did not go into the hysterics that the uninitiated four by twos did. They took any sort of agitation or molesting for the work of the Fascists. Who could blame them, when Mosley was trying to instill anti-semitism into the East End working class (though, from what I can remember with little success)?

It was no good telling the Jews that the boys meant no harm, and that it was just a mixture of boredom and high spirits. Try telling that to the owner of a Jewish delicatessen, who first heard, then saw, his empty milkchurns being hauled along the road, tied to the back of a lorry. Or the man who opened his door, to be struck on the loaf by a plank of wood that had been leaned against it. Or the little orthodox Jewish boys, who had their caps snatched off their heads and thrown in the canal by Cambridge Heath Road. The lads hoped to see them jump into the canal after their caps, but no such luck. The Jewish boys were too well brought-up to strip down to their birthday suits and jump into that filthy canal, like their more uninhibited tormentors.

This is how these young East Enders of the twenties used up their energies. But as for hating Jews, I don't think they did really. They hadn't a clue about politics, so they had no convictions one way or the other. I think that is very sad. What views they did have, if any, were the Conservative kind, picked up from parents, aunts and uncles.

They would sometimes sit on the stairs in Craven Buildings and play cards. Sometimes with money, sometimes not, depending on what they were able to lay their hands on. They would play Toss, throwing pennies against the wall, to see who could get nearest. The winner would get all the other coins on the ground.

At one time, Uncle George moved to Russia Lane, one of the most notorious streets in Bethnal Green. It used to run from Bishop's Way through to Globe Road, but now only half of it remains, since they built council flats across it. Like Poyser Street, Russia Lane had terraced houses and a block of flats several times larger and dirtier than Craven Buildings. The flats took up almost a quarter of the length of the street. The terraced houses were just as bad as those in Poyser Street, but compared with the flats, over a century old, they were like the Dorchester.

You entered the flats through a black opening in the wall. There were two dwellings on each landing. The two doors faced each other, and in between was a shared toilet plus a sink with one tap. Some people used to wash on the landing, to save carting the water into the flat and back again to throw it away. The brick walls were a deathly mixture of black and grubby grey. They had probably been grey all over at one time, but nearly a century's exposure to the London air had turned them black. The stairs were grey stone, and had iron railings covered with chipped black paint to match the morbid black and grey of the walls.

Only a fool would enter Russia Lane after dark. The Law always went in uniform and in twos, to ward off potential attackers.

George Brown's gang was the toughest and shrewdest in the district. If there was nothing else to do, one gang would pick a fight with another and enjoy the excitment of busting each other's noses. Russia Lane was exclusively the gang's terrirtory, now that George had moved there. Any strange young face turning into the Lane would be politely stopped. Or, if the mood took the boys, the intruder would find himself tripping over a protruding stiff leg.

He would be interrogated as to who he was, where he had come from and where he was going. The boys might go down his pockets and claim such articles as a bag of sweets, a wooden top, or even a halfpenny if the victim was a wealthy one. They claimed these items as a sort of toll for allowing the stranger to pass. He might get off with a punch in the ear, or a kick up the rear, depending on how the gang felt at the time. If, on the other hand, he was a member of a gang that George's mob had recently tangled with, the next ten minutes of his life were made unpleasant for him indeed. If he was a member of a recent rival gang, he had to do his best to hide the fact until he was clear of George's boys and out of the street.

They say that youngsters are violent today, but I think violence was in vogue during the twenties in all the working-class areas. The only thing is that the generation of that era are rather shy of admitting such violence existed. Personally, I do not think that violence is caused by poverty alone. The main influence these days is the mass media. It is true that the young have many more advantages now. But are they given enough encouragement to use them? Are there enough evening institutes, and if there are, are they close at hand for youngsters? After being at work all day they have to rush home, rush through their tea and rush out, if they are going to be on time.

The only source of pride for an uneducated youngster is how tough he is, 'like that James Bond bloke', or some other unlikely character; a figment of someone's brain. It doesn't matter whether the violence is dished out by the goody or the baddy. It is still violence. It has a degrading effect on our young, gullible people. The media could do so much for our young. In areas like educational films they do a worthwhile and important job.

But it is a pity that they put out so much rubbish, in addition.

In the summer, George, Dad and the boys would acquire bikes and ride down to Southend. They were not able to buy new bikes, or even second-hand ones. So they did the same as my mates and I did, when I was in my early teens. They went down the Kingsland Road Waste on Saturdays, or Club Row of a Sunday. They'd buy an old frame here, a pair of handle-bars there and something else somewhere else. Each week they would buy a different part, until they had all the pieces, right down to the brake blocks. The frame was painted up in some outlandish shade. A piece of thin plywood, obtained from one of the local cabinet makers, was fixed to the frame so that the spokes of the front wheel would just tip it. This made a sound like a propellor, giving the rider a sense of speed and excitement.

These piece-by-piece bikes had to have names. After all, the others did: Triumph, Raleigh, Macleans and, of course, BSA. Well, these home-made machines were given equally grandiose names. They were called 'ASPs', standing for All Spare Parts. For the first few weeks or so, these ASPs would, as expected, give a bit of trouble. The brakes might not work properly, or the chain might be too long or too short. A mechanic might find that one of his wheels was slightly buckled. But once all these set-backs were overcome, they were ready for the long Southend trips. A group of boys would sit on the curb, sorting out each other's mechanical problems until it was all put right. One would be putting on a pedal. One mending a puncture, his bike turned upside down. One would be nursing a bleeding finger, from catching his hand while undertaking a job of work. A piece of rag, which served as his handkerchief, would be bound round the wound.

I remember finishing one of my works of art, one Saturday. All I wanted was two inner tubes. Foolishly, I had allowed myself the extravagance of a visit to the local cinema the night before. My father was out of work at the time. I realised that it was worse than useless telling Dad about my financial set-back, but my need for the inner tubes seemed to activate the optimistic side of my nature. Dad, of course, was unable to help me out financially, but all was not lost. He conveyed to me some of his vast experience in getting over such deficiencies of capital.

'Well,' he said. 'Do what I used to do. Stuff two tyres out with paper. That'll last you till next Saturday. You'll get some more money then.'

I took his advice. Although my summer evening tours of the

district with the boys were not as smooth that week, culminating in a sore behind, I did have the advantage of being able to ride over any surface without fear of getting a puncture. This was a common enough disaster for all riders, whose second-hand tyres were well and truly worn.

To get back to Dad and Uncle George, in their young cycling days. They rode through the night, on a quiet country road. Once they were passing an old cemetery and Dad spotted a white figure sitting on the back of George's bike. George looked round and saw it too. He took fright, and pedalled harder to get away from it. After they had passed the cemetery, the figure disappeared. George is convinced to this day that it was a ghost. 'I suppose he wanted a lift,' he says.

This was not the only thing that happened to poor George on this particular trip. They were going down a steep hill. At the bottom, lay a sharp bend. George was picking up more and more speed. Head almost between his knees, leaning well forward over his drop handle-bars, he sped at full tilt down the hill. Now he was coming towards the bend, and started to apply his brakes. But it seemed that his brakes had decided to fail on this particular Saturday, at the moment when they were most needed. Need I say any more?

Well, I needn't, but I just can't resist it. George sailed full steam, right through this poor woman's wooden fencing and almost into her front room. He stayed with his bike, right through the downhill, high-velocity plunge. Yet he emerged unscathed. Once again, proof that George was made of some unperishable, undamageable material. Up he got, apologised about the fence, and away the boys all went. Naturally, this was not until they had expressed their merriment, in strange, inaudible, fitful sounds that might pass for laughter, ranging from a deep bass to a high-pitched whistle. As they pedalled off, they mocked him something terrible. But although George was the governor, he could always take a joke.

'It's a wonder you didn't break your bushel and peck there, George.'

'It'll cost that poor old cow a good handful to repair that fence, George. I reckon you ought to go back and give her something towards it. Don't you, boys?'

'*Yes.*'

'Thought you was gonna go right through her burnt cinder, I did. Don't know how you missed it.'

They went on like this at George until the novelty wore off.

As George got older, he went into his father's sweep business. Some women preferred the son, some the father. The reason behind the preference was cleanliness. Some sweeps made more mess than others. Some thought George was cleaner, some his father.

One Saturday night, George had just come home from his round. He had knocked at every door. He had his usual nightly bath in the old, oval, zinc tub that hung by one of its handles on a nail in the back yard. He plastered his obstinate forelock with brilliantine and water, to keep it in its proper place. He slipped on a lavender shirt, a green tie and his beautiful pink suit, with thirty-six-inch trouser bottoms. He was dressed for the kill. His father had just rolled in. He was always a bit later than George. Perhaps George, being young, worked more quickly than his father, if less thoroughly.

'You can get that lot off,' says his Dad. 'Old Mother Ellis wants her chimney done tonight. Must have it done for the week-end. Better get round there as quick as you can.'

'Bleeding hell,' says George. 'I already knocked there today, and she didn't want it done.'

'Well, I don't know about that. I just seen her and she wants it done.'

George had to go. He couldn't argue with his father. The old man was only a midget. Compared with him, George was a giant. But George respected his Dad too much to argue. Not only that, his father was the senior partner, as well as founder of the business. It was he who had supplied the sacks and the brushes, and made the wooden carts for the game. So George went.

'I done the job all right,' he told me. 'But did I leave her some mess. She didn't ask for me no more, after that lot.'

For a short time, my father planned to go in the business with George. The old man was getting a bit past it now, so my Dad was going to help out, if you could call it that. Let me give you an example of my father helping out.

They both started off from Peacock Street, about ten o'clock in the morning.

'Now, you know where to go, don't you, Bill?' George asks. Dad tells him he does.

'All right, Bill. I'll come round to you later to see how you're doing. Don't forget, take your time until you get used to it. Give a good sweep and be as clean as you can.' With that, the two sweeps parted.

Dad called on his first customer. 'Mornin', Mrs. Roberts. I've come to do the chimney.'

'Oh, come in, son. Do you want a cuppa Rosie before you start?'

'Thanks very much,' replies Dad. 'I'll bring me brooms in.'

Dad starts putting a sheet up, covering the whole of the fireplace and mantelpiece. Then he joins one of his yard-long rods to the broom handle.

''Ere y'are, son. Drink that first and then you can make a start.'

They both have a few words about money and the weather. They finish the tea and Dad gets to work.

He shoves his broom up the chimney, joins the on a rod and shoves it up again. Dad just didn't realise how many rods he had joined on. The most he needed was about eight, before the broom came out of the chimney pot.

'Can you go and have another look for me, Mrs. Roberts, and see if it's through now?'

Mrs. Roberts went out, looked and came back to report that there was no sign of the broom-head whatsoever. Dad was bewildered. He only had one rod left. He scratched his head with his black, sooty hand.

'Well, I'll have to go find George, and get some more rods off him,' he said. He got up from the floor and went to look for George. He didn't have to look far, for George was coming up the road the two met.

'All right?' said George.

'Well, I don't know,' Dad replied. 'I've shoved up everything I've got and I still can't see the broom-head poking out.'

The whites of George's eyes grew larger, standing out against his soot-blackened face. His jaw dropped. He raised his hand to it, as if to give it some support.

'Everything you've got? You had fifteen rods there, Bill. You mean to say you've used the sodding lot and you can't see the broom-head poking out yet?'

They both stood outside the house gazing up at the chimneys, trying to seek out the vanished broom-head. With all his experience, George was at a loss to understand what had happened. He crossed the road to get a better view of the roof from a distance. At once, the problem was solved.

'Gorblimey.' George let out, using his full lung capacity. 'It's come out all right, and gorn down the chimney next door. Her place must be a right old mess. We're in for something now.'

Dad looked at George sorrowfully.

'Well,' said George. 'We've got to get up on the roof now and try and git the sodding thing aht.

Of course, although George said 'we', he knew who it was who would have to go up there. Dad couldn't stand heights. So up he went, dislodged the broom, took the wrath of the lady next door, cleared her place up, apologised, and that was that. George always did the straightening out in any crisis like this, while Dad looked on, wearing a very faint grin. I can't help thinking of them as a Cockney version of Laurel and Hardy.

After one or two set-backs like that, Dad decided he had never been cut out to be a sweep. So he went from a black, sooty overall to the hygienic white coat of an ice-cream salesman. By this time, George had also made a clean sweep of things and gone into the wood game. To make a few bob extra, he set up a dolls' house workshop in his front room. He would borrow (as he called it) his materials from his firm. Dad would help out on the delivery side, with his ice-cream trike. He would make his way round the factory at a given time, and George would be waiting with a few pieces of wood. Dad would then put the wood on top of his vehicle and take them round to George's place.

My father was never a devoted ice-cream salesman, either. He was no more enthusiastic about this job than he had been about sweeping chimneys.

'Too much work for the old pegs, pedalling that old thing,' he would say. 'Too much for the old plates of meat if you walk. Not only all the walking and pedalling, I've worn out Gawd knows how many pairs of Almond Rocks and about four pairs of boots. What I earn hardly keeps me in footwear.'

One can understand Dad's attitude to the job.

George was out of work again, which was nothing unusual in those days. But he found he needed an assistant, part-time; and need I say who that assistant was to be? Dad's trike stood outside George's house more than it did outside Polikoff's tailoring factory, where he was supposed to stand in the afternoons. He would be in the workshop, still wearing his white coat and with his cash bag over his shoulder, helping George out in his new venture.

Benny Rood could see by Dad's takings that his feeling for selling ice-cream was cooling off. He had Dad in the old shack he called an office and questioned him about it. Well, Dad made some excuse and promised to do better, a promise he had no intention of fulfilling. He was much more interested in dolls' houses, now that George had made a sale, and had given him an Oxford out of his takings. Of course, he wanted to hang on to the

104

ice-cream job, for his remuneration was regular, if small. But his love for the manufacture of dolls' houses couldn't fail to have a detrimental effect on his ice-cream job.

On one extra hot summer's day, Dad had left the trike out in the heat for so long that all the ice cream melted. Rood went nuts, and Dad's job went bang. He didn't really care, though, for his interest in the job had melted away, just like the ice cream. But then the dolls' house venture gradually fizzled out, like all Dad and George's enterprises.

When they were in their teens, they decided to hit show-business, as comedians. Comedians they most certainly were, on or off stage. Their first performance was a talent contest at the Museum Cinema, in Cambridge Heath Road. The first prize was a pound, but they never got it. Dad dress up as Dr. Jelley in a frock coat and a high hat, which he had snatched up down Club Row. George was a patient, and came on swathed in bandages. They cracked a few jokes, but unfortunately George could only remember one joke. It went like this. Dr. Jelley would say,

'Well, what's your name?'

'George Brown,' the patient would answer.

'Where you from?'

'Kent.'

'What part?'

'All of me.'

At the end of the act, they finished up with one of their songs. It goes like this:

> 'Now you know me as a doctor,
> I'm one of great renown.
> I only charge a tanner cash,
> Instead of half a crown.
>
> Well, I'm Jelley, good old Doctor Jelley.
> No matter what complaint you've got
> I can cure you on the spot.
> And if you've got a nasty pain
> Down in your Darby Kelly,
> Just pop your tummy round to me.
> I'm good old Doctor Jelley.
>
> Last night the door bell rang
> As the clock was striking two.
> There upon the door-step sat
> A cock-a-doodle-doo.

He said "Oh, doctor. Come at once,
The hen she's on her back.
She's twisted her bazooker
And cannot get it back."

I gave her boiling water,
Chloroform and smellie.
Now she's laying hard-boiled eggs,
I'm good old Doctor Jelley.

This morn upon the telephone
Three doctors asked me round.
They said they wanted a specialist
To share a thousand pounds.
They think the case is quinsy
 And find they're in a hole.
 So come at once, because the old
Man's going up the pole.

Well, I'm Jelley, good old Doctor Jelley.
When they saw me, those doctors three
They took off their hats to me.
I said if the case is quinsy
I'd eat my umbrella.

Sometimes they would change the act, and render another of
their compositions, like this one:

'Not so long ago in an old washtub,
Mother made a puddin' for a lovely bit of grub,
While father stirred it with our yard broom.
The neighbours got jealous
And came knocking at our room.
One bloke looked, he pointed with his thumb.
He said "Half a ton of flour
And a pennyworth of plums."

Out went the light,
While mother took her knickers off.
Danced on the floor,
While father took his slippers off.
Scouting about for the rolling pin to find
They couldn't find the rolling pin,
So down came the blind.

Once we had a beautiful Barnet Fair.
We bought a lot of cannon balls
And covered them with hair.
"Roll, bowl a pitch," you could hear them cry
He thought he had a coconut
Because he had a bloke shy'd
He caught it such a treat.
Hit my sister Polly
Who was holding up the sheet.

Out came her brains,
While a fellow stood behind.
Blimey, what a milky one.
And down came the blind.'

These were just a couple of may renderings. Composed and sung by W. Barnes and G. Brown

They won two or three small prizes at the talent contests. Then, the thought of extra lolly spurred them on to better things, like doing the clubs. They started working all the clubs in the East End, and eventually aspired to the West, where the money is.

Dad used to take a hell of a time to get ready of an evening. So he used to put his gear on at home and walk through the streets with his stage make-up on, dressed in his Dr. Jelley gear. All the kids had a good laugh, until the novelty of seeing him like that wore off. They had a complaint from the Entertainments Board or some place like that. They had to change the name from Jelley to Shelly. Perhaps the real Doctor Jelley had put in a complaint. You couldn't really blame him. But Dad and George had worded the song as a mark of affection for the doctor, rather than ridicule. Dr. Jelley was considered the local philanthropist. He had some odd ways, it's true, but the poor respected him.

Of course, those who had a few bob wouldn't lower themselves to call in the threepenny doctor, as Dr. Jelley was called. They thought, as people do nowadays, that the more you pay, the better the goods. It may be true in the majority of cases, but not in every case. I suppose it lowered their prestige to pay only threepence for medical treatment.

It was good to have a friend like George. He was a bodyguard as well as a friend. In those days, when people were quicker to flare up and settle the smallest dispute with a punch, it gave you some comfort to have a mate like him. Gran Barnes' drinking friend was Mrs. Black, wife of the caretaker in the flats. In my day, it was Mr. Shore. Mr. and Mrs. Black had the appearance of two seasoned all-in wrestlers. Mr. Black was certainly the man for the job of caretaker. He was afraid of nothing on this earth.

'Nothing could put him down,' Mrs. Black would boast. One could see by her appearance that the statement could quite well apply to herself, too. She seemed more man than woman. Coarse in her ways, plump, tall and wide, in a long black coat that never seemed to come off her back.

One day, one or two of Gran Barnes' seventeen kids had been playing in the flats, just like I used to, on the landings and the stairs. Mr. Black came over to Gran's place, pulled the latch on her street door and shouted, 'Oi, Mary. Get your kids out of our flats. They're driving us made over here.'

Gran was a bit occupied at the time as she was just getting up dinner for nineteen people. 'Oh, piss off, will you. I've got enough to do here, without your problems.'

Bill's temper was up now — it didn't take much. 'Just wait till I see your old man,' he shouted down the dark passage.

'Balls,' Gran answered, and carried on with her dinner.

Bill Black waited for one of the kids to come down the stairs and when he reached the bottom he hammered him round the ear. Right, Mr. Black had thrown down the gauntlet.

Now Grandfather was well aware of the bulldozer strength of Black. He didn't exactly rush across to the caretaker's house. Eventually, he did summon up his strength and willpower and over he went. What he had forgotten was that Mrs. Black always fought alongside her husband. After all the usual preliminaries, Grandfather started to slip off his jacket. As it was half-way down his arms, it restricted his movements for a second or two. Over came the combined sledgehammer of both Blacks. Down went Grandfather.

When Dad came in, Grandfather was nursing a black eye. Black in every sense of the word. Plus a swollen jaw. The eye was Mr. Black's handiwork and the swollen jaw was his wife's feminine contribution. Dad knew that Grandad and he (tough as they were) were no match for the resilient Blacks. The only answer was Dad's heavy man, George.

Black was no novice in disputes of this kind. He knew that revenge would be diligently sought, and that retaliation would most certainly ensue until the offended party was satisfied that he had inflicted sufficient damage upon the agressor. George and Dad tried to waylay him time and again, without success. His years as caretaker had involved him in many similar situations. He had learned from experience just how to dodge any likely assailant.

It was on a Saturday night that he met his Waterloo. Dad and George had no belligerent thoughts on Saturday nights. But it just so happened that they were standing outside Dad's house when Black came burping along one evening. He was making for home, after a bladder-full at the Wheatsheaf. As he came unguardedly by, they made a grab for him. The shock seemed to sober him up. He struggled free and ran as fast as his twenty stone would let him to his flats.

Dad and George were hot on his heels. Their victim could not get his door open quite fast enough. As he fumbled with the key, he turned to look. He should not have done that, for as he did so, he caught one right under the Vera Lynn from George's great mauler. It was a punch of such momentum that the door collapsed as Black was thrown against it. With that, the pair ran downstairs. Black lay there, motionless. They watched the performance from a darkened doorway, and saw the funny side of it, as the neighbours carried Black in, using the door as a stretcher.

In his young days, George used to visit the 'Premier Land' boxing booth on Sunday mornings, hoping for a fight so that he could buy himself a pair of shoes. That is gospel. For a win, he would get seven-and-six and for a lose five bob. There was the occasional added bonus, win or lose, of a fantastic black eye. Or again, he might get off with his jaw being somewhat enlarged. But if you had the physique of Uncle George, you didn't have much to worry about. One punch from him was like being hit with a hundredweight sack of coals.

Hard times they most certainly were. The quality of life of those in work was hardly any different from those who were not. In those times, women had to scrape for a penny to put in the gas meter. If their husband had a job, they didn't have to start scraping till about Wednesday. If he didn't, they were scraping all the time, in varying degrees. It was an every-day thing then to see children with no shoes on. Some kids even had to have their heads shaved to get rid of fleas. I can remember that still going on in my school days.

They call them the Good Old Days. Good for the well-to-do perhaps, as ever, but not for the likes of my family. The Good Old Days? They can stick that up their Jaxie as far as they can get. Even after all these years, we are still only on the brink of what you might call good days. Kids are better dressed. Better housing is being built, although many are still living in shacks and some don't even have a roof over their heads.

Yes, a good percentage of the working class are certainly living better today than they did in the twenties. But this really isn't the way to look at it. We always seem to be looking back when we should be looking at what we could have. We could compare that with what we've got now, instead of looking at what it was like years ago and thinking how lucky we are. By looking at it this way, we will advance much more quickly. All I hope is that we never have to go through what our ancestors went through. Don't let us kid ourselves that it could never happen. It could happen all too easily in this unstable, dog-eat-dog world.

I can only write of my own observations and what I have heard about these great East End people. They don't have dreams of fast cars and jet planes (at least, the more mature ones don't) or a life of luxury hotels and big cigars. All they want out of life is a decent living, without the worry of paying high prices week after week for the most essential things, like rent, food, clothing. They have no desire to join, and indeed have no chance of joining the middle-class rat race. Almost all the working-class man's wages go on his family's keep. Anything left over is for a holiday, or perhaps the occasional new suit. He could never join the rat race, even if he wanted to. But all he wants is a fair wage and fair prices. If people are suffering from nervous tension and all the other ailments that modern society has produced, it isn't because the working man has joined the rat race but because he is finding it more and more difficult to live.

7 From 1940

It was now 1940. Nothing was to be the same again. This was for the better in some respects and for the worse in others. Women were to smoke, the same as men, wear overalls and chew gum. These would have been shocking things to do in the past. We were in modern times now. Things were beginning to change. We even had a brand-new, modern war. It was this that changed people's whole way of life. The war brought about much unfaithfulness between husband and wife. Families were broken up for ever. Not so much through unfaithfulness; that could be forgiven. The real disruption came from the bombing and killing.

I was about seven, and more aware of what was going on around me. There was one thing I can remember liking about the war. This was that I no longer had to sit outside our flats in Holly Bush Gardens eating chips with my Aunt Winnie (who was about fourteen at the time) waiting for my Mum to come home from work. I used to hate that, especially in the winter when it got dark early.

That was all finished. Dad was out of work and now so was Mum. We all moved to Hill House in Downham, Bury St. Edmund's. When I say all, I mean all my father's family as well as us. It was a smashing war for me in that respect. My parents were always around, plus the rest of Dad's family. They weren't all there. There was Gran, her daughters Rene, Hettie, Winnie, Betty, Florrie and my Uncle Johnny, who was only eighteen months my senior. Down the road was Gran's eldest daughter Polly with her children. So no one was lonely.

It was a great time, apart from the scrimping and saving. The house was large and gloomy, more of a mansion really. No one dared to go up to the top floor. It was much too creepy. At the back was the biggest garden I have ever seen. Rather different to the old back yards down Poyser Street. There were apple trees everywhere. The only thing that spoiled it was the cemetery next door. It's funny when I think of it now, because us kids didn't call it a garden or that other posh name of 'lawn'. It was so big that we called it the 'field'. Well, I suppose it was really.

I remember seeing my first mole, emerging from the ground. 'Look out, John,' I shouted. 'There's a rat over there.' Well, John was scared stiff, wasn't he? Anyway, we told my Dad about it.

My Dad knew everything. He certainly had a nut on him. How he knew so much about everything, I don't know. We got him to come and have a look and right away he says, 'It's not a rat. It's a mole.' He picked it up and got us to stroke it. We loved moles after that. We used to amuse ourselves for hours with them. We had such deep respect for those moles that if we found a dead one we would give it a proper burial, and stick a small, wooden cross on its grave.

Once I fell out with John and it developed into a bit of a fight. He got the better of me. When I got home, I told Dad all about it.

'All right,' he said, 'I'll see to him.'

I got home earlier than John on this particular afternoon, and Dad and I went into the field. Dad selected the largest apple he could find. It was an enormous one. We stood on some bricks so that we could see over the fence onto the street, and waited for John to come along. Dad hung fire till he was well in range, then blimey, what a shot. It caught John right on the top of his napper. The apple burst into a million pieces. He hollered, more with shock than pain. He went on holding his bonce, looking round and wondering where in the world it had come from. Me and Dad were in stitches. We slid down the fence onto the grass, helpless with laughter, hardly able to draw breath. John never found out who had shied the apple until years after, but he never forgot the incident.

Once we were out walking in the countryside and it was the time of year when the farmers left their sugar beets at the side of the road, ready for collection. I started to pick some dandelions. 'Don't pick them, Ron,' John warned me. 'You'll piss the bed, you will.' Whether or not the superstition is true, I don't know. But I did wet the bed for a whole week after. It must have been psychological.

Dad took a job on a coal lorry while we were down there. He put on his best suit and stiff white collar, to make a good impression. He was the smartest coalman Bury St. Edmunds had ever seen. You should have seen him when he came home. What a mess. He was as black as a Newgate's knocker when he came in. He came home in a different spirit than when he went out.

'Sod that job,' he said. 'No more or that for me.'

That was the end of Dad's coaling days. He hardly ever did a stroke all the time we were away.

One weekend we managed to get back to London. We went in Dad's coal lorry, before he finally packed the job in. All the family and other London friends climbed on board, and away we went. It was an open-backed lorry, and it was freezing. By the time we got to London that night, we could hardly move. What a ride that was. We stopped a thousand times to relieve ourselves. We had nothing at all to eat. We were cold and miserable, but the thought of getting back to London, even for a couple of days, cheered us all up. We sang songs all the way to keep our spirits up: 'Run, Rabbit, Run', 'Take Me Back to Dear Old Blighty', 'When the Lights Go On Again', all the songs of the day and many other older ones.

We dropped everyone off at Bethnal Green and arranged to meet them on Sunday for the rigorous journey back. Then we made for Gran Gullis' flat. By now, she was living in Quantock House, in the very posh neighbourhood of Stamford Hill. She stayed there for the rest of her life. Stamford Hill was a much cleaner area than the Green. It had more green than Bethnal Green ever had. There were even trees along the streets. There were some very nice-looking private houses in Stamford Hill, too. Though very old, Gran's flat was like a palace, compared to her place in Poyser Street. She settled down easily in Stamford Hill, because the flats had balconies like Craven Buildings. The neighbours could stand out there and talk to each other. There was the same communal atmosphere in Quantock as in Craven Buildings, though the neighbours were a little more reserved. Of course, it isn't quite like that now. The people are just as nice as they were during the war, but they don't seem to communicate like they did then.

On the Saturday night, there was a knock at Gran's door. When she answered, two great big Law were standing there.

'We're looking for your son-in-law, William Barnes,' one of them said. 'Have you seen him at all?'

'No,' Gran answered. 'He's down at Bury St. Edmunds with his family, as far as I know.'

This seemed to satisfy the Law, and away they went. Dad's firm had informed the police that he had stolen the lorry, when in fact he had only borrowed it for the weekend. What they didn't like was Dad using their petrol, as well as the lorry, for his short vacation. Petrol was strictly rationed then. When we got back to Bury St. Edmunds, Dad just dumped the lorry and kept himself out of the way till it all blew over.

As I had such a long journey to school, Dad made me a box on the back of his bike. In winter, he would sit me in it and take me to school. Dad wasn't very good at balancing with me in the back and I would have much preferred to walk, but he wouldn't hear of it. I used to hang on for dear life as I sat in that box and always felt relieved when we got to school, especially when the roads were icy.

In winter, Dad would amuse us kids by making snowmen or by rolling a snowball along until it was about six foot round. We would watch it gradually get smaller and smaller as the warm weather came along. If it hadn't been for my Dad, we kids would never have known what to do with ourselves. One Christmas we didn't have a pot. Dad was always boracic, now his betting job had gone. About three weeks before Christmas, he said, 'Right now. We're going to rehearse a play for Christmas night.'

With all us kids, Dad wasn't short of actors and actresses. We used old curtains to dress up in. Our hats were made of old cardboard. The play had something to do with an orphan boy who was sold to a master tradesman by a workhouse master. I was the orphan boy. We didn't do bad at it. It gave the adults a laugh, anyway.

There were no Christmas decorations for us. No Christmas tree, no pudding, nor turkey. Nor (strange as it may seem to some) did we get any toys. Gran Barnes did what she could by knocking up a giant-sized bread pudding. All her puddings were outsize, but the best was a suet pudding she made once. That gave her quite a problem when it came to getting it out of the pot. On this occasion, she managed to make some custard to go with the bread pudding, using half milk and half water. The dinner itself was so ordinary that I can't even remember what it was. My father got some pennies from somewhere and wrapped them in coloured paper. He gave one to each of us, for being such great performers. This was also our Christmas present.

Despite our lack of possessions, we managed to enjoy ourselves. Dad organised some games. We were all sent out of the room.

'Now, I want you one at a time,' said Dad. Of course, we were all eager to be first. If we had known what was in store, I don't think we would have been so eager. John was first. The kids waited in silence, trying to hear what was going on. Suddenly, there were roars of laughter. We waited, looking at each other, puzzled. We couldn't wait to get in and see what was happening. In went the next one. The same hilarious laughter again.

'Right, next one,' Dad called. The next one was me. In I went, full of enthusiasm. One the table stood a plate. On the plate was a mound of flour and right on top of the mound rested a penny.

'Right,' said Dad. 'You've got to pick up the penny with your mouth, without getting any flour on your face.'

I was keen. Too keen to realise the danger I was in. Down went my head to the plate and I tried carefully to lift the penny. Suddenly, my head was pushed flat into the pile of flour. I got a mouthful as well as a faceful. They loved it, especially the previous two victims. This was my Dad all over. If he hadn't been there, it would have been one of the worst Christmases. Instead it was the best. It hardly seems possible that you can say that about a Christmas with none of the trimmings.

Things were beginning to get a bit hot for Dad, so we decided to come home to London before the Law could grab him. Everybody knows everybody else in the country. Much to Dad's disadvantage, everyone knew the local Bogey, and vice versa. As the locals were none too keen on us Cockneys (I think we were too rowdy or something) he decided to take refuge in the one place he knew would be safe.

Back we went to Holly Bush Gardens. The first thing we had to do was get our furniture out of storage. We had next to nothing in hard cash at the time.

'Well, you'll have to pay the five quid you owe before you can have your stuff, Madam,' said the pot-bellied boss. What a riduculous way to address someone. Madam. We've got some diabolical words, us English.

We just didn't know what to do.

'Can't we pay you off so much a week?' asked Mum, a little nervously.

'No, can't do that,' he said emphatically. 'Tell you what, though. Let me have that piano of yours and we'll call it a day. I'll deliver all the stuff to your place, as well.'

'I should think you would,' retorted Mum, sharply. Then she remembered that she had to control herself. She had hardly any money and at least she had been given the chance to get back what was ours.

'Well, it's up to you, Madam. Take it or leave it. It's entirely up to you.'

Mum and Dad looked at each other in defeat.

'All right, then,' Mum decided. 'Can you bring it round right away?'

'Certainly, Madam,' Fat-guts answered, piously.

Me, I could have cried. I loved bashing that piano, the first and last one I ever had. Not only that, Gran has bought it especially for me, and had kept up the payments on it until it was ours. It was a great loss to Mum and Dad, but an even greater loss to me.

I cheered myself up with the thought of having all our furniture back. Also, Gran had a piano at her place in Quantock House. I could go up and have a go on that. There were times, though, when I went up there that Gran was unable to stand the strange tones I used to produce. After suffering a good five minutes of it, she had to ask me to give it a rest.

I think Dad realised how disappointed I was. One Sunday dinner time, he came home from the Lane (Club Row) with his winkles and shrimps under one arm, a ukelele under the other, and a slight tinge of beer on his breath. The ukelele was for me. A couple of strings were missing, but they could be bought at the one and only music shop in Bethnal Green, on Norton Folgate. That shop is still there. I was thrilled with the instrument. Two strings missing or not, I strummed away like a lunatic. I didn't have a clue how to play a scale on it. I think if I had had someone to show me how to get the notes I wanted, I could have mastered it. But we didn't know anyone in the neighbourhood who was musical. I just contented myself with strumming away as I sang a tune.

The bombing got worse each night, so Dad sent Mum and me away again. He stayed at home and made what money he could. This time we went to St. Ives in Cambridgeshire, not far out of London. I can still remember the name of the street: Penny Farthing Close. The place belonged to old age pensioners. They were quite nice people to live with. The only trouble was, that the wife didn't seem to realise that you could have other things for dinner, besides spam and potatoes. Food was short, it's true, but blimey, you could get dried egg powder and sometimes a beetroot or a piece of meat off your ration book. But not her. It was spam and potatoes for ever, with her. Even now, I detest spam. It reminds me too much of the war.

It was at Penny Farthing Close that I had the experience of getting a bag of sour cheese sploshed in my face. The old dear we lived with used to hang a linen bag from her clothesline with sour milk in it. She would leave it there, dangling and stinking, till it turned to cheese. Whenever I went out to the carsey, I couldn't resist poking at it from underneath. I would even pretend to go to the bog, just to give it a poke with a rigid index finger. Now and again, she would catch me at it, peeping out behind her curtains.

'Stop that, you little devil,' she'd bawl, almost losing her teeth in the process.

This time, I overdid the old poke. *Splonk.* I was covered in stinking cheese. I smelt like a cheese factory gone wrong. At least the saturation saved my skin. They were so delighted with the sight which met their eyes, and so helpless with laughter, that they forgot to clout me. I never came within poking distance of a cheese bag again.

I had my second romantic experience while I was at St. Ives. I suppose I was about eight at the time. I had not one, but two admirers. They were just crazy about me. That was understandable, seeing how I was the only boy in the street. There was Joyce, a tubby blonde, and Melinda, who had the most beautiful brown hair and eyes. They would both hold my arm when we went to play on the swings in the forest. They fought for my attention. It was smashing. Nothing pleases the male more than two females fighting over him.

It was a pity that I broke Melinda's arm, for I think she was really the one I preferred. It happened like this. We were having a go on the see-saw. Melinda sat on one end, so Joyce immediately came round to my end. Melinda's end was on the floor, so Joyce and I had to push our end down before we could get on. Now Joyce was no light weight. Just as our end was level with our waists, we both jumped on together. Our end crashed to the ground, and Melinda fell off. So Melinda had to stay at home for a couple of days and Joyce had me all to herself. Mind you, this didn't stop Melinda handing me one of her little notes whenever I passed her window.

In the summer, my mother and my aunt might go down the local. That's all there was to do round there. Before the war, it was a terrible thing for a woman to go into a pub, but since the war people have more liberal views. Those who had been evacuated had to do something or they would have gone nuts.

The country life was not at all to the taste of many Londoners. It was too quiet and dull, compared with the life they had been used to in East End areas like Poyser Street. That is why many of the older ones stayed in London right through the war. Bethnal Green was a part of them: the pubs, the people, the shops. Even those decrepit old terraced houses, that had seen so much hardship. Nothing that Hitler could do would drive them away from the place where they had been born and bred.

They loved Bethnal Green, yet sometimes they hated it. The old people could remember the Bishops Way Workhouse, with the inmates being let out at certain set times, dressed in their grey workhouse clothes (an appropriate colour, I should say). Then

117

there was the smell of the horses in the stables opposite the houses, and the cry of the winkle and shrimp man, punctually every Sunday afternoon. This was their place. They were so attached to it that the fear of bombs never overcame their love of Bethnal Green. Many stayed there and many died there during the war.

The war was drawing to a close. Although Hitler was almost done for, there were still air raids on London. But Mum decided it would be safe to go home now. Dad had been kicked out of Holly Bush Gardens for not paying the rent. He was staying with Gran Gullis. Our furniture was once again back with the pot-bellied warehousemen. I must have been ten-and-a-half by then and times were very hard. Yet we had some good moments.

Gran Gullis' brother George was a real comedian. He'd come in pissed every Saturday night, and sometimes during the week as well, and tell us how many coppers he'd done over that night. I think he must have done at least one every Saturday. Whenever George was pissed, out would come this tale. Whether there was any truth in it or not, I don't know.

One Saturday night he said to me, Come on, Ron. Get your ukelele. I'm taking you down the pub with me tonight.' Away we went to George's local, the Wheatsheaf in Windus Road. I stood just inside the pub, behind the draught curtain out of sight of the governor. George brought me a muscado. I liked them. They were the same colour as beer and it made me feel more grown-up than drinking lemonade.

'Come on, Ron,' George said, when the men had finished their darts session for the night, 'give us a song now.'

Having convinced myself that I was intoxicated enough on my muscado, I stood behind the curtain, just letting my head pop out. Then I let rip. I was a bit shy of course, but Uncle George encouraged me by joining in with his mates:

> 'This old coat that I've got on,
> The inside is all right
> But the outside has seen better weather,
> So I cast this coat aside.
>
> I don't work for a living,
> I get on all right without.
> Don't toil all day,
> Simply because I'm not built that way.

Some people work for love,
Others for sunshine or rain.
But if I can't get sunshine
Without any work,
I'd rather stay out in the rain.'

'Hurrah,' they shouted at the end of my performance, 'more, more.' This drew the governor's attention.

'Get that boy out of here,' he shouted. He was slopping pints of mild and bitter over the counter, his shirt sleeves rolled up. He looked as if he could have done with a drink himself, judging by the way he was sweating.

I withdrew my head, until George came back-stage with another request for me to sing. After hearing the governor's fog-horn, I was a little reluctant to chance another of my off-key renderings like 'Lily Marlene', or 'We're Gonna Hang out the Washing on the Siegried Line'.

'Don't worry about him,' George egged me on, 'he's only the governor.'

So away I went again. By now, the governor realised that Uncle George was the one behind all this joviality and music. He called him over and had a word with him in the nicest way he could, concealing his discontent at my presence as much as possible. The reason for these unaggressive tactics was that George was a great drinker. All publicans like great drinkers, of course. Who can blame them, when it's their livelihood? The governor didn't want to lose a consumer like George, so he conveyed his feelings about my voice and musical accompaniment in the nicest possible way, adding that the pub was not licensed for music.

Uncle George listened patiently while the governor told of his distress at having to put the block on his new musical discovery. 'OK, guv,' answered George. Then he came straight over to me, poked his head through the curtain and said, 'Go on, Ron. Let's have "I've Got Sixpence".'

The governor was continuing his splashing act at the bar. He heard my voice and caught sight of my head, poking through the curtain. His shoulders drooped in defeat. George had won the battle. From then on, I made frequent appearances at the Wheatsheaf, and I no longer had to hide behind the curtain. The hat would be sent round at the end of the evening, which was of considerable financial benefit to me. It was then that I realised the value of musical talent, although my own was never very far advanced.

Although the war was on, I enjoyed those days living with the Gullis family. I remember Uncle George coming home one night, in his not uncommon intoxicated condition, with a giant beer bottle on his shoulder. Where he had got it from, heaven knows. It was a display prop from an off-licence, about four foot high and two foot in diameter. It always came out when we had a party at Gran's.

What turn-outs those parties were. There would always be one boozed participant who would lock himself in the carsey for a couple of hours, causing a queue of desperate drinkers outside. Sid, a family friend, would make the piano rock back and forth, his head down and his elbows high, as if he was going in for the kill. I would stand and watch, fascinated, as he shook his sweating bald head and stamped his right hoof in doubtful time to the music.

I used to think, 'Blimey, he sounds good. I'd like to play like him. But I wouldn't want to look like that while I was doing it.'

The air-raid shelter in Gran Gullis' flats was a rectangular brick building, about twelve feet high. It had four windows, set very high up in the wall. You couldn't look out of them, and it wouldn't have made any difference if they'd been built lower, for they were of smoked glass covered with close-mesh wire. These windows measured about four foot by two. Just big enough to let in enough daylight to see by.

It was a depressing place, with half-a-dozen forty-watt bulbs running down the centre of the ceiling. The floor was grey concrete. Around the walls were bunk beds, three high. A couple of old 1930 armchairs stood at each corner in the yellow dimness. On one wall hung a dartboard. A few upright wooden chairs were scattered around, plus small tables and beer crates. These were used for playing cards on, or for meals. We played draughts, dominoes, tiddly-winks, snakes and ladders; anything to take our minds off the bombs.

A depressing atmosphere indeed. Uncle George would liven it up, though; especially of a Saturday night, when it was odds-on he'd be pissed. He didn't care a sod about the bombs. He'd walk home from the Wheatsheaf during a raid, full of Truman's ale. Bombs would be exploding, anti-aircraft guns booming away, and down the road swayed George, still clutching a pint beer bottle and singing at the top of his voice:

'This is the army, Mr. Jones.
No private rooms or telephones.

You had your breakfast in bed before,
But you won't get it there any more.'

He would then go to bed and sleep through the lot.

Some people would pack down on one of the bunks. Others were unable to sleep at all, and would sit up playing cards or dozing fitfully in the armchairs. As a result of these sleepless nights, people would go to work (and children to school) unable to put in a good day. Families became irritable with each other. Most of the arguments were only minor ones, though. Everybody knew how the others were feeling, and most of the differences were quickly smoothed over.

Every night we got into bed, knowing full well that we would be up again before morning. All, that is, except Uncle George, who would continue his nasal symphony till daybreak.

Despite the way of life at that time, I rather liked it at Gran Gullis! I liked the clean freshness of her home, her self-sufficient nature, her fantastic apple pie, her unmatchable curry and, most of all, her Berry piano. However, our life with Gran ended quite soon, when Mum and Dad found a place in Brooke Road. That was in 1944, at the end of the war.

8. Brooke Road

Brooke Road is a rather long street, running from Upper Clapton to Stoke Newington High Street. When we moved there, it was just like the country, with trees all along the footpath. It was a mainly Jewish area, with large, three-storey houses. There were three families in the houses that were rented out. We were lucky; our flat overlooked Stoke Newington Common. This was certainly a much better place than Bethnal Green.

We moved into number forty, right at the top, on a Saturday morning. The two families below us were Jewish, and related. Boober lived directly underneath us with her husband, Mr. Alex or Zeider. 'Boober', or 'Buba', in Yiddish is equivalent to 'Gran' and 'Zeider', or Zayde, means 'Grandad'. This is how I addressed them, right from the time we moved in. Boober and Zeider were a dear old couple and stood all our Cockney antics very well. On the ground floor lived Mr. and Mrs. Hamburg, with their two sons. Charlie was about my age, and Cecil must have been about fourteen.

Well, we moved in. We didn't have much, though by some miracle Mum managed to get her bedroom suite back out of storage. This was the most valuable possession we had. It had been bought in about 1930 and was still going strong in 1960, the time of my parents' divorce. I had no bedroom suite at the time, so I slept with my parents. The kitchen doubled up as a sitting room. We had three rooms in all. The large one was our bedroom. The one next to it was to be mine, when we could get a bed.

The three flights of stairs up to our flat were killers for those over forty. There was a strut missing at the top of the first flight. On Boober's landing stood the shared toilet and, next to that, Boober's wooden food cupboard. Although Mrs. Hamburg had her own outside toilet, they were none too keen on using it, especially in the winter. So they would use the one on Boober's landing, making three families all using the same WC.

We were well pleased to see the bathroom, next to the toilet. We had a bath every time the geezer was working properly. If it went wrong, out would come the zinc bath in the kitchen, and in I'd go. My mother and father would each wait till they were alone, before taking the plunge. They would make a quick job of it, for fear one of us might come in.

In the kitchen we had two old armchairs, an old, unpolished, unpainted table whose legs had been used as a scratching board by a cat. We had a sideboard at one end of the not-quite-square room, which my father had made before the war. To fill up the space under the window, there was a dressing table with the mirrors taken off. Mum used this for her linen, and on top of it stood our utility accumulator wireless set. The case was made of plywood, polished in its natural colour. It was a rectangular shaped box, with a little window in it to see where the stations were: the Light and the Home. You could get 'Dick Barton, Special Agent' and 'ITMA', with that great comedian Tommy Hanley. Plus that master of rhyme, Cyril Fletcher, with Stanley McPherson at the organ, and band leaders like Victor Sylvester, Geraldo and Harry Roy.

Our food cupboard was rather small, but what with food being rationed and Dad out of work, this was no problem at all. At the top of the cupboard Mum kept her innumerable pots and pans. Cooking utensils were one commodity we seemed to have plenty of. If you wanted to get the salt cellar or the jam pot out of this cupboard of ours, you were exposed to a double hazard. Either one of Mum's heavy pots would come down on your bonce, or Dad would suddenly open the flat door which was at right angles to the food cupboard. As it opened, the door sent you flying.

We had a small fireplace, surrounded by a brass fender. In front of the fire was a coconut mat, the one and only with a dirty great hole right in the centre. There was a mirror above the mantelpiece. When you had finished combing your hair in the mirror you had to be very careful. As you walked away you would find your feet tangled up in the hole in the mat, sending you arse over tip.

About this time, I realised that my mother was pregnant. I learned from the other kids in the street that when a woman's tummy got big it meant she was going to have a baby. I asked one on my informants, who had a rather fat mother, why his mother hadn't had a baby yet. 'Well,' he said, 'my Mum's just fat, that's all.' This left me wondering to what proportions she would expand if she became pregnant.

On October 20th 1944, my friends' theory was proved correct. At the age of eleven, I had a sister. Everybody said I would be jealous of her, but I don't think I was really. I felt good to be able to say to people, 'my sister done this,' or 'my sister said that'. I had gone eleven years without a brother or sister, hearing other kids talk about their sisters and brothers. Now it was my turn, and at the slightest opportunity I would talk about 'my sister'. Of course, the age gap did put us on somewhat different planes.

My Aunt Mary looked after me while Mum was in St. Bartholomew's Hospital. I had one of my earliest asthma attacks during that fortnight, though Aunt Mary looked after me like a mother. I got more and more excited as the time drew near for Mum to come home with the baby. Dad put up some new wallpaper, which he bought with the money Mum had earned doing some home work. The work was called making dollies. Let me tell you about it.

Dollies were not little pink things in white dresses, as you might imagine from the name. They were the insides of torch batteries, black carbon cylinders. Mum's job was to wrap a piece of gauze round the cylinder and tie it with cotton. My Aunt Flo had started Mum on this job. They used to work in what was supposed to be my bedroom. Mum had just started carrying when Flo persuaded her to do dollies. What with Dad out of work and a baby on the way, things looked very black indeed. So Mum and Auntie Flo took on the dollies. Things really were black then, from the carbon dust.

They would sit all day, tying the gauze round the batteries. They were then placed back in their boxes, which measured about two foot by eighteen inches. When full, each box weighed 56lb. The carbon dust got ingrained in their hands and was almost impossible to wash off. Their finger nails were continually black. The dust would be all round their noses and mouths, all over their clothes. It eventually clung to the wallpaper and everything else in the room.

The dollies came in three sizes. The small ones were the hardest work, and paid eight shillings for two hundred. One box would be a full day's work for two people. Then there were the easier ones, the large size, which paid three and nine per hundred. They only took half a day. The very large ones were fifty for one and nine. That took a couple of hours.

The workers had to collect and deliver the dollies themselves. For this part of the job, Mum and Flo acquired an old pram, a very common mode of transportation in East London, even today. They would load the small pram to capacity, and even then they never had room for the last three boxes. Then there was the journey to Stamford Hill. When they got to the factory they had to carry the 56lb boxes up a long, steep flight of wooden stairs. Then they picked up another box, ready to take home on the pram. Finally, they would collect their two quid or so, and make off for home with the two hundredweight of dollies. On arrival, they unloaded the cargo, and made two or three journeys up and down our three flights of stairs. On the last trips down, they would bring the other finished work that they had not been able to get on the pram for the first delivery. Then they went marching back to Stamford Hill, to repeat the process once more.

Time passed, and Mum knew she had to stop this work now she was seven months gone. It wasn't only the physical strain. The carbon dust, which seemed to get into everything, was not the sort of thing to bring a baby into. A couple of months with no dollies would just about give the black carbon which was ground into Mum's nails time to fade.

By the time Mum came home from hospital, the place looked like a new pin. The baby made our lives so much brighter. I would come in from playing in the street every night at six, to see my sister being bathed. I was proud to push her out in her almost-new, utility pram. Before, when I'd seen other boys pushing their siblings in prams, I'd taken a right piss out of them. I used to call them 'nancy boys', or something like that. Now I was one of them, and enjoyed it immensely. I had a sister and was quick to let everyone know about it. I loved her; until, that is, she ate half my stamp album when she was three months old. That was the first bit of antagonism I felt towards her. I had to accept that this was one of the drawbacks of having a young sister.

At Christmas time that year, I was officially told that Santa Claus was a myth. I knew really, long before my parents told me, but by acting ignorant I had always been sure of getting something in my stocking. This Christmas had been a really bad one as far as money was concerned. On Christmas Eve, Dad only had a ten-bob note in his pocket. Within my hearing, he said to Mum,

'Well, Hett, he won't be getting much this year. All I've got is ten bob.'

Then he turned to me and said, 'Well, you know there isn't really a Father Christmas, don't you?' I neither nodded my head nor shook it at this bit of unwanted information.

'Well, look, I tell you what,' continued Dad, 'Mum'll take you round the toy shop and buy you something with this ten bob. How's that?'

I wasn't too pleased. Usually of a Christmas, I hadn't done too bad. I was used to getting one good present, like a wooden aeroplane, as well as a small Christmas stocking and some sweets and fruit. Mum put her coat on and we went round to the toy shop. I picked out a wooden machine gun, which fell to pieces in a couple of days. The toy didn't come to the full ten bob, so Dad was able to get himself a packet of Gold Flake cigarettes with the change.

After that Christmas, Dad managed to get a lorry-driving job with a transport firm in Stamford Hill. He got £10 a week, plus tips. This made some difference, but we were never to see the luxury of his bookmaking days again. Dad tried everything imaginable to make money in his spare time, so many things that I couldn't possibly go through them all.

Mum, Dad and the baby moved into the dolly-making room, now it had been done up. I slept in the large front room. My own bedroom at last? Well, not entirely. It was now a sort of bedroom-cum-workshop. I slept by the wall in my newly-acquired single bed, opposite the two large windows. I hated sleeping in that room. It was large and cold, especially in the winter.

We would all get sweltering hot in the kitchen, where we had the heat of the gas oven as well as the coal fire. Then we would retire to our freezing beds. My large room would be like a fridge. I used to lie there shivering for ages, till my body warmed the sheets. Then I dropped off.

Mum could never keep a coal fire in every room. It was hard enough to keep one in the kitchen. Even now that Dad was at work, she couldn't always afford to buy a hundredweight, or even half a hundredweight, from the coalman who called on us. Instead, out would come Old Faithful, the pram, and she would go down to Manor Road coal depot for a quarter hundredweight. She sometimes had to do this after a full day's work.

This is no figment of my imagination. I am glad to say that my mother is still around to confirm my words. I feel that she does not like me writing about this sort of thing, but she has helped me a great deal with putting this book together. I think people hide their hardships too much. This applies to quite a few people these days, too. If people do not come out with their experiences, we will get a picture of everyone, from peer to pauper, living a happy contented life. All right, things aren't as bad as they used to be, but there are still poor people about. Some have been poor all their lives and have grown so accustomed to it that they don't even realise how poor they are.

It is only now, in my forties, that I realise, looking back, just how hard-up we were. It was this poverty which caused my father to pursue his futile efforts at trying to make good. No-one could have done more to try and free themselves than Dad, sitting in that room which turned into one kind of workshop after another. He mended wirelesses, he made toys, teddy bears, leather purses, belts, aprons, plaster ornaments, imitation jewellery. He bred budgies in my bedroom-workshop. When all this failed, he cleared people's gardens, decorated their rooms, mended their cars, french polished their furniture, gave them driving lessons, taught them ballroom dancing. He also worked weekends for a local catering firm.

Sometimes I would go to the catering firm with him. I used to earn myself a couple of quid, good money at twelve years' old, working in the kitchen: humping boxes of plates, cutlery and silver, washing up, packing all the gear back into the cases and loading them onto the lorry. I worked from eight in the morning till about one the next morning. At that age, I loved it. Well, there was plenty of lovely grub, like french fried potatoes. I ate them as fast as the poor woman could cook them, till she would wave her metal slice and swear at me in her foreign tongue.

By the time we got home, with our bags full of cakes, fruit, creams and anything else that was going, we were whacked. We had our last cup of tea and got into bed. It was all right if we did the job on Saturdays. We could lie in till two in the afternoon on Sunday. But if we were working on a Sunday night, I'd be falling asleep all next day in school and I expect my Dad felt the same driving his lorry. It's no wonder he hardly ever had time to go out for a drink with Mum. He was obsessed with the need to make good and start his own small business.

Mum and I would sit of a night, painting wooden toys. This venture would last about six months, die a natural death, then be replaced with a new idea. Next, we would be assembling imitation jewellery or painting plaster ornaments. Dad's mind was never still, continually planning and scheming how to make money. 'If you're lucky,' he'd say, 'you can become rich in a very short time.' Then he would quote pieces out of the News of the World, about rags-to-riches blokes who started with one penny and finished up making a million, or an empire, even.

My Dad's efforts taught me what a lot of bull-shit that all is. No one could have tried like he did. He was devoted to making good as one might be devoted to an ideology or a religion. He was still trying when he was sixty-three, and was well into the antiques game just before he died. At a generous estimate, he left £200. People run away with the idea that there is big money in antiques. There is, if you can spend big money. It is just because it is so rare to pick something up for a penny and sell it for a thousand quid that the newspapers make such a thing of it.

At one time, Dad was doing quite nicely mending cars. He started putting away two bob a week for me, in a drawer. 'Now,' he said, 'when you start work you can put to that yourself each week. That will give you a bit of capital.'

The idea soon faded, as Dad thought up another scheme.

'There's an old V8 pilot up the road.' he said thoughtfully, one day. 'Fourteen pound. Now if I bought that and did it up a bit, I could get twenty-five on it. The only thing is, I've only got a cockerel. Another four nicker and I'd have the fourteen.'

Dad looked at me, knowingly. The two bobs he had put away for me came to exactly four quid. They were in a blue cash bag in the sideboard. Dad went to the sideboard, fought with the ill-fitting drawer, put his hand in and pulled out the paper bag. He turned apologetically to me and said, 'Look, I can make a good eleven quid profit on this. When I do, I'll put the four nicker back and another sheet besides, OK?' I was not over-enthusiastic about this plan. I nodded slowly, but something seemed to tell me my four nicker was gone for good. I was right.

We had the car in the front garden, much to the delight of the other resident! They stuck it well, though. Dad was underneath, repairing and swearing. At last, the heap was ready for the road. Dad had a mate who drove a break-down wagon. He hooked us on. As we turned the corner, something went crunch. The near-side front wing had snapped. Dad sweated and swore like nothing I had ever heard before. He soon remedied matters by replacing the broken spring with a block of wood.

One Sunday morning, Mum and I got a real shock. 'Coming out for a ride in the car this afternoon, Hett? I mean, we might as well get a bit of use out of it, before I sell it.' This was Dad talking. We couldn't believe our ears. Dad spent nearly all his spare time in the workroom, making something or other, but this new venture seemed just up our street. This could be the beginning of Sunday afternoons in Epping Forest. We hoped it would last long enough to give us a few outings, anyway.

I was quite excited about us going for outings in Our Own Car. It cheered Mum up, too. It would make a nice change from our usual Sunday afternoon lay-down: Mum in bed and Dad sitting in a battered armchair, his feet hanging out of the window in summer (the best place for them, I may say) and his News of the World over his face.

We were all set for the road. We had had our dinner, and Mum had made up some sandwiches to take with us. In her bag was a bottle of lemonade. We made our way downstairs. I kept a look-out for dangerous holes in the lino, an instinctive reaction by now. If you caught your foot in a worn part, over you'd go.

Mum and I got into the banger. I had never understood why old cars were called bangers, but I was soon enlightened as the engine detonated into life on Dad's thousandth turn of the starter handle. Dad jumped in as fast as he could. To keep the engine ticking over, he pumped the accelerator like mad. It was not dissimilar to a surgeon pumping oxygen into a patient who he had just brought back to life, in an obstinate battle to make him live on. The old car seemed to tremble as it moved off, like a greyhound suffering from malnutrition. We turned right into Rectory Road, intending to do a left into Downs Road and then up Lea Bridge Road towards Epping. Alas, we never got that far.

The banger coughed and choked its way almost as far as Downs Road, like a chronic bronchitic. Suddenly there was an ear-splitting explosion. I had heard plenty of explosions in London, but never of such combustive force as this one. The car was now enveloped in the blackest smoke imaginable. It hung around for two or three minutes, then cleared. No longer were we surrounded by black fog. Black faces, wide-eyed with astonishment, encircled us now. Dad opened the bonnet and fiddled about. His head emerged from the works, black and sweating.

'It won't make it,' he announced. 'You'd better go home.'

We did, leaving Dad to perform another miracle on the old heap which should have been pensioned off long ago. That was our afternoon out. Mum put the kettle on and made a cup of Rosie Lee. About an hour later, Dad came chugging home.

Not long after, Dad rid himself of this load of trouble. He found someone willing to take the car off his blistered, cut and greasy hands for £14. Dad forgot to tell the purchaser about the block of wood under the front wheel. He also forgot to repay the four nicker he had taken out of my savings. But then Dad was always absent-minded about things, especially when it was to his advantage financially.

Next, he bought a dozen box tricycles, with the idea of setting himself up in the ice-cream game. He left the trikes in the front garden while he got them ready for the road. Of course, we had no fridge or anything like that. But Dad was now carting fish on his lorry. His idea was to make up a lot of ice cream in a big container, hump it onto his van and take it to the cold store, where he picked up his fish. But Dad was unlucky. The cold store bloke wouldn't hear of it. That was another of Dad's businesses frozen solid.

Then he got interested in ballroom dancing. He got on so well that he won a medal, and the principal asked him if he would like to teach. Dad said he would, and helped out two or three times a week. He enjoyed having the extra money, but he just could not get the idea of having his own dancing school out of his head. So, to put his mind at rest, that's what he did. He rented the hall once a week and charged half-a-crown entrance fee. He needed a radiogram, but he was blowed if he was going to pay out for one.

Not long after, Dad rid himself of this load of trouble. He found someone willing to take the car off his blistered, cut and greasy hands for £14. Dad forgot to tell the purchaser about the block of wood under the front wheel. He also forgot to repay the four nicker he had taken out of my savings. But then Dad was always absent-minded about things, especially when it was to his advantage financially.

Next, he bought a dozen box tricycles, with the idea of setting himself up in the ice-cream game. He left the trikes in the front garden while he got them ready for the road. Of course, we had no fridge or anything like that. But Dad was now carting fish on his lorry. His idea was to make up a lot of ice cream in a big container, hump it onto his van and take it to the cold store, where he picked up his fish. But Dad was unlucky. The cold story bloke· wouldn't hear of it. That was another of Dad's businesses frozen solid.

Then he got interested in ballroom dancing. He got on so well that he won a medal, and the principal asked him if he would like to teach. Dad said he would, and helped out two or three times a week. He enjoyed having the extra money, but he just could not get the idea of having his own dancing school out of his head. So, to put his mind at rest, that's what he did. He rented the hall once a week and charged half-a-crown entrance fee. He needed a radiogram, but he was blowed if he was going to pay out for one. They were expensive enough second-hand, let alone new. It would have made too large a hole in his already pint-sized capital.

He still had some electrical stuff up in his workroom, the remains of a previous venture. He scooped the lot together, took the drawers out of a cabinet he had made in about 1928, and converted it into a radiogram. It took him about a week to finish. He was all set now, and every week he would cart the lot round the hall on our old faithful pram. In the end, for reasons I cannot recall, that undertaking went down the pan, like all the rest.

Now Dad was carting fish, he was able to make certain gains at someone else's expense, mostly his governor's. He started collecting empty fish boxes and would stack them up to the ceiling in the bedroom-workshop. He came home with his van and then delivered the boxes to local factories. Mum gave up moaning about this after a while, and just took it as a way of life.

There was no knowing what Dad would get up to next. He'd come home with rolls of gelatine, two-hundredweight sacks of sea shells, bags of white plaster, boxes of this and sacks of something else. Mum was no longer interested what Dad had in them. She had grown so accustomed to it by now. If ever a man tried, my father certainly did. He did it to make life better for us, but really it had the opposite effect.

I used to play the hop more times than a flea on a dog's arse. I hated school and my asthma was a good excuse to stay away. That is why I was put into a convalescent home. If I had been fit, I think they would have put me in a school for truants. I liked it at the convalescent home, but it took me a long time to settle there. Some mornings I would wait outside Dad's garage for him to come out with his stinking fish van. He'd always have a moan at me for not going to school, but he invariably let me come with him.

The wet fish shop was owned by three Jewish brothers. Now and again, one of them might come out with us on the van. I didn't mind this much, so long as it wasn't Wally. The cab was rather small, and sitting between Wally — all twenty stone of him — and Dad was no joke. Wally would force his way through the door, heave himself onto me (causing me to become about a foot wide) and then go through the almost impossible process of shutting the door. His face was fat and red. It went rather well with his black hair and overcoat. Once in, neither of us could move an inch. We were packed like the tinned sardines that Wally sold in his shop. In fact, Wally's black coat and vast size made him look more like a whale than a sardine.

When we reached our destination, Dad would have to get out first and open Wally's door for him. Wally went through the same contortions as when he got in. He was a good bloke though. He used to give me half-a-crown every time I went out with Dad.

I'll never forget the time Dad was humping a barrel of bloaters off the lorry. They were in some sort of sauce. The lid of the barrel was rather ill-fitting. Dad humped the barrel off the tail-board onto his back. As he walked forward, he tripped slightly. The oily sauce spilled over the rim, right down his bushel and peck. I jumped into the cab, out of sight, and almost died laughing.

You should have seen Dad when he lost his temper. I remem-

ber going to a posh hotel with him once. He humped in about
four boxes of cod. Then he went to the bloke in charge with his
chit which had to be signed, and for a more important reason: his
tip. The man signed the chit and handed it back. Dad stood there,
waiting and watching the bloke's hands, hoping that one would
find its way into its owner's pockets, dive in and emerge with a
two-bob bit. The hands seemed lifeless.

'Er, all right?' prompted Dad.

'Oh yes,' the bloke answered.

Day rubbed his hands down his sides. 'Well, I'm glad it's all
right then,' he said, undaunted.

'Yes thank you,' replied the other. Still no sign of hands moving towards pockets.

Dad could see it was useless. 'Come on,' he said to me,
grumpily, and we made for the door.

'Just a minute,' the bloke called. We turned, and saw one of
his hands going into his pocket. Dad brightened at this new turn
of events. The bloke produced the lowest silver coin of the realm,
apart from the silver threepenny bit.

Dad's eyes bulged with contempt. 'A sprat,' he said, with hatred. 'Well, you can shove that up your dirt box, as far as you can
poke it. Four bleeding boxes of cod I've humped in here. You're
supposed to have your own staff for that. If I breaks me neck
while I'm in and out of your hotel, I can't claim a halfpenny. I
could be off work for a month and neither you nor my governor
would pay me that,' Dad snapped his fingers.

'Well, that's all we ever tip drivers.' the bloke replied.

Dad snatched the sixpence from his hand. 'All right,' he said.
'But don't expect me to hump your stuff in next time.'

We made our way out. As we got a few yeards away from this
poor tipper, Dad turned and threw the tanner at the bloke. The
poor fellow dived behind the fish boxes for protection.

Why was Dad so keen on his tip? There were two reasons. First,
it supplemented his poor wage. Also, if you refused to hump the
stuff in, the customer might phone your boss about it. The boss
would then have you in the office and give you a talking-to. If
you persisted in this gross misconduct, you would be given all the
shittiest jobs, with heavy humping and light tipping. You might
even be sacked, though they would never give this as the reason.
That was the strength of it then, and it may well apply even
today. So you humped. That way, you got your tip, small as it
might be, and kept your job, badly paid as that might be. It is
surprising how few people realise that a driver is not insured for

injury if he has a fall or something, while not actually inside his vehicle.

I used to love those days out on the van with Dad, especially when we went into the country. I took in the vast spaciousness of green fields: cows lying on the grass, golden haystacks in the distance, lambs leaping among brilliant yellow buttercups, a horse with its mane ruffled and flowing in the gentle breeze, its young foal following close behind. The smells of the country brought on my asthma, but that didn't worry me one bit. It was well compensated for by the beauty of this green land round about me.

When we finally got back into the smoke, it looked ten times worse than before, just like when we got back from being evacuated.

Germany had surrendered unconditionally now. We no longer had to black out our windows at night, or put sticky brown paper over them to stop them shattering in the air raids. No longer did the air raid wardens tramp the streets at night, like town criers. The wardens' cry was slightly different from their predecessors', though. Instead of 'Twelve o'clock and all's well,' it was 'Turn that bloody light out'. We discarded our gas masks now, instead of having them hanging over our shoulder wherever we went.

There were pictures of Hitler's handiwork in the newspapers. Skeleton-like corpses piled four high in vans. Pictures of shocking concentration camps.

Then there was the surprising gesture of Winston Churchill shaking hands with Joe Stalin. Generals like Eisenhower and Montgomery were household names. Men that ordinary people had never heard of before. But the shelters and the ration books were to remain for some time yet. The iron railings that once stood outside some town houses were never to be replaced. They had been turned into guns, bullets and bombs.

Large white sheets hung outside windows with 'Welcome home, Jim' (or Bob, or whatever) on them. The name doesn't matter to the reader. The thing is, it was their sons, their husbands, their daughters, uncles and aunts that they were welcoming home.

People could hardly wait for the official declaration of peace. On 7th May 1945, the East End sky was lit up with a fiery glow. It wasn't the incendiary bombs now. The fires were not there to kill or maim anyone, but to celebrate Britain's victory. We had won that war of bombs and killing – the physical war. But for the working class it had been just one war in many. They still had the battle of trying to live just above subsistence level, and the continued rationing didn't make that fight any easier. As least we chairs and bedsteads stood almost as high as the trees. In the West End, they went mad. People thronged the Mall and Trafalgar Square. They climbed lamp-posts and let off rockets (the peaceful kind); if they had them, that is, for all fireworks had been banned during the war.

We stayed at home and celebrated down our streets. There wasn't a street without a celebration going on down it. You could go from street to street, joining in with all of them. It was fantastic. People were so elated, free from the apprehension and tension of war. They seemed to be all as one, hugging each other whether they were close neighbours or total strangers. Everyone had forgotten their little differences of opinion. They were irrelevant now.

Tables stood in the middle of the roads, piled with sandwiches, lemonade and buns for the kids. Out came pianos, armchairs, kitchen tables. Men and women stood in the street, talking and drinking, singing, joking and laughing. The kids kept the fire going, stuffing themselves with buns the while. At one end of the road, a pianist played 'The Lambeth Walk', while at the other end it was 'Yes, We Have No Bananas'. Singing, dancing, screaming, shouting, drunk with the joy of victory, it was an anything-goes atmosphere now, all over London.

Some people were not able to share the joy of relief. Those who felt that now they had lost everything, a husband, son or daughter. It was no celebration for them, only heart-ache. They saw other women dancing with their sons, husbands holding their children in their arms and trying to kiss their wives at the same time, the whole family demanding their attention at once. Not a pleasant experience for the strongest, and one that time alone would heal.

Dad had always been a staunch Imperialist and head over heels about Churchill, so he was well pleased at the way his idol had handled the war.

'There y'are. I told you, see. You've got to have those Conservatives in. They've got the money and the brains. He's done a wonderful job, that man. A real gentleman and a hero, he is. There'll never be another like him, I tell you that.'

True, Churchill had a hand in the war, but blimey, to hear Dad you'd have thought Churchill had won the thing single-handed. Both Dad and Churchill were to get a nasty shock when Labour got in by quite a good majority.

'That's it,' Dad ranted. 'That's the bleeding thanks the man gets, after all he's done. Attlee? What's he done then, eh? Nuffink.

Nuffink at all. Yet that Labour lot take office. Gawd help us now.'

Labour were to remain for about ten or twelve years, but whether they were any worse than the Tories we don't know. The country was in a right old state at that time. We finished up owing Harry Truman a right old screw.

Now the HP boom started and people's homes started to look better than ever before. Not ours, though. We still seemed to be back in the thirties. One or two people had cars now, and things did seem to be improving gradually. There were more jobs available, so more money to spend. But not for Dad. According to him, money was to be saved and then speculated, not thrown away on trivialities like clothes, furniture and carpets.

'They all take you on anyway, with the HP lark.'

So Dad saved, and continued with one exploit after another. He still pulled out his own teeth, cut his own hair and mended his own boots. His politics always stayed the same: Socialists and Communists were the cause of all our troubles and set-backs. 'What we want in this country is a dictator, like old Franco. He'd put them all in their place. If they want to cause trouble, shoot them, that's all. That's the only way to get this country on its feet. We're too easy on everyone in this country. You've got to have people in Parliament who've got the money. The ones who've got it are the Tories, so it's them that's got to have the power. It's only common sense. I mean, what's the Labour Party got? Nuffink.'

Dad and I would go down Club Row together of a Sunday. He would stand and look on the stalls for ages, seeking out something cheap that he could make a few bob on. It might be an old duplicating machine, a battered wireless or perhaps a lawnmower. He would clean them up, make the necessary repairs and sell them.

It was all hustle and bustle down the Lane. An old Jewish woman used to stand with a million carrier bags over her arm, crying, 'Kaiser bugs, Kaiser bugs'. At first I wondered what Kaiser bugs were. I thought they were some kind of bug I hadn't seen before, until Dad translated for me. On one corner stood the chestnut man with a white-hot fire. We would get a warm-up while he served us. Then, as we progressed along, there came the smell of cockles and whelks. Further up Cheshire Street was the cordial drinks stall. In the winter the drinks were hotted up. It was smashing.

After the drink, came the need to relieve myself. 'Gor blimey,'

Dad would say. 'You're not having any more drinks when we come down here.' Privacy was not an easy matter in a Sunday market. We had to make our way to one of the bomb sites on the edge of the market. There, I would burst forth, my tension and anxiety vanishing in liquid relief.

Back to the market we'd go, to watch an East End craftsman selling little envelopes. 'Here we go, you jolly old lot,' he'd shout. 'Here y'are, a tanner for one of these packets. There may be a tosheroon in it, or nuffink. Who'll buy one?' He would pick up packet after packet and open them. Every one he opened had a half-crown inside. It looked convincing, but it didn't fool Dad. He knew all those kind of capers. Plenty of people got caught, though.

Dad used to stand for ages, trying to tumble the trick. At last, he spotted it. The bloke had the one packet with the coin in it. He must have practised for hours before the trick was perfect. What he did was to conceal the packet in the palm of his hand, pretend to pick it up from the box, and cleverly bring the genuine packet into view as his hand came out of the box. Crafty? Deceiving? Yes, but it took guts as well to run the risk of being sussed in one of the toughest areas of London.

On another corner, the Fascists would be shouting the odds. Further up the road, an African prince in full regalia sold racing tips for half-a-crown. If his predictions failed to live up to his boastful claims, he would disappear to some other market, till all was forgiven but not necessarily forgotten.

It was one mass of life and movement. Pressing, pushing, shoving, shouting, bargaining and bartering. Everything and anything could be bought in Club Row: jewellery, second-hand clothes, fire-irons, back-scratchers, hats, umbrellas and furniture, to name but a few.

On the way home, Dad would stop for a pint while I waited outside with a glass of lemonade. Then we made for home with our bargains. We would sit down to the baked dinner Mum had ready for us. Dad carved the meat as always, after sharpening the knife on the window sill. After dinner, it was bed for Mum, the armchair for Dad and out in the street for me.

Dad's head was full of games. He would put his hand in his pocket and draw out his fist. 'Now then,' he'd say to me, 'will you give me a penny for what's in there?'

'Well, what's in there?' I always asked.

'Ah, that's for you to decide. It's a chance you either take or leave. Now, come on. Do you want what's in there for a penny or don't you?'

A penny was a lot to me then and this was a hard decision to make. 'No, I don't want it,' I said.

'You don't? Dad answered, in a way that made me think there was something substantial in his fist. This confused me, but I was still determined to hold on to my penny.

'Right. You don't want it then, eh?' Dad concluded. He then opened his hand and in his palm was a shining half-crown.

I was choked. 'Next time I'll have it,' I told myself.

'Here you are. Try this one,' said Dad. 'Do you want it this time?'

Well, of course, I fell for it. I parted with my penny. Dad opened his hand to reveal nothing but his empty palm. Now I was even more choked, almost on the point of tears. Dad kept the penny.

'That'll teach you to be shrewd with money, won't it? It'll make you more alert where money is concerned. Now next time I make you an offer, you'll be more careful, won't you?'

He wasn't really as severe with me as that story implies. Dad was a man who could accept a loss as well as a win, albeit with more enthusiasm for the latter. If I decided to buy what Dad had in his fist and it turned out to be a two-bob bit or a half-crown, I would get it.

'You deserve it,' he'd say, 'for being shrewd and using your own head, and not being influenced by other people's crafty words.' I suppose this was Dad's contribution to my education.

Now that Mum had had the baby, she started doing a bit of cleaning for Boober's daughters. They were a bit middle-class if you know what I mean. They were nice enough people, but they got every ounce of their five-bob-an-hour's worth out of Mum. That was good money, though. Chars were not easy to come by. The job suited Mum because she could take the baby with her. But as my sister got older, she was minded by this woman and that, like I had been, while Mum went out to work.

I used to envy those kids who had their mums waiting for them at the school gate, to take them home to a nice tea. When I left school in the afternoon I went straight home to Brooke Road. Dinner times, I went to Gran, an aunt, or perhaps a neighbour. When I got home in the afternoon, I would push the street door three times. The ill-fitting lock would give, and the door would open. I didn't have a key, but then I didn't need one. I always told Mum that Boober had let me in.

The kitchen always looked dim and lonely. I would become

aware of a strange feeling inside me. I was too young to understand it then, but I know now that it was a feeling of insecurity and loneliness. It was as if the kitchen was not real, as if I was not real. I was behind a glass screen, looking at the kitchen before me. All my inner feelings were my very own, not to be told to anyone. They were my secret. Even if I had wanted to convey these inward experiences to anyone, I would not have been able to. I did not even understand them myself.

Anyway, I used to put the kettle on, make a cuppa, and light one of Mum's dog ends which she left carelessly on the mantle-piece. I'd have a wash and then go out to play until Mum called me in for dinner.

9. Friends and School

I had plenty of mates down Darville Road, off Brooke Road. My best mate was a Jewish lad called Larry. We were so close that he even shared his ringworm with me. Ringworm is a scalp infection, which eats away the hair. It grows again though, and the new mop is usually curly. Larry went as bald as an ice-rink but mine was caught in time. Mum had kept on telling me to keep away from him, but my affection for the boy overcame my fear of a bald napper.

We played on the bomb sites, reliving the bombing and fighting that went on in the war. There was always an argument about who was going to be the Germans.

'I'm not being a German. I was a German last time.'

The main reason for not wanting to be a German was that they always had to lose. Lumps of wood served as our guns, dustbin-lids our shields. We collected all the old rubble together to make a camp, which had to be attacked. The girls played tamer games like hop-scotch, skipping, or one of their stupid ball games. Our war would go on until another, more realistic one developed.

'You're dead. I've shot you twice.'

'No I'm not. You only wounded me in the leg.'

'No I didn't.'

'Yes you did.'

'All right, I'm not playing them.'

So our war game would finish and we'd play cricket until another dispute developed, making it necessary to find another pastime. One of our gang, Poshit, was not an easy boy to play with.

'I mustn't lay on the ground,' he would say when we played soldiers. 'My Mum'll tell me off if I go in dirty.'

Poshit couldn't climb the trees (what was left of them) on the bomb site. He wasn't allowed to pick up bricks to help us build our camp, he mustn't kneel on the ground, he always had to wear his cap, and wear it at the right angle, he had to go home as neat and tidy as he'd come out. He didn't suit us one bit, the poor little sod. He used to stand and watch more than he joined in. He was lucky, though. One snob of a family wouldn't even let their kids out to join us lot at all. It must have been the equivalent of child imprisonment. That was just one of the differences between the Green and Stoke Newington.

The boy Charlie, who lived downstairs, was as thin as a needle. No matter how cleverly I tied him up, he always wriggled free. It was impossible to hold him. It was like watching a second Houdini.

My parents never allowed friends indoors. I think it was because we had so little space to call home, and what we had did little for our prestige. If Boober came knocking on our door to see if Mum could change two bob into shillings for the gas meter, Mum would keep her out on the landing and out of sight of the kitchen. Friends and acquaintences were strictly taboo in our house. The only ones to gain entrance were close relatives, and they did not come very often, or the UAB man. What a panic the latter would create.

'Hide that wireless. Take off that watch. Hide the bag of coal.'

All this just to give the UAB man the impression that we were poor, a fact that hardly needed emphasising. Not only that, Dad always said that if they saw you had something of value they would tell you to sell it. Whether or not this was all in Dad's mind, a left-over from the thirties, I don't know. But if he was out of work and the UAB man called (always without warning) there would be one mad rush to get all our valuables, such as they were, out of sight.

Another of my friends was called Dezy. He was brown and furry, with two dark brown eyes and four short legs. He started following me home from school, and we grew very fond of each other. After I had been meeting Dezy and playing around with him for a few days, the neighbours told me that someone had kicked him in the head a few months back, and that he was now vicious. They said he had bitten a number of kids in the district. Now I knew why none of the kids would go near him. Yet I played and romped with that dog, and he never so much as growled at me. He was one friend that Mum and Dad did allow in the house, which pleased me. But as I grew older, Dezy just seemed to fade away.

By this time, Aunt Poll and Uncle George had come back on the scene. They had moved in next door with their children, Audrey (twelve), Iris (about my age) and little Georgie (only five).

I was never keen on playing with girls. Their games made no sense whatever to me. I could never make out what they got out of skipping and playing ball. But Audrey and Iris were different. They were right little tom-boys. They played with me like boys:

142

fighting, playing cowboys, Knocking Down Ginger, blowing raspberries at people as they passed our house, joining in at cricket and football. I didn't need the boys who played down Darville Road now. These two sticks of dynamite provided all the fun and adventure I needed.

Dad smashed a small hole through our wall, so that we could communicate with Uncle George and his family. Us kids used to long for Saturday night to come. Uncle George would call through the hole, 'You ready, Bill?'

'Yes, we're ready,' Dad would answer. Mum and Dad would meet Poll and George outside the street door. Then away they'd go to the Wheatsheaf, the Coach and Horses, the Birdcage, or some other pub along Stoke Newington High Street.

Right, now we were on our own, free to enjoy ourselves. First, Audrey would demonstrate her skill and daring by sitting on the window sill with her legs dangling outside. This was smashing, better than any circus act. We had a first-class view of this performance, and I was filled with excitement as Audrey's legs dangled in mid-air. Iris and I enjoyed it immensely.

Then, suddenly, that miserable old cow across the road would spoil our fun. 'Get in,' she'd scream, 'get in.' You could see this poor woman at her window, trembling with the shock of this public performance. Her eyes used to nearly pop out of her head. The poor soul must have had a thousand heart attacks.

That was only the start. Next, we would tie a piece of cotton to a penny and dangle it out of the window. When someone passed by, we pulled the cotton. They would think they'd dropped a coin and would go searching up and down the pavement, while we killed ourselves laughing.

We'd make up little brown envelopes that looked like wage packets. We stuffed them with bits of newspaper, cut to the size of pound notes. One of us would drop an envelope outside the house and watch the reaction of the victim who found it. Inside we would put a note, saying something like, 'Hard luck'.

We loved it when our parents went out. It was the best night of the week for us.

We used to play aeroplanes, too. We would each get a chair and lay it on the floor. We sat on the back part of the chair with our backs resting on the seat part. We were now three Spitfire pilots in a dog-fight with the Jerry.

One night we passed the time by playing Cowboys and Indians. Audrey and Iris must have got a little carried away. They were the Indians and I was Roy Rogers, the Western hero of the day.

They captured me and wanted to roast me alive. They stood me the mantelpiece, which was covered with a runner. Audrey had found a box of matches. She struck a match and was just waving it across the mantelpiece, when suddenly the whole lot went up in flames. We smothered it with a cloth before it got too far. Mum would go mad when she got home, we thought. So we did a quick repair job by cutting off the burnt edges of the mantel-cloth. Luckily, we got away with it.

Our next bit of fun — or rather my cousins' — could not possibly have gone unnoticed. This was the night we played barbers' shops. In my innocence, I agreed to be the customer. It is hardly necessary to elaborate on that episode. To say that I ended up looking like one of Hitler's crew-cut Stormtroopers would be putting it mildly.

The only cinema we could get in to was the Vogue, in Stoke Newington High Street, just opposite the nick. They nearly always seemed to show 'U'-cert films. In the summer holidays we would pay our eightpence and spend the whole day in there. If we had the money, we would go and see the same film two or three times a week. We would sit through three showings on each occasion. Of course, we had to make sure the manager didn't catch us staying there all that time. He chucked us out once, explaining as we walked up the gangway that it wasn't a lodging house. If we had the cash and the coupons, we'd take a few sweets in with us.

At night, after school, we sometimes went to play on Stoke Newington Common, or down the shelters that had not yet been filled in. Or in the summer we might go and have a splash in a great tank of water. This had been for emergency use, in case of fire, during the war. We also used to go and play in the now obsolete air raid wardens' hut.

I always wanted to go swimming, but my father would not hear of it. 'No,' he'd say. 'It's too dangerous.' I wasn't even allowed to go with the school. I finally learned to swim when I was thirty-eight. I had to fight a by-now intense fear of the water. I fought that fear and beat it. Now I enjoy the pleasurable exercise of swimming.

One boy in particular sticks in my mind from those Stoke Newington Common days. For the sake of anonymity, I will call him Jimmy. To see the change in this boy, as I did, was a terrible, terrible thing. It was almost as distressing to the onlooker as to the victim.

Jimmy was a handsome, fit agile youth, expert with a football.

144

He was about seventeen when I knew him. Before long, he would have to go in the army. This was probably for the last part of the war. Jimmy it was who had all the say on the football pitch, and Jimmy it was who always seemed to have the ball during the course of the game. He was a robust, sturdy boy. The change that I was to see in that strong and handsome youth is an episode in my life that I shall never forget.

It is a most distressing experience, and one that I hesitated to write about. But the experience has persistently crept back into my mind while I have been writing this book. I feel I must relate to my experience, or, more correctly, someone else's experience.

Jimmy suddenly went missing from the Common, without warning. It didn't take me long to find out from the other boys where he had gone. He had been called up at the age of eighteen, almost at the end of the war. It must have been about two years later that I saw him again. I wish I hadn't done.

I had walked into a local cafe during lunch break. My eyes encountered the profile of an old man, sitting sort of hunched up. At his side, resting against his chair, was a walking stick. I didn't pay him much attention at first, until I sat down opposite him. Then I had the most sickening experience.

'It can't be,' I thought. 'Not Jimmy.'

The young features barely showed through in the lop-sided face. The trunk was bent forward and to one side. The face was pale, with the look of age. The features were still young, yet at the same time old-looking. He was even dressed like an old man, in an old cloth cap and a shiny mac.

'No,' I told myself. 'It couldn't be him. He looks too old, anyway. People don't age that quick.' I didn't reckon with the rigours of war.

He sat in front of me in a sort of semi-consciousness. He didn't recognise me, so there you are, it couldn't be Jimmy. Mind you, he never noticed me in those days over the Common, anyway.

Eventually, the old man got up and limped out. I could not get him out of my mind. I felt I knew him and yet I didn't. I had to find out, and the one to ask was Alf, behind the counter.

'Yer that's him. Jimmy.'

I was speechless. I walked off without even thanking Alf for his information.

'Oi, you haven't paid for your tea and sandwich.'

I turned slowly back, as if in a trance, took a coin from my pocket and placed it on the counter. As I walked out of the door,

I could hear a voice (I suppose it must have been Alf's) shouting after me, ' 'Ere y'are, yer change.'

War. All the bombing I had gone through in London. All the devastation I had seen around me: houses, factories, schools, churches. None of these had brought home to me in such vivid horror the consequences of war.

This young boy probably hardly knew what he was fighting for. This young, strong, agile body of a youth had aged thirty years in two. A boy of no more than twenty, with the appearance of a man of fifty. There would be no more football now for boys like Jimmy. He had been blown up and had spent a considerable time in an army hospital. Now he spent the best part of his week sitting in Alf's. No doubt he found it difficult to get a suitable job.

I hated school. Everything was so orderly, correct and restricting. Self-expression seemed to be alien to the whole grey, antiquated building. The male teachers were nothing like my father and the female ones nothing like my mother, or any other relatives, come to that. My lot sounded, and even looked friendlier than these beings. They looked as though they had just been taken out of a showcase. Their tone and accent had an aloofness about it which made it impossible to strike up any sort of relationship whatsoever. We were as remote as shit from sugar.

When I was there, I had to be a good boy. A good boy is one who sits quietly, however unnatural that may be. A good boy is one whose hand shoots up at almost every question the teacher asks. He is the one who gets noticed, among other well-behaved, intelligent boys.

I was among those who didn't merit a second look. There were two ways of getting noticed. One was by being clever. The other was by playing merry hell and getting the cane. The latter had a sort of prestige for some. It was an adventure for those who were curious as to what it was like, getting the cane and having your name in the book. You had the consolation that at least the Head knew you by name and appearance. I would have loved to have been noticed, but I was neither clever nor brave enough.

I did eventually make my mark, though. This was one unforseen advantage of having a weak bladder. Ernie had the same trouble. He was cross-eyed and wore steel-rimmed glasses. He had a mass of dirty-looking, blonde hair which grew in all directions. He mumbled rather than spoke, like they do in nick. Ernie had an old look about him. Even at the age of twelve he had bags under his eyes. I thought I was fragile, but beside him I felt like

Hercules. His skin was rough and white as a corpse.

Us two weak-bladdered customers were sat right at the front of the class. I had felt a bit ashamed of being allocated the first desk in the row. All the rest of the class knew why I was there. I felt a little better after Ernie joined me. Mrs. Adams hated us disturbing the lesson. Well, it must have been annoying, right in the middle of a subject. We used to be in and out three or four times in a morning. This is why she sat us two sprinklers in the front desk. Yes, I got noticed then all right, but it wasn't quite the thing. I wasn't over-keen on getting that look of contempt from Mrs. Adams every time my hand shot up.

There was one particularly embarrassing time when she had asked a question. I shot my hand up. She looked at me with joyful surprise. 'Yes, Barnes?' She waited.

'Can I be excused, Ma'am?'

She shot her index finger towards the door. 'Go on,' she said sharply.

Mrs. Adams wasn't as hard on Ernie and me as some of the teachers. I remember one bloke in particular who would never let you go to the toilet during the lesson. If you dared to ask to go ouside during school hours, he would refuse your request and give you a telling-off into the bargain. Ernie and I found ourselves in this teacher's class one afternoon. We were not compelled to sit together. It was only Mrs. Adams who preferred this, when she took us for Scripture. We liked sitting together, though. It wasn't because we were particularly well-matched as friends, but because we both had the same problem. Being together made us feel more secure and less prone to ridicule.

I wasn't particularly keen on Ernie at all, in fact. He was just a support for me, like I was for him. Those thick glasses of his made his eyes look big and staring, as though he was continually surprised. I tried to avoid meeting his gaze head-on. That made my eyes feel funny and out of focus. Perhaps I appeared just as peculiar to him, through thick lenses, as he did to me. The thing was that we needed each other. Ernie was a good fighter, and if any of the kids made fun of us, we could soon put a stop to it. He was thin, but he was pliable and strong as wire. He was a good friend to have in that respect.

On this paritcular afternoon, we were in McGlaughlen's class. We both sat together, breaking our necks as we squirmed this way and that in an effort to hold back the urgent stream. We knew McGlaughlen was strict and that it would be useless putting up our hands to go outside. He would only refuse and tell us off.

One of his excuses was, 'If one goes, the whole bloody class wants to go.' I'm sure there was some truth in this, but it did make Ernie and me feel we were a bit of a nuisance to everyone.

We were both at bursting point now. 'I tell you what, Ron,' Ernie said, 'let's both put our hands up together, and whoever he points to first will ask for the two of us.'

'Good idea,' I said.

A good idea it was, but it didn't work. Ernie had thought that by speaking for the other and keeping together, we could solve the problem. That might have worked if there had been more weak-bladdered children in the school. As it was, this was just one more occasion when we both walked home with our shorts and underpants soaked.

Eventually, Mum began to realise that there was something wrong with a school that only allowed its pupils to perform their natural functions at certain times of the day. She wrote a note to the headmaster. He never answered, but there was a marked difference in the teachers' attitude to us two water babies after that. It fizzled out as the months went by, though, and Ernie and I began arriving home with soggy pants once more. Another letter was written, our pants stayed dry for a few weeks, and the never-ending circle continued. Finally, when I was about fourteen, the problem solved itself.

I was still at High Street School (now Fleetwood). Fortunately, not all the teachers were disciplinarians. I found two that I could approach, out of about a dozen in my part of the school. The first was Mr. Herbert, who was not as foolish as his name implied. I learned more from him in six months than I did in three years with the other lot. The atmosphere was so casual and relaxed. Mr. Herbert never used the cane; he had no need to. He was a Jewish teacher, and though he spoke well, he didn't have that plum-in-the-mouth accent. You could talk to him, just as you would talk to the milkman, postman or tally man. No fancy words or thought-out sentences. You could speak with ease and not feel conscious of your 'ain't's, 'nuffink's and 'ain'it's.

In the other classes, those who got their sums wrong all had to line up at the teacher's desk. It looked like the Labour Exchange, which I had seen once when I went with Dad to keep him company. You got a bit of a telling-off, then a quick explanation of what it was all about, with an admonition to do better next time. I never left the teacher's desk any wiser than I was at the beginning. Well, they couldn't take all morning over it, with a queue of twelve boys waiting to be seen. Some teachers didn't even take this much trouble, especially if you were dim like me. For kids like us, there was no hope. You were just not up to it, so there was nothing more that could be done.

Mr. Herbert was different. He was a slow, thorough man. He would have a pile of arithmetic books on his desk, the work of the slower boys. He would spend as much as a whole hour with one boy, till he had got it correct and clear in his brain. I suppose he thought it was better to spend a lot of time on one boy and put him right, than to give each child two minutes, bashing them off one after the other and getting nowhere.

I was never any good at reciting tables. I suppose it was too uniform for my brain. Due to Mr. Herbert's efforts, I was finally able to add, multiply, take away and divide, and get it right at least a third of the time. My confidence was boosted considerably when ticks began to appear in my book. I even got one or two stars. I was not a bright boy at school, even at my peak, but what I learned I learned from Mr. Herbert.

There were no clouts round the ear from him, no ridicule. If a kid played up a bit, he was not allowed to go to football or swimming. Or he might be made to stand on the landing for a whole morning. These punishments were far more effective than the cane. This was because there was such a happy atmosphere in the class that you felt you were missing something if you were left out. It was no hardship at all to be chucked out by the other, stricter teachers. On the contrary, it was a relief to be out of their way for a while, away from their rigid conformity.

We had nicknames for many teachers, as kids always do. Miss Bristow was Bisto. A prominent Adam's apple protruded from Mrs. Adam's neck — a perfect match. She was known as The Apple by the kids. Mr. Herbert was known as Old Herbie. This nickname, unlike the others, was applied more in affection than ridicule.

Every morning, one of the boys was sent over to the baker's to buy hot buns. These cost a halfpenny each and we were all allowed to eat them during our milk break. I think you paid another halfpenny for the milk, unless your old man was out of work, sick, dead, or had left home for some reason. There were school dinners, but I preferred to go round to Gran's or buy some chips or a couple of raw carrots.

One Christmas, our class was rehearsing for a show. Mr. Herbert asked for volunteers. I raised my hand, a thing I would not have done in another class. Generally, I preferred obscurity. Mr. Herbert was pleased, and he liked the song I sang to the class.

It was the one my father used to sing in his club turn days, called 'Not So Long Ago in an Old Wash Tub'. It was OK till I came out with the bit about 'While mother took her knickers off'. Mr. Herbert advised me to change it to 'While mother took her pinny off', and this I did. The kids killed themselves every time I rehearsed it. At the finish, they knew it by heart and joined in with such enthusiasm that Mr. Herbert had to tell them to keep their voices down.

As the time for the concert drew near, Mr. Herbert gradually squeezed me out of the show. I suppose he was thinking of the other straight-laced teachers and the effect my song would have on them. It was too Cockneyfied for them. So I lost my big chance.

Being in Mr. Herbert's class, I began to feel more a part of the school. I felt more relaxed and free. I wasn't afraid to put my hand up to ask a question in other classes. Before I had been afraid of the teachers' ridicule. It seemed a different world in Mr. Herbert's class. He wasn't everlasting bawling out to the kids to be quiet, sit straight, stop this, stop that. We used to have a jaw in between doing our sums. Mr. Herbert took no notice. I suppose he felt he would get better results this way. He only told us to be quiet when the mumbling and whispering developed into a crescendo. Then, understandably, he had to put the block on. It is a pity there were not more teachers like him about in those days. Although people told us otherwise, the schools really were still Victorian.

My long sought-for contentment with school soon vanished. It was time to move on to the secondary school in Northwold Road. If Old Herbie had come with us, it wouldn't have worried me at all. At last I had become happy at Fleetwood, after experiencing one impersonal teacher after another (and one or two, downright rotten). But they were to appear as angels, compared with some of the teachers at Northwold.

The headmaster reminded me of an under-nourished bullfrog. He had dark-brown piercing eyes. His brows always took on the shape of a question mark when he looked at you, as if he was on the brink of going into a rage. All the new boys were lined up at the front of the hall at assembly, the first morning. The Bullfrog stood on a high platform, grasping a five-foot-long cane. His cohorts stood behind.

He said a few words. I can't really remember what. I suppose my mind was concentrated on that outsize cane he kept with him. I expect he told us the rules and regulations and wished us luck. The same routine as with so many other kids over the years. Kids whose faces he had long forgotten, never mind their names. Year in, year out, one batch in, one batch out. It must have been like working on a conveyor belt, only using human beings instead of raw material.

Williams was another teacher who always had to carry a cane, like an army officer. No doubt it made up for his feelings of inadequacy.

Bullfrog used to take us for science. While we wrote in our books, he would stand on sentry duty, scanning the class. If anyone looked up, even to stretch their neck, Bullfrog would say, 'Come on, get on with it.' Down the boy's head would go. The idea of the Frog's extra-long cane was that he could reach over to the back desks with it. If anyone dared whisper to his partner, the cane would come slashing down on his fingers, unless he had remembered to keep them out of sight.

Bullfrog was strict. He had no friends among the pupils, and didn't want any. He had a craze for tweaking ears, shaking boys by the scruff of the neck, and other endearing habits. I learned nothing at all from him. The atmosphere was too tense for learning.

Perhaps others of my age could give an entirely different view of their school days. But as far as I am concerned, the teachers were as remote as hell. They understood nothing whatsoever of us kids. They knew how to keep a class in order. They knew the curriculum by heart. They knew how to put a lesson over. But all this was to no effect, because there was something they didn't know. Something to do with us.

The Bullfrog did not rule alone. There was another, just as inflexible as him: the tall, grey-haired, neat Mr. Palmer. There were other fairly strict teachers, but they came nowhere near the notoriety of Bullfrog and Palmer.

All was not lost, though. I was lucky enough to find one teacher of the same high calibre as Old Herbie. I had been put in a higher class (I think it was 4A). The reason for my promotion was not my high standard of academic achievement, but my age. I knew that if you were too stupid they kept you in the lower class. I knew I was no whizz-kid and dreaded the ridicule of the other kids if I was not put into a higher class with them. I could just imagine it:

'Ah, little baby Barnesie. Don't know what two and twosie is, does he, wuzzy?'

Well, I was lucky. I was put up with the rest. At first, I felt as though I had fooled my teachers and fellow pupils alike, but then I felt unsure of myself again. I would have to learn harder subjects now. I hadn't even begun to master the easier ones yet.

Mercifully, Mr. Clydeman was one of those teachers who seemed to possess all the understanding that the others lacked. I was only about twleve then, but right away I could sense a kind of goodness, even saintliness, in this Jewish teacher. He was the complete opposite of Mr. Palmer. I often wondered what sort of relationship these two differing personalities could have struck up in the staffroom. Not a very promising one, I should imagine.

Mr. Clydeman was like Mr. Herbert. He explained everything. Nothing was too much trouble. He had no favourites and no whipping boys. There were no regular class monitors. Everything was as informal as possible. Clydeman never lost his temper, though at times he had good cause to. He was what you might call the psychological type of teacher.

I began to pick up again. I knew almost as much as the average boys in the class. I even regained the confidence to stick my hand up now and again in answer to a question. I gave some ridiculous replies sometimes, unintentionally of course. This caused some of the boys to laugh and chatter among themselves. Clydeman would be down on them like a ton of bricks. 'Silence,' he called.

They knew they had overstepped the mark. Mr. Clydeman gazed firmly down the middle of the class, his head slightly forward and a determined look in his eye. 'Why do you laugh?' he said at last. 'Does it give you a feeling of superiority? Does it? You, Mason. Stand up.'

Mason stood. He was long, skinny and now nervous-looking.

'Now then, Mason. You seemed to be enjoying yourself at the back there. Perhaps you could enlighten Mr. Barnes on the matter.'

Mr. Clydeman's thumbs sought his braces, found them and hooked themselves comfortably through them. 'Well, come on, Mason. Mr. Barnes is waiting.' Clydeman began to sway back and forth on his heels. Referring to me as 'Mr' seemed to give me a higher status than Mason. Mason looked quite embarrassed as he turned his head towards me, then back again to Clydeman.

'Don't you know the answer, Mason?' inquired Clydeman. Mason lowered his head and shook it.

'Then what are you laughing at?' shouted the teacher. 'You, Finklestein, stand up. Wright, you stand up. Golding, on your feet.' Clydeman sorted out all the merry-makers. 'OK, Wright,' he said. 'See if you can answer the question. You may not be as

Wright as you think you are.'

He had a go at each of them in this way. It was most amusing. Mr. Clydeman is one of the few teachers that I can look back on with deep affection. If a teacher can achieve that, he is a teacher indeed.

At break, we played the usual games. Conkers, bobs and bobsters, cigarette cards. I was never enthusiastic about these games, or any other games, for that matter. I always seemed to be a loner. Not that I wanted to be. I really needed a best friend, but for some reason I never managed to get attached to any one boy. When I did take to someone, which was very rare indeed, it turned out that he had a friend or friends already. Most of my time at school was spent alone, except for my alliance with Ernie which was just to give each other mutual support in class. We were not like other boys. We had to go to the toilet every five minutes. We were both ribbed about this by the other kids. As soon as the boys started we would find each other. Together we could stand up to them. But apart from these occasions, we were never what you could call real mates.

So I wandered aimlessly around the playground, watching the others playing leapfrog. Or the girls skipping. It really used to fascinate me, the way they twirled that rope and the speed they got up. I didn't feel a bit left out of things. I was quite happy to watch.

Once I did make an attempt to join the conker-happy crowd. I got myself some conkers and string. After a few challenges and several sore knuckles, due to my opponents inaccuracy when making a strike, I got fed up with the whole pointless business. My conker was now a tenner, having smashed ten opposing conkers, not to mention their owners' knuckles. It was beginning to be looked on as a potential champion. That was before the fatal day when it was obliterated by a giant-sized opponent. As the assembled boys witnessed the pulverisation of my conker, a cry of 'Ahh,' went up. This was a demonstration of their collective sorrow at its passing. Individuals came up to me and expressed deep regret at my conker's violent ending.

'I never thought he'd beat you, Ron.'

'It was an 'ard sod, yours, Ron. Didn't bake it, did you?'

'No, course I didn't. Anyone can tell if they've been baked or not.'

'Well, it's a pity to have lost, Ron. Still, better luck next time.'

For me, there was no next time. I couldn't have cared less about my esteemed and now vanquished conker. I had participated just for something to do. I never had much enthusiasm for games, anyway.

By now, I had got well used to Mr. Clydeman and my hatred of school had subsided. It was a treat to look at the attendance register, over Mr. Clydeman's shoulder, and see with my own eyes a full row of red ticks beside my name. Mr. Clydeman was pleased;

'You've done well, Barnes. Now, keep it up.'

I certainly would have kept it up, if only to be in his favour. But with Mr. Palmer came a renewal of my hatred for school. I reverted to absenteeism, many times due to my asthma and many more times due to my fear and dislike of Mr. Palmer. No one dared to show the slightest sign of high spirits in his class. The boy Smee wouldn't have dared do what he once did in Clydeman's class.

Clydeman was calling the register. 'Gerry Mason?'

'Yes, Sir.'

'Ernest Slade?'

'Yes, Sir.'

'Derek Smee?'

'That 'Smee.'

Mr. Clydeman dealt with him, but not in the same way that Palmer would have done. It may have been his influence that taught me to dislike harsh and unfeeling discipline. Harshness is bad enough when dished up to adults, let alone children whose impressions and feelings about the world are not yet formed. Palmer was no teacher. He would have done better as a prison officer. Better for himself, that is, not for the inmates. How people like that are allowed to have complete control of children, I don't know.

Well, Palmer put the bubble in and I was sent to Geere House Open Air School. I was lucky. Palmer had done me a favour. I was now at a safe distance from his cane, away from his down-the-nose look. I felt strange at this new school, but at the same time safe. There was no hard discipline here. The whole place vibrated with an air of freedom and happiness. I can only put this down to the humanitarian and sympathetic (but not pitying) qualities of the staff.

Yes, I was a lucky boy indeed. Much as I had liked Clydeman, I hardly missed him. I realised now that it wasn't Clydeman alone who was necessary for my well-being. He had become a sort of refuge in a large, dull, ancient building, inhabited by equally old and dull, but also severe, teachers. Greer Houses didn't need a Mr. Clydeman. They were all like him. There was no caning here, or only very, very rarely. There was no feeling of difference between teacher and pupil. This was truly a happy school.

10. Kippers, Oxo and the Utility

One afternoon, I walked in and was surprised to see all the other residents of the house in our kitchen. Right away, I knew something was wrong. No one was ever allowed in our flats like this. They were standing in a rough circle. I pushed my way through. There, sitting on a chair, was my mother, crying over my little two-year-old sister. 'She must be dead,' I thought. She lay in my mother's arms, white, limp and lifeless. I looked round at all the apprehensive faces.

'What's wrong?' I asked.

My mother just sat there, rocking and crying over my sister's little limp, soft, still body. I was dazed and confused with fear.

'She fell through the banister rail,' someone said. I knew immediately which rail they meant. It had been missing for the whole three years that we have lived there.

'We're waiting for the ambulance,' I heard again.

Fortunately, Glenda pulled through. But for weeks afterwards one side of her head was as soft as jelly. It wouldn't happen again, though. Dad tied one of his neck-ties across the rails, and that's how it stayed.

Glenda was now being looked after by a woman in Sanford Terrace, and Mum had gone back to her smelly tobacco factory in Commercial Street. On several occasions I caught a chest cold or had an asthma attack, and my mother had to leave me alone in bed till she came home in the evening. They were lonely, sad days for me, but it was this loneliness that started me drawing and reading. I was never a regular reader as a child, but I became one as I got older. Drawing, painting and music have been with me since my childhood. Though my musical talent, such as it was, has almost faded now, due mainly to lack of those two precious commodities, time and money.

As I got older, I became more saucy to my mother. I also became proficient in the art of swearing. One day, (probably a Saturday) my mother had brought home a piping hot loaf of bread. I loved hot bread. Mum gave me one slice, then another.

'Could I have another slice, Mum?' I asked. Mum cut a third, and then a fourth. It was my request for a fifth that done it. She picked up the remaining third of a loaf and aimed it at my head.

'You want bread?' she shouted. 'Take the sodding lot then.

Here y'are.' As she bawled the last two words, I could see the crusty, hot loaf coming towards me. I did one of my Tommy Farr ducks, as Dad had taught me. The bread hit the gas stove with a clatter, knocking saucepans and frying pan to the floor with a crash.

'That's all it is with you,' Mum moaned. 'As soon as I bring a hot loaf in, you can't leave it alone. I ain't got money to spend like that. I'd need two loaves a day with you eating it at that rate, not to mention the marge, an' all.'

I picked up the frying pan and saucepans, and put them back on the stove. I took very little notice then of my mother's reaction to my gluttony. She had never got as agitated as this before, but I never gave it a second thought. The day-to-day pressures in the home, in the market, in the factory, making ends meet, all these meant you had to come to the end of your tether eventually. The nearest at hand is always the one to cop out. That one happened to be me on this particular occasion. It wasn't my continual consumption of the bread that had got Mum hot under the collar. It was how to pay for another loaf when that one was gone.

Butter was a real luxury then. I acquired my taste for this creamy commodity during a visit to Gran Gullis. I was privileged, for Gran was the only one who had butter on her bread, on account of her health. This time, though, she gave me a slice of bread with real butter on it. At first I didn't even know it was butter. I had never tasted its succulence before. But I could not help remarking to Gran how smashing it tasted.

'It tasted different, Gran,' I said. 'More creamier, or something. Can I have another one?'

Gran hesitated for a moment. 'All right,' she said. 'Just one more, then that's your lot.'

She cut the bread, and applied the butter with a chrome-handled knife. I noticed the butter was spread a little more sparingly this time. I did not remark on this point, telling myself, 'Beggars can't be choosers.'

When I got home, I told Mum about my experience up Gran's and the rich taste of butter. 'Oh, all right,' said Mum. 'I'll see if I can get a bit for you.'

It must have been weeks later that she came home with a stingy two-ounce piece of butter. 'Blimey, Mum,' I said in astonishment. 'Couln't you get a bigger piece?'

'No, it's too dear,' she answered.

I could see that I had no chance of getting butter on my bread

158

every day, so I reconciled myself to being content with marge, and having butter maybe once a month. It wasn't just the price, for Mum could sometimes afford a whole quarter. Things had not yet got back to normal after the war. Many things were still rationed.

Then there was the morning I tasted my first egg in six years. I'd thought all the hens in England had stopped laying. I never expected to see another egg, as long as I lived. I couldn't believe it. A real, a real – yes, I felt it – a real egg. I sat entranced, just looking at it in the egg cup.

'Well, go on then,' Mum prompted. 'Eat it.'

I raised my spoon slowly, ready to deliver a short, sharp crack to the brown shell. It seemed a pity to treat a long-departed friend like this. Down came the spoon. Then, as I removed the top of the shell, the mouth-watering smell. It was fantastic. I could stand no more. The egg was gone before you could say 'chicken run'.

'Cor.' I smacked my lips and wiped my mouth on my sleeve. 'Got any more, Mum?' I asked, my eyes wide open and bright.

'I have,' Mum replied, 'but no more this morning. You'll have to wait till tonight, then you can have another one.'

This was great. Two eggs in one day. Things must be getting better, I thought. I suppose I was right. Even so, Boober still locked her food cupboard on the landing, by the lavatory. Who could blame her? Eggs, butter, bacon and many other foods were like gold then. Fish was also in short supply. This was to my father's advantage, though, as he was carting fish.

Oranges started to appear. As the rationing gradually came off, prices increased. Those with the money went mad and bought up everything in sight. I suppose they were afraid that the government might slap on rationing again, for some reason or other. My Dad was a bit choked, for fish was quite easy to get now. None of it made much difference to those who were hard up, though. They still had to endure another kind of rationing: the one that comes of poverty.

'If we buy so much of that then we'll have to go without something else. If we buy a quarter of coal, we won't have enough for the gas to make a cuppa tea, or hot the baby's milk up.'

Yes, there was still plenty of that kind of reasoning about, though it wasn't long before Macmillan was telling us that we'd never had it so good. Gawd knows who he was talking about, but he certainly couldn't have meant us. True, some people could afford fridges now, or twelve-inch black and white TVs. But there were many more families like mine. Many men were still unable to find work, despite all the talk of their being jobs for everyone now. Families like ours couldn't afford a coconut mat, let alone a fridge or a telly.

My parents had none of these new mod cons. Everyone was HP mad in those days. Everything, from safety pins to pianos, was on HP. This gave people the impression that they were better off. They forgot that all this HP would cost them the best part of their lives to pay off.

So we were all amazed when Mum finally got Dad to sign for a new dining suite, promising him to pay the instalments out of the housekeeping. Whatever Mum earned was never her own. It all went in food, rent, gas, electricity (the last two have been cut off more than once). She kept me in boots, after seeing how quickly I could get through shoes. She also began to smoke very heavily, which Dad disliked intensely. But who could deny her this one simple pleasure to help her through a week of toil and pressure? She could have done a lot worse and gone on the beer. Plenty of women did, though more in my granparents' time than in the forties.

I was nearly fourteen now. I began to knock around with some older boys over Stoke Newington Common. We played football or rode home-made bikes, or perhaps knocked about with girls who lived along Sanford Terrace. We never went out with the girls on our own. We were always in a crowd. If a girl and a boy decided to go to the pictures together, it would always be the same two. Mostly, though, we stuck together, boys and girls both. This didn't bother me, for the girl I was matched up with was Italian and couldn't speak a word of English. Not only that, you couldn't get anything out of her, not even a kiss. Her not talking English made my task here even more difficult. So really I was courting and yet I wasn't.

Sanford Terrace was small and dark. The bricks of the dolls-house-like abodes were dark grey to black. This was due to the smoke, car fumes and factory stench. At the end of the turning, hung a crucifix. Underneath was a home-made wooden box in which flowers were put every Sunday. It was a memorial to local people who had given their lives in the two wars. The crucifix hung on the wall of a block of old flats. Drab as the district was, that memorial was kept as clean as a new pin. You would see the old ones every Sunday, putting a few flowers in or giving it a clean over with a cloth.

Sanford Terrace and the surrounding houses made a sort of small village. I liked it down this end of the Common. It was more communal than Brooke Road. The people in Sanford Terrace seemed more like those who lived in Poyser Street before the war. There was a little grocer's shop where the women would wedge themselves in, with hardly room to open their purses. Babies would be left outside in pushchairs. Mother Morris would waddle down the road with her shopping bag, and then have to come all the way back for the pint of milk she'd forgotten. She'd got one foot onto the shop step and then could make no more headway. The place would be crammed out, with a least four people.

'May,' Mother Morris would call to the shopkeeper. 'Can you pass a pint of milk out to us? I'll pay you in the morning, when it's quieter.'

'All right, gal,' answers May. She passes the pint to the customer at the counter who then hands it to the one behind, till at last Mrs. Morris has got her pint.

'Bleeding crowded,' she says to herself as she walks home. 'Good job old Queenie wasn't in there.' Queenie was the local eighteen-stone flower seller.

It was 1948, and the women still sat outside their houses in the summer, as their mothers had done in the twenties. It was a dying practice now, though. Sanford Terrace was one of the few streets where you could still see this. The kids played in the street under their mother's watchful eye, while the old man went round the Cricketers' for his pint. Saturday night, the old woman would go with him and he would take his accordian, to liven things up a bit. But the juke box was on its way in, so another local habit of making your own music and entertainment began to die.

My love of the piano and accordian was growing even greater, despite the fact that we had neither of these instruments at home. The more I listened to Mr. Smith in Sanford Terrace playing his accordian, the more urgent became my desire to acquire one of these expensive commodities. My need was not met. I had to wait till I went out to work, and then save what I could to get one.

The antagonism between Mum and Dad was beginning to break the surface. There was never any rowing or fighting like some people go in for. There was just an uneasy, unfriendly, cold, indifferent atmosphere. As time passed, these feelings (or non-feelings) grew worse. Even when my parents got on all right, there was little outward show of affection, though they must have felt it — for each other and for me. The only thing I regret is that it left me unable to show my feelings, or to understand my parents feelings.

I didn't realise that even a simple question like, 'How are you tonight, love? Tired?' could mean the difference between a happy home and an unhappy one. It took a long time, but I began to realise that you must not expect perfection in your partner (or in anyone, for that matter). I began to realise just what a rotten deal some women have: a husband to wait on, housework to do, their factory job, shopping, babies. It's not exactly a bed of roses being a man, either, but I'd rather stay as I am.

At one time, they were digging up the road in Sanford Terrace. This was smashing for us kids. We played in all the dirt and muck with our little metal shovels which were really meant for the beach. I didn't have a shovel. It would hardly have been worth it. I saw the seaside once in the whole of my childhood. That was the time my mother went to Canvey Island for a week with the girls at her firm. Now I could sample the pleasures of the seaside by digging into this heap of clay and dirt with my lump of wood. It certainly gave us kids a change and we loved it. The best was yet to come, though. A time when we were to abandon our shovels altogether.

The night-watchman was called Bert. He was a Cockney, an old merchant seaman. He used more Cockney slang than I had ever heard. All the kids got friendly with him. After tea, we would all meet at Bert's hut. This was in the winter, and it was a real joy to sit round Bert's coke fire, listening to his inevitable seaman's tales. We sat in the dimly-lit hut while the warmth of the fire moved over us. It was really cosy, a cosiness that no amount of money could buy.

Bert told us about Africa, its ways and customs and the poor living conditions there. He had weird tales of China. He recounted stories about all the different wives he had had; one in each port, or so he reckoned. They were interesting tales, if not altogether true, and we sat listening for hours. Just as we had got totally immersed in an episode of Bert's sea life, he would say, 'Here, look at that Jeremiah. Gi'us that Lord Lovell, and I'll put some more coke on.'

A sigh of 'Ahh,' would go up from the kids. Now they would have to wait for the end of Bert's tale.

After he'd put the coke on, he would go on with his story. The damp coke would crackle as an accompaniment to Bert's reminiscences. After an hour or so, it was time for a cup of Oxo and a slice of bread all round. This was the highlight of the evening. Some nights, old Bert would have a pair of kippers.

'Righto,' he'd say, as he got up from his wooden platform seat which ran right round the hut, 'who's going to get the can of water?'

He'd push his greasy, creased cap to the back of his head and hitch up his drooping, baggy trousers. He kept his thumbs tucked down the waistband, and stood up as straight as he could. This brought his full height to about five foot. Bert was about seventy. He had a walking stick, which he could have done without had it not been for the wound in his leg. He had received this during the war, on one of his merchant ships. They got it worse than anyone, Bert told us.

No one like walking across the Common to the horses' trough to get the water for Bert's Oxo. It was warm and cosy in the hut, and bloody freezing outside.

'Now, who's going, then?' Bert asked again.

When he cooked his kippers over the fire, it smelled delicious. It made you feel starving. He got the fish out of a piece of newspaper, put them on a bit of rusty metal and laid it over the fire. This kipper cooking was a strategy of Bert's to get someone to go for the water. He would wait for the heat to get to the kippers. Gradually, the fantastic smell glided into our nostrils.

'Well, who's going?' Bert would ask yet again. There would be no response. Our minds were full of kippers.

'I'll tell you what. Whoever gets the water can have a bit of me Jack the Ripper.'

Shouts of, 'I will, I will,' came from us, and Bert had more willing hands than he needed. He would send two of us together, giving us his can, and calling out after us something like:

'Now mind that frog and toad. Keep that cherry hog of yours on that piece of string and don't take him off it till you get back.'

The journey back to the hut was the worst. By now we were freezing. The cold water had splashed from the tap onto our shoes, and what with that and a full can of water to carry, we could not get along as quickly as we would have liked. On reaching the hut, we handed over the water. The kippers were done now, and we sat waiting for our reward. If it was raining outside, Bert would give us an old shirt.

'Here y'are,' he'd say. 'Dry yer Barnet on that.'

Bert would bring the can to the boil, drop in three or four Oxo cubes, then douse the lot with pepper.

'Here y'are,' he'd say. 'That'll warm yers up, it will.' He

163

poured it into enamel mugs and handed it round with a lump of bread, torn from the loaf. The water fetchers had the extra treat of a piece of kipper.

He was a marvellous old man. After the meal, he would have to go round and check his lamps. 'Gi'us me nanny goat off that nail, will you, son?' he would say to one of us. 'It's a bit cold out there tonight.'

Bert would leave the hut with his army of kids following. We would all check to see that his lamps were alight. Our night was almost at an end now, but it was hard to leave the warmth and cosy atmosphere of the hut. As Bert came back inside, his great nostrils gushing steam into the cold night air, he made straight for the blazing fire and warmed his hands.

'Freezing. Should have put me turtles on. Well, come on, boys. You've got to push off now. I'm going to read me linen and then get some Bo-Peep.'

We would have loved to sleep in that hut ourselves. Some day we would become night-watchmen, we hoped, and have our own hut, kipper and Oxo.

It was a sad loss when Bert finally departed. He had been there for almost a year and now he was gone. He had become the centre of our life in Sanford Terrace. After school, it was always at Bert's hut that we met. We had turned it into a sort of community centre. All the neighbours knew Bert and greeted him as he came limping down the road with his walking stick. After he went, the street never seemed the same again to us kids.

A few weeks ago, I passed Stoke Newington Common and was sad to see that all the little terraces had been pulled down. It was as if the war was still on. The sight of those devastated, quaint old houses brought back the same feelings I used to get as a youngster when I saw parts of the East End bombed.

In these old houses people had been born, had celebrated their weddings and had mourned the death of their dear ones. These places had seen the conflicts that can enter into families: the arguments, the rows and perhaps sometimes the fights. The houses had also seen the other side of life. The happy time when Dad had come home from the war and they hung a sheet out of the window with Welcome Home Alf written on it. The Saturday night parties after coming out of the Cricketers' in Northwold Road, with Alf playing his accordian all the way along the street. The birth of a baby. The loss of a mother. The new hope brought by Dad getting a job, while the family next door were sick with worry because their father had lost his. This is what those old houses saw; not in one generation, but in two, three or maybe more.

Now they are gone, never to exist again. They were small houses. Little light came through the dwarf-size windows. They had no bath, and only an outside toilet. The walls were made of wood and plaster. The criss-cross, narrow strips of wood were a god-send for bugs. These houses were not exactly the Dorchester, but to those who lived there, they were home. Their inhabitants kept them as clean as possible in such conditions. They papered the walls regularly, which helped to keep the bugs down. It doesn't matter how clean you are, it is a full-time job keeping insects out of this sort of building.

These people had been uprooted from the locality they loved. Of course, this also had its advantages. The new flats us East Enders now enjoy (and I am one of them) have a bath, inside toilet, larger, brighter and cleaner-looking rooms. For me, at least, this is adequate compensation. But without the old houses, I think a district loses its character somehow.

To get back to my days. It was 1949, almost time for me to leave school. Our battle of the bugs continued, and my father's business-like brain was still working overtime.

'Pity we can't sell them bugs. Make a fortune on them, we would, the amount we've got here.'

Of course, Dad was joking. He was in one of his jovial moods.

'Yes.' Mum replied, 'but I don't think there'd be much call for them.'

'I can just see the advert now.' went on Dad, full of wit, ' "Barnes for Bugs".'

That was one of the lighter moments in our life at Brooke Road. It is a good thing when people can make light of their problems once in a while.

There was a Government advert at the pictures in those days. It was a song to educate us into saving. That was a laugh for a start. It went like this:

> 'Make your aim a bob in the pound,
> A bob in the pound today.
> Make your aim one in twenty.
> Mind how you spend,
> You'll find nineteen more than plenty.

The bit I really liked went:

> 'Play the game, don't throw it around.
> A bob in the pound from your pay.
>
> You'll be glad in the brighter days tomorrow

That you learned to save today.'

There were other songs coming out too, just as fanciful if a little more romantic. 'Heartbreaker' was one; 'The Woodpecker Song', 'Feet Up, Tap him on the Bobo' by Guy Mitchell. You put a threepenny bit in a juke-box and it would cry out for more, with 'Put Another Nickle In'. We had Bill Haley with his Rock and Roll. There was also Ted Heath (the band-leader, not the politician). You could listen to Winifred Atwell playing 'Twelfth Street Rag', 'Moonlight Gambler', 'Dixie Boogie' or 'Brittania Rag'. Then there was Frankie Lane, who sang of the infidelity of a girl call 'Jezebel', and all Johnny Ray could do was 'Cry'. What's more, within five years or so we were all to be shocked by the bikini.

On the bridge in Northwold Road stood a rickety-looking cafe. It was really just a wooden shed. The locals called it the Utility Cafe, though this wasn't its real name; in fact, I don't think it even had one. Utility goods were on the market then and they were very poorly made. The cafe was constructed in a similar way, and that's how it got its name. It used to open late at night. When my parents left the Wheatsheaf with Uncle George and Aunt Poll, they would make their way there.

The Utility was about fifteen feet long and seven wide. Its walls were a sickly green. As you went in, the counter was facing you. Every so often, all activity had to stop while a train went rushing past. People would hold on to their cups of tea, while others just managed to save their sandwich as the plate went sliding along the wooden table top. The small windows rattled, the whole place vibrated, and the pin table tilted.

When Mum, Dad and all their friends got in the cafe, they seemed to turn it into a pub. Uncle George would bring out a pint of beer and a glass that he had knocked off from the pub. They would order hot pies, cheese sandwiches, saveloys, Eccles cakes. In between eating, they burst into song. You don't see that sort of thing now. They'd have the Law in.

Someone would be on the pin table while the musical enter-entertainment was going on. When the steel ball hit a buffer, it made a noise like 'boing'. It struck me as rather funny when during a chorus of 'Nellie Dean' you would hear this 'boing'!

> 'There's an old mill by the stream
> Nellie Dean . . . . *boing*'.

Uncle George never went short of anything, rationing or not. One night, they came home from the pub to find there was no milk. George came promptly to the rescue.

'Come on, Bill.' he said. 'We'll go and get some.'

The dairy yard wasn't very far from us. George climbed over the gate while Dad kept weeny. A few minutes passed, then Dad heard George:

'Here y'are, Bill. Cop this.' Dad expected George to pass a pint of milk over the gate. He should have known better. From over the top emerged not a pint, nor even a quart, but a full-sized churn. Dad looked up at it, wide-eyed and open-mouthed.

'Come on, Bill. Take it, for Gawd's sake.'

Dad pulled himself out of his stupor and let the churn slowly down to the ground. As George jumped from the gate, there was a *riiippp*. He had caught the seat of his trousers on a nail.

'Sod it, I've torn me Rowton Houses,' he proclaimed.

By now, my parents' subdued grievances were coming to the surface.

The tension at home, the work, the shopping, the money (or lack of it) were all beginning to tell on my mother.

One evening, I got real mad and let rip with one of my swear words. Dad had just come up the stairs. He was drunk, a most unusual thing for him. He pushed the door open. On the table lay the carving knife. He grabbed it. I ran downstairs into the toilet and stayed there for at least an hour. This was certainly not like my father. There was tension between my parents. Dad had come in drunk, and hearing me use this sort of language at my mother had just about done it.

Not long after this, I left home. I had left school and was in the french polishing trade. It was about 1950. I went after this furnished room, where you lived with the family. I told the landlady I was eighteen. Anyone could have seen I was lying. I didn't even look fifteen. Anyway, she let me come. Her old man seemed curious, always pumping me about where I had lived and where I worked. One morning I caught sight of a Bogey's helmet on the sideboard. That did it. I was away. Apparently, though, the bloke had investigated me, found out who my parents were and assured them that I was all right.

I made for Gran Barnes' house. She looked after me all right. But when I had one of my asthma attacks, she was scared stiff, and worried about me.

I soon had enough of being away from home. I thought, 'Well, that's taught them a lesson. They'll go mad when I walk in. They'll be all over me.'

I pushed the street door open with my shoulder, as always, made my way up the three flights of dark stairs and pushed open the door. My mother was clearing up; my father must have been at work.

'Oh, hello,' Mum said, as she swept. 'Want a cup of tea.'

11. The Boys

By this time, I had got in with a gang of boys. Some came from Hoxton, some from Dalston, Hackney and Stoke Newington. We called ourselves the Dalston Boys. Our ages ranged between thirteen and eighteen. We were the junior mob. The senior or upper mob were a different kettle of fish altogether. Us young-sters were just out for fun and birds. The older gang were the real McCoy. Some of them had done time in remand homes and Borstals. Some were downright thieves and layabouts. They would have nothing to do with us inferior beings. One or two of our gang tried to get a bit of prestige by hanging round with the seniors. They were promptly told to piss off until they were eighteen.

Few of us could afford the drape suits of that time. Those who did buy new gear bought the cheapest on the market. I fancied myself as one of the lads now. I had my hair styled in a DA, and took up my father's practice of putting margarine on my locks. Dad was rather amused at this.

'Taking up my lark, eh?' he laughed. 'Don't forget, marge all week and butter on Sundays.'

I wasn't sure if he was joking or not.

I wore a white, high-collared shirt, with a flashy tie in a giant-sized knot. My trousers or jeans looked as if they had had a row with my thick crepe shoes and fluorescent yellow socks. Dressed in this fashion I would make my way down to the Dalston Fair, the boy's meeting place. The fair used to lay up there every winter. In the summer, we would go to Clissold Park.

I began to buy cigarettes. Smoking used to kill me, with my asthma, but I was a man now and did all I could to prove it to myself and others. Everyone else smoked, so I had to. I dressed and acted as much as I could like my favourite gangster film star, Alan Ladd. He wasn't the only one I wanted to imitate. There were much more vicious bleeders than him, like Humphrey Bogart and Paul Muni in 'Scarface'. One film I never tired of seeing was 'Angels With Dirty Faces', starring James Cagney, Pat O'Brien and those slummy Dead End Kids. This was one film that I could relate to. I suppose those Dead End Kids were a bit like us, even though American. That's why we loved them so much. The film was about a gangster, who the Dead Enders worshipped. He is tried for murder. The priest (Pat O'Brien) tells him to scream when he goes to the electric chair, to show the kids that he is not as brave as they think he is. The idea was that if they lost all faith in their hero they might be saved from a life of crime.

I had my arms tattooed, to make me more of a man. Some kids didn't dare have it done. Their parents would have murdered them. The tattoo shop was the size of a toilet. The tattooist was an old man in shirtsleeves and braces. He had a walrus moustache which looked a bit worse for the wear, due to his perpetual smoking and tea drinking. It was damp, limp and had a yellowish-brown tint. On the tattooist's nose rested a pair of steel-rimmed glasses.

On the wall were tattoo designs to choose from: flowers, patterns, nudes and crests. I picked none of these. I went for a heart with a dagger through it. On my second visit, it was a serpent. My third choice was even more gory: a dragon that looked as if it was coming out of my arm. I wonder now if there is something psychological about my choice. Perhaps it was my reflection on life. I have never been an aggressive person, though. It would have been more in keeping with my nature to have chosen something like flowers, birds, or perhaps a crucifix. What could have been going on in my young head to have chosen such morbid tatoos? Anyway, I was certainly a man now, complete with a drape suit, styled hair, a fag on, and my tattoos.

Ginger, one of our gang, was of the small, stocky build characteristic of East Londoners. He was a tough'un. There were bigger boys among us, but he assumed the leadership of the gang without opposition. When he walked, he leaned forward as if he was looking for something. He had piggy eyes, fringed with heavy lashes. A snub nose was set over thick lips. He had red hair — appropriately, for his father was a Communist and a docker. Ginger himself, like the rest of us, didn't know the difference between a Communist and a Buddhist monk. We knew who the Fascists were all right, though. We had had enough of them during the war, and they were still preaching at us in Ridley Road, of a Saturday night.

We used to have a bit of a laugh over the Fascist meetings. which were held near the coffee stall. Us boys would throw out our right arms in the Nazi salute and shout 'Heil Hitler.'

'Oi,' old Joe would say. 'You know you can get done for that nowadays.' 'By 'getting done', he meant that it was against the law and you could be had up in court for it. Whether that was true or not, I don't really know. It didn't stop us, anyway. Some Satur-

170

day nights you would see a scuffle and a bit of a fight between those at the meeting; nothing serious. We kept out of the way. We had no idea what they were fighting about, and we didn't care.

We had our own battles to fight. They were never over-violent, though. At one time, there were three antagonists. This only involved the young boys, not the senior gang. They had much more important business to attend to.

On one flank we had to beware of the Hoxton gang, on the other the Stamford Hill boys. There was another fair that used to lay up for the winter along Hoxton Street. It was probably the overflow from the Dalston fairground. It was fatal for a Dalston boy to venture into the Hoxton fair alone. The Hoxton boys might recognise you as a Dalston lad. Or they might not recognise you at all, which was just as bad, for strangers would be set on just as easily as Dalston boys. The Stamford Hill boys were a little more refined. They left Hoxton and Dalston boys alone. This may have been for fear of retaliation, for there were times when the Hoxton and Dalston gangs combined forces. This would happen when one of us had sustained a good hiding from a Stamford Hill boy one Saturday night at the Royal. We would all march on the Hill in full force, looking for Stamford Hill boys to bash up in revenge.

This may all sound very blood-thirsty, but it was nowhere near as bad as might be inferred. Blows were struck, certainly. There was plenty of horse-play, but not to the extent that it could be called out-and-out violence. It was not like the cowboy and gangster films. We did not join in the scuffle with any deep convictions or ideals, like those at the Fascist meetings. It was just one of the ways we knew of having fun. A good scrap, or meeting a couple of girls apart from our regular birds, broke the monotony of the Dalston streets. At first, the fair was a novel meeting place, but we soon got accustomed to that, and then of course boredom set in.

Eventually, the Hoxton and Dalston boys became one gang. It It was inevitable. Ginger, who led us Dalston boys, lived in Hoxton and so did a few more of our members. The great alliance came suddenly one night. The Dalston boys descended in full force on the Hoxton territory. Ginger came to an agreement with the leader of the Hoxton gang. They would share the power between them. This meant that the large gang met some nights in Dalston and some in Hoxton. If you forgot where you were meeting the boys, you would make for the nearest hang-out first (in my case, the Dalston fairground). If they were not there, they

171

would be at the other place for sure.

One night, this kid strolled into the Hoxton fairground with a whole large stalk of bananas. We didn't know where he'd got them and we didn't care. We just got stuck into them, and that was that.

One night, one of the fairground blokes caught Ginger while he was breaking into one of the machines at the fair. The bloke was a tough, big'un, and Ginger was getting the worst of it. We joined in, then more of the fairground blokes entered the contest. We fought them off, and made for Kingsland Road, Ginger had got a right pasting. His eye was swollen and his lip was bleeding. As we marched down the road, Ginger's mother came in sight. You could tell her a mile off, in her Victorian-style black hat and thread-bare black coat. News of the fight had reached her. She went straight up to Ginger and swung a flat hand to his right ear, making such a smack that I could feel it myself.

'Get home, you little bleeder,' she shouted.

It was unbelievable how passively Ginger took this treatment. He was a good fighter, and tough as nails. He stood no nonsense from anyone; except, apparently, his mother.

Us Dalston boys spent every weekday evening tramping up and down Dalston till one in the morning. This was after the fair closed at midnight. We would have a bit of a change at the weekends. This is how my typical weekend went.

I finished work (my french polishing job in Kingsland Road) at one o'clock on Saturday afternoon. I had a stroll down the Waste to see if there were any bargains to be had, like a modern shirt with a cut-away collar or a pair of crepe, blue suede shoes. On my way, I stopped at the apple fritter stall. That stall is still owned by the same family today. I think they have been there for over sixty years.

I stood and watched the fritter man charge a dozen small metal cups with a liquid flour mixture. The cups were fixed to a frame which had a long handle. When he had filled each cup, he would drop in a piece of apple. Then the whole frame was immersed in the tank of boiling fat. The fryer moved the frame up and down, and the fritters gradually became more and more golden. By this time, my stomach was doing somersaults, as though eager to get out and make a grab at the fritters. The smell they gave off was fantastic. If you were down to your last tanner, you just could not pass that stall by. You got four in a bag, sprinkled with sugar, for sixpence. The last time I had them, they were a shilling each.

Now I was all set with my fritters. I made my way further along the market. I passed the usual group of three-card trick boys and wondered why they bothered to work the Waste. Surely there were more punters down Leicester Square, and more money too? I suppose they knew what they were doing. I passed the toy shop. If my luck was in, I might see Pat, a bird I got friendly with over the fair. She lived over the shop. But no luck.

Hello, there was Ronnie Clarke, one of the boys. He was in the polishing game and all.

'Watcha, Ron.'

'Watcha,' he replied.

'Just finished work, Ron?' I said.

'Yes,' he replied. 'Going down Conicks to get me suit.'

'Cor, smashing,' I exclaimed. 'Want me to come with yer?'

'If yer like.'

I about-turned with him and we made our way to Conicks, a modern clothes shop along Kingsland Road. Ron told me all about the struggles he'd had trying to save for this suit.

'Put a pound in one week, I do, and take out two quid the next. Well, it's that Shirley I'm taking out, ain't it? You know, pictures, pie and mash in Cooksies. You can get through ten bob in one night. I'm gonna pack it in. I enjoy meself better with the boys, anyway. We pick up plenty of birds an' all, don't we? I nodded in agreement.

We made our way along the market, walking in the fashion of the time. Jacket undone, hands in pockets, feet pointing slightly to the side as they shot out. This gave the walker a slight swaying motion, creating an impression of toughness. It also made you walk with a sort of a bounce, indicating a couldn't-care-less attitude. Why the boys felt they had to walk like this, I can't say. I think the gangster films had a lot to do with it. I could never kid myself that I was tough or uncaring. I put on a bit of a bounce, but I could never acquire the exact amount of sway to go with it. It seemed daft to me, so I left that bit out. We never discussed or even mentioned the way we should walk. It was something that seemed to come as you got into your teens and became more conscious of dress and hair style. I suppose your way of walking had to improve (if you could call it that) with the new style of teenage of dress you had adopted.

We were almost at the shop now. Just as we got there, we spotted a smashing-looking bird, just our age.

'Cor, look at that,' bawled Ron, like a town crier who has just had a month's rest from his work. He is helpless. He can't take his eyes off her. 'Fantastic. Cor blimey, Ron, just look at those.'

I quickly assure him that I am doing so, that I have been doing so since he first pointed out this teenage Jane Russell. Our view was soon obscured and the spell broken by some fat old dear pushing a pram with a great bundle of gear on it. The young beauty was gone from our lives as quickly as she had appeared. We went into the shop.

After I had been with my mate to get his suit, I decided it was time to go home and get some grub. Then I would get ready to meet the boys down Dalston. From there, we would go to the Royal Ballroom in Tottenham.

I had my tea, washed and then shaved off what bum bluff there was on my chin. I hadn't bought my own razor yet, so I used Dad's. I plastered my hair with margarine and water, to make sure my DA stayed in place. Then on went my new shirt.

'Oh, that's nice,' exclaimed Mum. 'You can't beat a white shirt on a man.'

Now I was ready to hit the town. I made my way down the stairs and into the brightness of the summer evening. I made my way down Brooke Road to the High Street, where I would catch the number 647 trolley bus to Dalston. I looked swell in my knee-length jacket, thick, crepe-soled shoes, bright yellow tie in the most gigantic knot. I wore nice, well-pressed trousers on Saturday night. During the week it would be jeans or denims.

At Dalston Junction, a group of between ten and twenty boys would congregate.

The Royal was a large, luxuriously decorated ballroom. It was full of atmosphere: dimmed lighting, a licensed bar and small tables round the dancing area. This was the luxury we had seen on the films. Now we had the setting, so we became the actors. One boy might fancy himself as Errol Flynn, and chat up one bird after another. One might be a second Bob Hope, cracking jokes all night. Then there were the more aggressive ones: the Humphrey Bogarts, George Rafts and all the gangster types. It was this lot who sometimes caused a fight and spoilt the evening. Then the bouncers would chuck you out. Not because you had actually done anything, but just because you were with the fight-happy ones. Some of them would actually put themselves out to cause trouble. They would give another bloke's bird the eye, or keep asking her to dance.

After leaving the Royal, we would make our way down to Joe's coffee stall on the corner of Ridley Road. There, we would have a sandwich fit for a giant and a cup of tea. We would have a laugh and a joke among ourselves and with any girls we met.

We strolled up and down Kingsland Road every night of the week. Sometimes, a few of the girls we knew would come with us. At the end of the evening, we would pair off with a girl and go round the back of Woolworth's for a bit of a snog before we went home. Many's the time I've had a policeman flash his torch right in my face, with the order to 'Move along'. The girl would quickly button up her coat and, depending how far I had got, her blouse also. We would just walk away with the bogey following.

The boys used to brag among themselves about how far they had got with a certain bird, and of fruitless attempts with others.

'Like a bleeding ice-berg, she is. Nuffink doing there, nuffink at all.'

Or perhaps, 'Cor blimey. I thought me birthday had come.'

I have a feeling the stories of bitter failure were more genuine than those of success. We liked to think we were permissive, but it was mostly on film and paper rather than in reality. If a young girl became pregnant, she was quickly whisked off to an obscure home in the country, as though she had some contagious disease. Or, if she was old enough, she got married quick.

This sort of thing still goes on today, more than we are aware of. We are still living in the past to some extent. Girls still marry or are sent away if they get pregnant at the wrong time. All to save themselves from the terrible disgrace of the perfectly natural function of having a baby. No one is really to be blamed or praised in the matter. Like all old customs and beliefs, these are extremely obstinate and hard to dismiss from our way of life. Some old customs may be for the good of all. Those like the one I have mentioned, however, only help make the individual feel rejected by society.

Conscription had come in by this time, a godsend to any young male who had got his girl friend into trouble and didn't want to marry her. Due to my health, I was one of the happy unwanted. It wasn't easy finding mates now. I didn't want to romp around with the fifteen-year-olds, and I was still too young to be accepted by the upper mob. I had to be twenty or more to get in with them now. I could have gone to the club in Stoke Newington Church Street, but it was all birds and young kids there. I would have felt a right narna among that lot. Anyway, they had chucked us out once for throwing clay at each other in the modelling class. I had wanted to do clay modelling. I loved art. But of course the other boys didn't. They took the rise when they saw me in there with this apron on.

'Aw, look, he's gone queer. Didums don't arf look sweet, don't he? Koochee, koochee. Ah, he's lovely, ain't he?'

That was it. I sploshed a great dollop of clay at the nearest face. I got a faceful back. Then a lump hit the wall as my next, quick-thinking opponent ducked. The young art teacher, somewhere in her twenties, went scurrying for the boxing instructor. Out we went. No, I couldn't show my face there again. I was right pissed off.

All was not lost, though. I met an old mate of mine who I had known at the open-air school I went to when I was twelve. Bert had also failed the medical for the army. From then on, I was always on Bert's territory. He lived in a sort of miniature village in Shephard's Lane. A group of privately rented houses in a square at the end of an alleyway. They were dark, grubby old places. Everyone in Shephard's Lane knew everyone else. It was one of the communities that still had that old fashioned friendliness about it. People still sat outside their doors in summer, while the kids played games. It seemed as if the war had hardly changed the place at all.

Fortunately, it had been overlooked by Hitler's bombers. This was understandable. This little square of old houses, at the end of a narrow alley, was unknown to even the oldest natives, let alone Hitler. I was astonished myself when Bert took me down there. This little community seemed cut off from the rest of human existence. It was like living on an island, surrounded by concrete instead of water. As soon as you entered the place, you could feel the friendliness there. The smallness gave you a sense of security. It made me wish that I lived there. It would have been better than that tenement in Brooke Road.

I was rather interested in the opposite sex then, and it wasn't long before I was going out with Joyce. She lived in Sheep Lane, very near Bert. They all loved music down there, so I used to take my accordian and we would have a tune in Joyce's house or Bert's. If it got too crowded indoors, we would go outside and have a sing-song. It was smashing.

There used to be parties some Saturday nights when the pubs closed. It was all beer, sandwiches and pickles, if the host could afford enough of these luxuries to feed twenty people or more. One of these parties was held by candle light, which gave the place a somewhat exotic atmosphere. This was not intentional, of course. It was just that the family giving the party had had their electricity cut off, for not paying the bill.

Bert and I used to hang around Mare Street a lot then. When we got fed up with this, we would go to the Ritz, near Clapton Pond. Whenever we went to the pictures, it was always to the Ritz. This was not because they showed better films, but for economic reasons. Bert's mum worked in the cinema as an usherette, so we got in free. We'd see one film three or four times a week, enjoying the satisfaction of getting in for nothing. It was even better than bunking in. It felt good just to walk in the main door, without paying. When we bunked in with some of the other boys, we had to get one of them to pay. He would then open one of the emergency doors at the side of the building and let us in.

It was at the Ritz that I met Doll, my wife. Bert was courting at this time, and it wasn't long before Doll and I were married. We had taken a bigger step than either of us realised. Now I really felt the drawback of being asthmatic. It hadn't worried me when I was single. I had only myself to keep. My mother never kept on at me to get work. That was fine, for I detested it anyway. I could be out of work for months, just like all my mates. It wasn't because of my health, or that I couldn't get work. It was because I hated the monotony, the smell and stink of being in factories all day. So I had been single, out of work and free.

When I left school, I experienced a freedom I had never felt before. Greer House was the best school I ever went to. Everyone was great. My relief was not at being rid of the teachers. It was the fact of being able to suit myself as to whether I went to work or not. When I did decide to make a start, I could more or less choose what job I wanted, though I didn't realise how little I had to choose from.

Now all that was finished. I had to get a job and keep it. That wasn't easy when I was always catching chest colds. Doll was pregnant. We lived, ate and slept in the large front room at Brooke Road. Mum, Dad and my eight-year-old sister Glenda slept in the smaller room. But Doll and I were so young and optimistic. We were in love and happy. She looked even better to me, now that she was beginning to show. It's strange how women seem to look more attractive when they are carrying. As time passed, though, things changed. It was neither her fault nor mine.. It was the circumstances of our life.

When I see young couples getting married today and taking furnished rooms (if they can afford them these days) or living with their parents, I think, 'God, I hope they make out'. No matter how well-intentioned the parents are, it never seems to work out. Each is in the other's way, no matter how well everything is planned. Bad feelings get subdued. You can't say what you want. Eventually, the tension becomes so great that it all has to come out, and everyone feels sorry afterwards. This is how we started our married life. In one room in Brooke Road.

12. Work and Married Life

I was interested in art when I was at school. My ambition was to become a sign-writer. This ambition was not fulfilled. This was due to the innate selfishness of the older people I had the misfortune to work with and their contempt for the young. I say this without apology. Greer House ¸ave me a first-class reference to enable me to get a sign-writing job. It might as well have been a dog licence. None of my employers ever even asked to see it. When I produced it, an adult hand would wave it aside with the words, 'School references don't mean a thing!' All my ambition to be a sign-writer was quickly smashed when I finally did get a job. Alf, the foreman, oppressed me so much that I just had to leave. Luckily, I found an opening, but one mistake cost me that job, too.

After that, I couldn't get a job sign writing for love or money. I didn't bother after a while, and stayed at home for a few months. I couldn't care less now what I did. I roamed the streets with the other boys who had not got a job yet. We were a small contingent of the future unemployed.

Then I happened to wander into the french polishing trade. From there, I became a baker's roundsman, driving a horse and cart at first, then a motor vehicle. I had to be hard sometimes, to get those Hoxton customers to pay me. It wasn't that they wouldn't pay: they couldn't. I had a right job convincing my inspector of this. The stairs and the weather got a bit too much for me, so I took a job driving a tailor's van. The money was very poor, something like eight pounds a week. Doll wasn't working, so things were rather tight. They would get even tighter when the baby was born. I began to worry about my frequent loss of jobs. As soon as we saved a pound, it would go again when I was off sick.

There was just one hope: my accordian. I had always loved music. No one in our family had played a musical instrument, apart from my grandfather Gullis. But I had wanted an accordian as long as I can remember. While I was in the french polishing game, I managed to buy one on the weekly from this music teacher. She told me that if I wanted lessons I had to have an instrument, so she sold me this one. I used to go upstairs and practise for hours. It was all by ear. I couldn't get on with reading music. For weeks, I practised by candle light, all on my own. That was another time when we had had the electricity cut off. I was always a bit afraid of the dark in my younger days, and candle light can be rather bizarre. I was so engrossed in getting the right chords that it didn't bother me at all, though. Anyway, Mum wouldn't have me in the kitchen. The noises I was producing on my instrument were a little unusual.

Now I equipped myself with a cloth cap. This served the double purpose of keeping my head warm and being handy for collecting coins in after I'd played a few songs in the doorway of a pub. Buskers nearly always had to stand in the doorway of the pub, not inside. At the few places with a music licence, they were only too pleased to have you right inside the public bar.

Every Saturday night, I would leave Doll at home and make my tour of the pubs. I might make a couple of quid from about nine till ten-thirty. That was good money. In the winter the cold was a drawback, but all the walking and playing kept me warm enough. Now and again, I got asked back to someone's house for an engagement party or something. This was nice because I got another couple of quid at least. If I was lucky enough to land up at a party, I wouldn't roll in till two or three in the morning. I would be half drunk into the bargain.

I stuffed my earnings away in a drawer and tried to keep it for when I was off sick. I might put four pounds in there, but when I opened the drawer later to count it, there would only be three. Right away, I knew Doll had been at it. That would cause a right old row.

'You've had a nicker out of here,' I'd shout.

'Well, you can stop it out of my wages next week,' Doll would say indignantly. Why we called the housekeeping money I gave her 'wages', I don't know. It was nothing of the sort. It was money to buy food and pay the bills.

'Here I am,' I'd shout, as always, 'trying to save a bit of cash to get us over the bad weeks, and all you do is take it out.'

All this was due to my lack of understanding. I had no idea how hard it was for a woman to manage on the wages of an unskilled husband. I did not realise just how much money it took to keep body and soul together from day to day. I got my pay packet and gave Doll what I thought was reasonable. My calculations were obviously not very generous. Even if I had been more aware of the cost of living and more sympathetic to my wife's shopping problems, I don't suppose I would have been able to supply the necessary amount of cash. Week in, week out, my

180

busking money was saved, only to be broken into. If I became sick, whatever was left in the drawer was gone in no time.

In the summer, of a Saturday mostly, I was asked to factory workers' beanos. They would ask me to bring my accordian along. I was promised all the beer and food I could put away, and two pounds ten at the end of the day. I would play all the way to Margate. We would have a stop half-way. Out of the great boot of the coach would come bottles of beer, empty beer crates to sit on, jars of pickles, boxes of sandwiches. All conversation and song quickly died down while they refreshed themselves. While they sat eating and drinking, the boss would come up in his Mercedes and try to join in as best he could.

When we got to Margate, they would all disperse in groups and make for the nearest boozer. This was the day out: beer and grub. I would be on my own for the rest of the day. I didn't mind that too much. I needed a rest, after all that playing. On the return journey it would be even harder work. They would all be pissed and raring to go. So I used to make for the beach and try to get a bit of sleep.

I loved looking across that vast expanse of sea. It always fascinated me. I picked out little specks on the horizon. I took in the colour of the sea, in some places a muddy brown, in others a rich turquoise. There were the sea-gulls with their tireless, high-pitched cry; first streaming past overhead, then just hovering, weightless, in the majestic blue sky, then suddenly diving down to the water's surface to catch their prey. How I wished I was a free and as skilled at flying as these beautiful, graceful creatures. No job worries for them, no price rises either. They just hunt the sea for small fish, or scrounge off boats and holiday makers. What a carefree life, I thought. But I wasn't a sea-gull. I was a human being, and life had to be faced. Not now, though, not now. Now I would lie back in the sand and take in all the beauty, mystery and calm of the sea. Children were playing, paddling, digging in the sand. People were sprawled out in deck-chairs. They, too, were forgetting their urban worries and problems for a while.

People say that many urban children are deprived of the country. Personally, I never felt really deprived by not seeing much of the country. If you never see the country, you never miss it. You are brought up among factories and buildings, surrounded by the rush and hurry of city life.

During the course of my busking career, I picked up with a banjo player from Hoxton. He was elderly, and had made busking his living. He was quite well-known in the pubs round Hoxton.

181

Pairing up with him gave me a bit of a boost and made the job more enjoyable. I could see, though, that I was not going to find any security in the entertainment world. I wondered how my partner had survived for all these years. Something had to be done if I was to keep going, if I was to hit back at losing time from work.

I must have inherited some of my father's business acumen. I had the idea of buying up old onion sacks and selling them to french polishing firms. I had seen some of these sack merchants during my french polishing days. I reckoned it wasn't a bad idea.

The first thing was to get mobile. I hunted the East End high and low for a barrow. Asking stallholders if they had one to sell was like asking for a Rolls Royce. I was amazed how scarce barrows were. One afternoon (probably one of my out-of-work afternoons) I happened to walk down a small passage off Amhurst Road. On one side of this little street was some waste ground. I spotted a scruffy-looking bloke in a black overcoat there. He was doing something to a couple of tricycles. I was interested right away. I walked slowly over to the old boy and stopped a few yards away from him. One of these trikes would do me fine. The thing was, would he part with one, and for how much?

He spotted me. His big nose protruded towards me. His thick grey eyebrows were twisted upwards unnaturally. His cheeks were drawn, and he looked at me with pale, droopy eyes that watered continually. I could see now that his overcoat was dotted with burn holes. This puzzled me, but I would investigate that later, when I got better acquainted with him.

'What can I do for you, cock?' he called to me, choking on a cigarette hanging from his mouth.

'Er, well, I was looking at one of these trikes.' I moved closer now, eager to make my bargain.

'What, you wanna buy one, cock?'

'Well yes,' I replied.

'Well I've got this one here I don't use, if you're interested.' He pointed to a trike that was lying on its side. 'A good one, that. Hardly used.'

By the look of the vehicle, I could tell his last few words were the understatement of the year.

'Good springs, cock. Good solid tyres. Excellent body work.' He continued in his praise of this slowly decaying contraption on wheels, as if he was a seasoned car salesman. He walked over to the trike, and with one clever movement had it standing upright. He came over to where I was standing, his black overcoat flapping

182

around him. He stretched out his arm towards the article up for offer and opened the palm of his hand.

'There. Ain't she a beauty?' he asked.

I looked doubtfully, first at the tricycle, then at its owner. The pleasurable look left his face as he noticed my expression.

'Well, how much then?' he said, a little agitated. I repeated my look of doubt. I rested my chin on my hand, thinking deeply of how much capital I could afford to gamble on such an unreliable-looking conveyance. There seemed no hope of getting anything else. A clean-up and a drop of oil might make some improvement, if rather small. The rust had certainly got at it, but it would do me until I was able to get a more elaborate, sturdier type of vehicle.

'Well, how much?' the salesman was saying.

'Well, I don't really know what to offer you, I said. Seeing how trikes and barrows were so scarce, I felt he would want something like five quid. I didn't dare suggest that, though, in case he wanted less. Of course, he wouldn't name a figure in case it was less than I was willing to pay. For the next few minutes the conversation consisted of: 'Well, what do you think?' 'Well, what do you think?' In the end, someone had to give in. Perhaps he needed some cash more than I needed his trike. Anyway, he finally said, 'Two quid?'

'Two quid?' I asked, feigning doubt.

This was three quid less than I had reckoned, but there was no harm in trying to get it even cheaper.

'Thirty bob,' I said.

He shot me an indignant look. 'Thirty bob?' he sang in a high-pitched voice. 'Now, come on. It's worth a lot more than I'm asking. It's gonna earn you money, ain't it? Now, come on, two quid.'

'Thirty-five bob,' I bargained. 'I can't afford no more.'

'All right, done. Give us yer money.'

The bargain was clinched. The two of us were now more relaxed. He sat down on a rusty old drum. 'What you gonna do then?' he asked.

'Sacks,' I replied.

'Sacks?' Sacks is no good. I've done it myself. No money there. Got ter git too many. Got ter do that in a big way, with a lorry an' that. No, sacks is no good. Chestnuts, that's the game. That's what I do in the winter. In the summer I sells a few bikes. I get the old rheumatism. Had it all me life. So I does a bit of chestnuts. It helps out for when I lose time in the saw mill.

This last bit of information frightened me a little. I was in the same sort of position as he was, only I was younger. I could picture myself at his age (about fifty-odd) on a similar piece of waste ground, trying to make money to compensate for loss of work. Frightened of the future? Why, I was in that dreaded position now, never mind when I was fifty.

'The old fire keeps the old back warm an' all, when I stand on the corners.'

Now I knew where all the holes in his coat had come from. The worst burns were on the back of his coat.

'I does the Arsenal on Saturdays. Or Tottenham. Whoever's playing. I don't mind the push to Arsenal so much, but that Tottenham's a murderous push. Well, it's so much farther to go than Arsenal. The coming back's the worst, up that bleeding Stamford Hill.

'I goes down Spitalfields in the week and gets me nuts. Then I cuts them. That stops them exploding, yer see, cock. If they explodes in yer face, it don't 'arf give you something. Not only that, once they explodes you only have the empty shell left. You puts that in the bag, and corse they come back and 'ave a go at yer. Some people get very nasty if you happen to serve up bad ones, as well. What I does is, I puts 'em all in a bath of water when I gets home. All the bad ones come to the top. It's no good selling bad ones like some blokes. You don't save much by it. Not only that, people won't buy off yer if you start that lark.

'But you've got to be careful with your fire. If the wind gets too much, you could have your whole trike alight in no time. Keep away from the fire, too. Some of 'em stand right on top of it when the weather's cold. They don't realise the heat that one of those cans throws out. One girl stood too near it once. She had a plastic handbag on her arm. It wasn't a handbag by the time I had served her. More like the size of a purse. She started crying about it. "Well, I told you, love, didn't I?" I said. I mean you can only tell 'em can't yer?

'Look,' he said. 'Why don't you come down the market with me and do a bit of chestnuts? Better'n sacks, it is.'

'OK,' I agreed. I had nothing to lose.

Charlie showed me where to get a metal oil drum and how to cut it so as to convert it into a chestnut can. These roasters are not so easy to construct as you might imagine. First, I had to cut the steel drum in half with a hacksaw. It was hard work. The cut had to be accurate all round, to make a proper job of it. The fire grate itself had to be just high enough to get the wind under it, to

184

keep the fire going. But it couldn't be too high or it would burn the chestnuts. They rested on a plate drilled with holes, which you put over the grate.

After many cuts and blisters, I was finally equipped with my roasting gear. The trike was cleaned up and oiled. Now I was ready for business.

I met Charlie down Kingsland Road with his trike and away we went to Spitalfields Market.

'Made a nice job of that, cock.' said Charlie, referring to my newly manufactured chestnut can and my cleaned-up trike. 'Right, come on, then,' he said. 'I'll show you where to get the best nuts at the lowest prices.'

Charlie took the lead and I followed behind. We pushed our trikes. They were so old and rusty that it was a lot easier to push them than ride. Charlie leaned forward as he pushed. His thick black hair, streaked with grey, blew in all directions. His blackened and burnt overcoat tail opened out like a pair of wings in the blustery wind. I watched Charlie as he walked ahead of me. I felt a little sorry for him, and a little afraid for myself as well. I would see to it that I didn't sink deeper and deeper. I didn't want to finish up a fifty-year-old, scruffy, wrinkled, under-nourished old man.

Well, I had got into the chestnut game now. I began to go out on my own. Then one night my whole business went up in flame. I had no fire insurance. Still, what could I have claimed for an over-worked, rusty old trike, an old drum converted into a roaster, three bags of nuts and half a hundredweight of coke? I decided after that experience that chestnut selling was too risky for me. While roasting the nuts, I could quite easily have roasted myself. Not only that, it was too much work for the profit made. That was another business project finished.

By this time, we had moved to Warwick House, in Southwold Road, Clapton. We had taken our Put-U-Up suite, the baby's cot and a table with four chairs. This was the sole extent of our furnishings. Mum was pleased we had got this place on the third floor, overlooking the Marshes. Now she could get back to normal. She had her large room again. Our Put-U-Up settee, which we used as a bed, collapsed in the process of moving, so we just laid the bedding on the floor. We had to make do with that until we could afford a new (no, not new, second-hand) bedstead. In the tiny kitchen we had one small table. The toilet and the bathroom were together. I suppose this was of some consolation if you had an attack of diarrhoea while having a bath. But it could be nasty if someone was in the bath and someone else wanted to use the toilet. In the living room we had our table and four chairs. In the bedroom was what was left of the bed. In Lesley's bedroom there was one bed.

After we had been there some weeks, a neighbour gave us a small bedroom suite that she had no further use for. I gave it a paint up and it fitted nicely into Lesley's room. I also put some wallpaper up to finish Lesley's room off.

I had got a job delivering laundry. I knew it wasn't going to last long. I was having too much time off. The heat, the damp, the stairs and the weather were all telling on me. I just kept going until I was told that they had a business to run and could not put up with my absenteeism any longer.

While I was on this job, I had a stroke of luck. I happened to be down a side street with my van. I spotted two smashing armchairs lying in the back entrance of a well-known furniture shop in Amhurst Road. 'I'd like them,' I thought. 'Fill up our living room a bit more, too.' The armchairs of our Put-U-Up suite had just about had it. I don't know about Put-U-Up, but sitting in them now was enough to Put-U on your back. A brand new suite was unthinkable.

A bloke in a brown warehouse coat came out of the shop. He saw me looking at the chairs. 'Can have 'em if you want 'em,' he said, as if glad to get them off his hands. I needed no second offer. They were on my van in a flash, before he could change his mind. I threw the old ones on a dump. I was glad to see the back of them. Our luck seemed to be in now, Another woman gave me an old piano. She was going to smash it up, but my wife just caught her. The instrument was positioned in our bedroom. I was well pleased. It was old and out of tune, but I ignored that. At the worst it was something to practice on until I could afford a really good one.

I was on my travels along Kingsland Road, trying to find another job, any job where I could be secure for a few months. I spotted this notice, 'Driver Wanted'. It was a timber firm. I had never handled timber before, but I lied enough to put me in purgatory for ever and got the job. If it had not been for this West Indian Christian bloke who worked as a labourer in the yard, and who later became my best friend, I wouldn't have lasted five minutes.

Derek Dixon was only a young lad then. He was one of the first batch of immigrants into this country at the time. He never talked about it to me, but I felt that, being over here alone except for a few relatives, he needed a good friend, or friends, who he could visit of an evening and at weekends. He lived in a furnished room; not a very elaborate one, either. I introduced him to Mum and Dad, and they seemed to take to him. He was a big bloke, and as he walked into Mum's small kitchen, he looked enormous. His head was only about five inches from the ceilling.

We would sit together, talking and drinking tea. Then he would start to tell us about the Bible and all that. This part of the evening may sound boring, but it wasn't. The way Derek put it over made it quite interesting. Then we would all have to sing one of his hymns, and before he went he would say a prayer. At the finish, a few more of Derek's West Indian friends started turning up. This had the effect of turning the whole thing into a miniature church. This was all right until we started singing Negro spirituals. The noise and excitement would have made a frenzied crowd at a heavy-weight title fight seem like a monastery garden. Complaints were bound to follow, and they did. So these little gatherings had to stop.

By this time, I was also trying to be a Christian. I thought that perhaps all my misfortune − being poor since I could remember − was due to my evil ways. Well, that's what we learned at school, anyway. Right, now I stopped swearing. I no longer rowed with Doll about nicking a sheet out of the drawer from the few quid I was trying to save. Now we would get on. I must have been stupid to think that this was going to make any difference, but there it was.

Working on the timber job had done nothing to improve my physical condition, so I went back to the Labour Exchange again. I knew I had nothing to worry about now, because I was a Christian. Not only that, the Bible told me that man does not live by bread alone. Perhaps we could do without that, as well as all the other things. Things like a summer holiday, or a fridge like other people. The latter wasn't that important, though. We wouldn't have had much to put in it.

I could do without health-preserving foods like fruit. Doll used to buy cabbage, but I could never eat it. There were things like honey and crab, though, things that we could ill afford, that I could have eaten. Cheese was cheap, but I didn't appreciate the goodness in it. I loved kidneys, ox or pork, but it wasn't very often we could afford them. So I mostly ate things like potatoes, peas, cakes and biscuits. This was due to a combination of lack of money and ignorance about the importance of eating the right things. But now my faith would carry me through all this ignorance and lack of cash.

The Labour Exchange offered me a job as a chauffeur to a small businessman. 'Just the job for you,' they told me. 'Light, clean; no heavy work.' I was quite convinced that at last my luck had changed, and that the Dear Lord had answered my prayers. It was worth the effort of not swearing and rowing for months on end. Now I would keep it up.

Alas, the clerk had forgotten to tell me that my future employer was an alcoholic who wanted me to work twelve hours a day, six and sometimes seven days a week. I began to wonder if this was the Good Lord helping me or the Devil trying to hinder me.

Mr. Mason, my new boss, was a short man with a belly on him like a prize bull. His fat, flabby face had more wrinkles on it than a well-worn boot. I would arrive at his home in Stoke Newington at ten in the morning, ready to take him on his tour of his building sites. This, he informed me, was to make sure the bastards were working. His frequent appearances during the course of the day ensured full capacity working; or so he believed. The short journeys from site to site took something like five minutes. They were 'short' trips in more ways than one, for we stopped regularly at pubs on the route for his scotch. In the morning it was scotch. In the afternoon it was scotch.

After his rounds, at six pm, he went to the Cumberland Hotel for dinner. I would sit outside with what was left over from my lunch-time sandwiches. The coffee in my flask was a dirty brown by now, and nearly cold. There were other restaurants open, it's true, but what chauffeur could afford their prices? On my wages, even the more modest establishments were out of the question. They all know how to charge in the West End.

So I used to lie back in my luxurious padded car seat, push my peak cap to the back of my head, and content myself with my dry sandwiches and cold, muddy coffee. Afterwards, I would relax with my pocket bible. It was ironic when I turned to Genesis, chapter two, verse sixteen: 'And the Lord God commanded the man, saying, "Of every tree of the garden thou mayest freely eat." '

The job lasted nine months, during which time I never seemed to have any time at home. What with the financial pressure and my continual absence from the family, our troubles intensified. Lesley had to be minded while Doll went out to work. We were nothing like the family I envisaged three or four years earlier. So early one morning, as I got out of the limousine and mounted my bike for home, I decided: 'Shit or bust, I'm packing it in. Twelve pounds a week for all this work and no family life.' In fact, what there was of our family life was being slowly crushed, which was even worse than having it quickly destroyed. Christmas was on the way, but I had been there nine months. I was sure to have some holiday pay to come; at least nineteen quid, I reckoned.

Mr. Mason was most reluctant to take my week's notice. Well who could blame him? What a bargain he had. In one man, he had not only a chauffeur, but a car washer (who cleaned not only his car but his two children's as well), a shoe-shine boy and an errand boy. All these in service for as much as twelve hours a day, Monday to Saturday. If he wanted to go to Brighton on a Sunday morning, I did that too, with no extra pay.

So he was most upset and annoyed when he found I was determined to leave, Christmas or no Christmas. He tried pleading with me, and when this didn't work he came very near to losing his temper. He thought better of it, though. Instead, he tried telling me about all the advantages of the job. Things like having a nice, warm, luxury car to sit in while I waited outside boozers and restaurants for him; and that I didn't have to start till ten in the morning. When I tried to point out that we didn't arrive back at his place till one or two in the morning, he changed the subject quickly. I packed it up, but Mr. Mason had his revenge by not giving me any holiday money. That was the most terrible Christmas.

I phoned the Labour Exchange about my money. I was told I would have to go before the wages council, and would first have to make an appointment. I could tell this was going to be a long-winded turn-out, with nothing at the end of it. I was now desperate for cash. I needed it immediately to get the grub in for Christmas, not to mention Lesley's toys. I was trapped. I could do nothing. I paid Doll her money that Friday night, but next week I would be on the Labour once again.

That following week was Christmas week. I couldn't get any work for love or money. I tramped all over, but to no avail. I even tried to get a few hours casual down Spitalfields Market, like most alcoholic vagrants do; I was that desperate. I just couldn't bear to see my child's face if she woke up on Christmas morning to find nothing at the end of her bed. Something had to be done, anything. I even had the thought of nicking something, but I wasn't cut out for it. Not only that, if I had been caught Doll and Lesley would have been in an even worse position. Anyway, I was trying to be a Christian.

As I searched for work that week, I saw women with full shopping bags; men carrying large boxes. The shops were packed with all the good things of the season, their windows bright with coloured lights and tinsel. Everyone seemed so jolly in the market place. Along the High Street I saw workers who had just knocked off. They were walking very unsteadily along the road, as a result of their celebrations on the shop floor. They would be swaying and maybe singing, either in a group or on their own.

I hated Christmas that year like I had never hated it before. I hated these stupid merrymakers. All the fantasy of the coloured tinsel seemed to be there to cover up the realities of what people like me were going through: a Christmas of scrimping and scraping. It was a bad year all round. That could be endured. But to have no money at Christmas to make things what they should be for your kids was a most terrible and heartbreaking thing for any man with any concern for his family. I hated that bastard Mason. I hated everything and everybody that Christmas.

Wasn't this the season of goodwill, though? Shouldn't I have felt something other than hatred? Shouldn't I have had a feeling of well-being on this Christmas Eve? A feeling of brotherliness, perhaps, a mild excitement as I looked forward to a few days off work with plenty to eat and drink. I should have felt all these things, but with three or four pounds to come from the Labour Exchange and the prospect of being out of work in the New Year did little to give me the usual Christmas cheer. I thought of all the others in my position and of those in an even worse plight. This seemed to give me some sort of unnatural comfort.

I went home in a right mood and took my frustrations out on Doll. This wan't right, that wasn't right, why isn't the front room tidied up? Plus a host of other criticisms, until eventually Doll broke out and then we ended up rowing or even fighting.

Why?

13. In and Out of Jobs

I was back on the Labour Exchange once again. We had struggled over the Christmas and we couldn't care less about the New Year. We knew that this year would be the same as all the others. When people wished me a Happy New Year, I felt like laughing in their faces.

I had no industrial skills at all, but I was an expert at signing on. I knew that I had to go to Box One and fill in the usual form. I knew that I had to wait three days before I was entitled to my pay. I knew the Labour Exchange. I knew the clerks behind the counter. I knew when a new face turned up on the other side of the counter, or when an old one was absent. Sometimes the clerks would greet me with the smile of a Saville Row tailor's assistant, saluting Sir Cuthbert as he walks into the shop. They were more friendly if you were on the Disabled Register. They never pressed you to take a job you didn't fancy. I suppose clerks vary, like the people they serve. Some are good natured, some not. I never had a bad experience at the Labour Exchange, though. Those blokes have got their work cut out all right, when you consider how many frustrated and unhappy people they have to deal with.

I was told that they had nothing suitable for me, as happened more often than not on the Disabled Register. I didn't relish the thought of being out of work too long, so I tried my luck at the able-bodied section. There, I was told the same thing. I thought about going back to Price's bakery as a roundsman. I had had to pack this job in before. Climbing stairs while carrying a basket, plus the bad weather in the winter, had proved too much. I thought I'd give it another go now. Luckily (if you can call it that) I was taken on almost immediately. I was in business once more. By the end of the week, my financial problems would be well on the way to being solved, if I didn't get sick in the meantime.

The baker's round they gave me at Price's was the one that nobody else wanted. I started at about seven in the morning and finished at four or five. The round was in Muswell Hill, delivering bread and cakes to houses along Coney Hatch Lane, Pages Lane, King's Avenue and Creighton Avenue. One of my customers was Alfred Marks, the comedian.

Apart from the long hours, there was the disadvantage of the very steep hill. You would finally get to the customer's door, panting as if you had done the three minute mile. You would hand over the small brown load they had ordered. Then they would say, as casually as if they were refusing a cigarette, 'Oh, we don't need it today, baker. Call tomorrow, though. We might need it by then.'

This was a round in a million. When I first appeared at the door, all the customers greeted me with, 'What, not another new roundsman?' It was clear that the round had carried off quite an army of previous delivery men in the past. I had no intention of adding to that number, so I was soon off.

Instead of bread, I now delivered milk. I knew that although milkmen start very early, they get done between one and two in the afternoon. That job died a natural death, too. I liked the hours, but it was much heavier work than my bread roundsman's job. I sweated and cooled down. Then I caught cold and was off work. This circle continued, not only on the milk round, but whenever I did heavy work.

I had to try something more sophisticated. I applied to a brewery in the City for a job as chauffeur. This would suit me down to the ground, I thought. They had their own doctor. I tried to hide my asthma, but he was no novice. He found it.

'Does it give you much trouble?' he asked. I knew he wasn't asking out of any concern for me, but for the sake of the company.

'Not much,' I answered in my most convincing tone.

He rested his chin on his hand and sat there thinking for about ten years. Well, that's how long it seemed to me. I hated being out of work. At long last, he came to life. He leaned forward over a form, with his pen at the ready.

'OK,' he said. 'Your job will not involve heavy work or entail being out in inclement weather. You'll be all right.'

'Gor blimey,' I thought. 'He should have seen me in my two previous jobs.'

Now I was a dignified-looking chauffeur, all five foot four of me. I thought, 'Well with a cushy number like this, sitting in a comfortable room waiting to drive some director to the West End, riding in a nice comfortable warm car in the winter, my asthma won't cause me to lose this job.' I was right, it didn't. Something else did – my poor knowledge of the topography of London.

I used to sit in the Chauffeurs' Room, as they called it. 'Closet' would have been more descriptive. It was a rectangular box, filled from morning to night with smoke from the pipes and cigarettes of the other half dozen chauffeurs. They sat round this table playing cards, and at the end of each game took short swigs at glasses of ale or cups of tea. They smoked like an old steam engine that someone had forgotten to decarbonise. I sat in this opium den for almost a fortnight, until the fateful day when I got the push.

I knew from the off that I wasn't much good at driving from A to B, in or out of the West End, but I didn't let on to anyone about that. They didn't even test my knowledge when I started. If they had done, I wouldn't even have set foot inside that chauffeurs' smoke hole. I was bored to tears sitting there day after day. I didn't play cards. I've never been keen on those sort of games. Anyway, these old hands seemed a bit cliquey and classed me as some new, inferior being.

One morning, the head chauffeur gave me my orders. 'Barnes, you are taking Captain Smith to Paddington Station at 2 pm this afternoon,' he told me.

'Blimey,' I thought. 'It's only ten o'clock now. He's given me plenty of warning.' So there I sat for a further four hours, waiting to do my first trip in my new job. All I knew was that Paddington was somewhere near Marble Arch. The route was very vague in my mind. Perhaps if I had had a map it would have helped. But I couldn't have got it out in front of that lot, or they would have twigged right away. It was almost two o'clock. The head chauffeur tore himself away from his card game and told me I had better get my car and drive it to the main entrance to pick up the Captain.

I couldn't have had a worse passenger. He, if you don't mind, was not only an army captain but the mouth and trousers of the whole brewery. 'Gor blimey,' I thought. 'What luck. If I make one balls-up with him, it will be as good as suicide.' My assessment of the situation was correct.

Out he comes, his back as stiff as a poker and his face every bit the same. I opened the door for him, although I thought he was quite capable of doing it himself. But then, that was the job. I gave him a nice smile as he came towards me, which he ignored. 'Thank you,' he said, as he leaned forward to get in, and that was it.

The head chauffeur had told me to go the short way to avoid the traffic. I didn't even know the longest way, let alone the short one. So right away I makes for Oxford Street. Now any driver knows that Oxford Street isn't the best of roads to use if you

193

want to get anywhere, even on Sundays, high days and holidays. But I, the Captain's chauffeur, make straight for the swarm and battle of cars and pedestrians that were always to be found in that well-known street of London.

Right, we've sat in Oxford Street now for about half an hour. He's missed his train and is quietly doing his nut in the back there. Well, it must have been most annoying to have an ex-baker's roundsman cart you into a load of traffic and make you sit there all that time, while your train goes steaming out into the suburbs. But why the hell didn't he tap on the partition and stop me when he saw the crazy route I was taking? He had probably done this trip more times than I had been on the Labour. He could have put me right. But no. He was far above indulging in conversation with such a menial

At the death, he must have been well sick. He lowered himself enough to open the partition and tell me, 'Take me back to the brewery at once, please'.

Now I had to find my way back to the street where the brewery stood. Time passed, and after this second tour of London, I eventually stumbled on the street I was after. The car had hardly stopped when out he shot, slamming the door behind him. He disappeared into the dark opening of the two oak doors. Instinctively, I knew that my duties had not been carried out to the Captain's satisfaction. I prepared myself for my next visit to the Labour Exchange.

I went up in front of the personnel manager, who I am sure was a bit of a Ginger. They had sorted him out for taking on such an imbecile, and had ordered him to get shot of me in the politest way possible. He did. He told me I could never think of being a chauffeur for the company again. He offered me a nice little number washing out fifty-thousand gallon beer tanks. I thought this might be better than the Labour, so I asked him if I could have a butcher's at the job. One look brought me to a swift and final decision.

It was a massive copper tank, as big as a block of flats. Well, almost. This great container held quantities of beer. It struck me that this was the sort of thing an ardent beer drinker might dream about: beer in enormous amounts.

When the beer had all been drained out of these tanks and taken to the pubs ready to be poured into the stomachs of the British public, the tanks had to be washed out by hand. As I looked down into one empty vat, I saw three men dressed in oilskins, sloshing water from a hose all over the place. I thought,

'One day in that receptacle, wallowing in water, would put me on my back for a month'.

It was odd. The old doc knew I was asthmatic, yet here was this bloke from Queer Street offering me a job in a pool of water. Well, I had to twig it, didn't I? They knew I could never have done that job. I suppose it was a nice, polite way of saying good-bye.

I wasn't out of work for long. I got another job, and wasn't in work long, either. This time, I was off sick for a fortnight. I went back to find they had taken on someone else. So back I went to my old haunt, the Labour Exchange. By this time, we owned a second-hand, fourteen-inch telly. I had managed to buy it for Doll to watch while I was doing my twelve hours a day, six days a week, for Mr. Mason on my first chauffeur's job. Now I would have plenty of time to look at it myself.

I was out of work for six months. Relations between Doll and me got very strained. She still went to work at a tassel-making firm, while I stayed at home and did the housework. The shortage of money, the reversal of our roles as husband and wife did a lot to damage our marriage.

When you have no skill of any sort, it is demoralising enough having to take anything that comes along; but being unemployed is worse than imprisonment. It makes you feel that life is aimless, hopeless and pointless. The longer it goes on, the more intense these feelings become. Some people do overcome them if they have been out of work for a really long time. The feeling of having lost status gradually fades and is replaced by acceptance and apathy. Being out of work no longer worries you. You learn to get by on your restricted income you can see no hope of employment, so you accept it and try your hardest to dismiss all thought of work from your mind.

I hadn't got to that stage yet. I could not accept the fact that I would always be in and out of work, due to my ailment. I could not accept that I would always be hard up. Perhaps if I had been content with my lot, Doll and I would not have had so many disagreements. I was ambitious. We were going to have a nice living room, nicely decorated, with a three-piece suite and a fitted carpet. A bedroom suite, draped curtains, carpeted hall, all the modern gadgets in the kitchen for Doll, and (something we really needed) a fridge. There was also Lesley's bedroom to bring up to scratch.

'As soon as I get another job, I will make a start,' I thought. This is what I always thought. Little did I realise that it was like trying to catch a bus that had just left the stop as you turned the corner. At that time, I didn't even realise how strong the odds were against me. I kept fighting back, unaware that this fighting back was undermining my physical and mental health still further. I am almost convinced today that I would have been much happier and healthier if I had not bothered to fight back. I would have had peace of mind if I had been content with what I had — an old council flat, one bed, one piano, an old three-piece suite that nobody else wanted, an almost empty kitchen and a thrown-out plywood bedroom suite for my child. Unfortunately, I wanted too much out of life. I wanted the things I was physically incapable of getting. It was ridiculous thinking of such things.

Tension was now running very high in our home. I got a job with a well-known transport firm in Stamford Hill. I lasted four months, losing the job after three minor accidents with the three-ton lorry I had to drive. I sincerely believe that it was the worry and tension at home that caused me to have these three scrapes. After so much insecurity, it was very hard to keep my mind on what I was doing. That was the end of the job for me. Not because of asthma this time, but perhaps because of a mental confusion brought on by being in and out of work so much.

This may all seem rather dramatic. I suppose there are asthmatics who have done the same job all their lives. There are certainly asthmatics who are much worse than me and yet have had regular employment all their lives. I suppose it is just a question of how the dice roll.

Eventually, I decided to contact the training centre for the disabled. I put in for cab driving and got watch-making. I knew that if I got a cab driver's licence I would be more secure because I would be self-employed. Those three wasted months at the training centre were the worst I can remember. My diet at the time consisted mainly of tea and toast. The poor old instructor had to tell me what a wash-out I was at watch-making. I could have told him that when I first started the course. I was useless at any sort of fine measurement or calculation. So, back to the Labour Exchange I strolled once again. I was never going to get my place done up.

Then an envelope was slipped through my letter box. It was from the local church and told of the sorry plight of that religious establishment in acquiring a new bell. To read it would have brought tears to your eyes. But it brought the blood rushing to my cheeks and made me deeply angry inside. There was I, wondering where our next meal was coming from, and all the church was worried about was a lousy bell. Perhaps they hadn't been told that many of the doors they had slipped their envelopes through belonged to people who had enough on their minds, without trivialities of the church's problems. This church was run by a vicar, or parson, or whatever they call them, who no one down our street had ever met.

I kept my envelope ready to give to the collector when he came around. He seemed surprised that I handed it over, especially when he felt the paper bulge inside. Most people mislaid their envelopes. Those that didn't returned them as empty as they had received them. The old parson must have looked even more surprised when he opened my letter and read what was inside. However he felt, he never replied.

Of course, with me it wasn't always the asthma that made me lose jobs. There were other, unforseen circumstances as well. If I could have settled in sign writing, the job I wanted, when I left school, I am positive I wouldn't have gone through such a quantity of jobs later on.

If I went through all my jobs in detail it would take several volumes, and I am sure the reader would get rather bored. So let me just give you a few highlights.

I was able to hold down one job for a whole year. Boy, did I feel proud of myself. I reckoned I deserved a gold watch for that twelve months. The firm I was working for reckoned differently. They reckoned I deserved the sack. This unjust conclusion was reached because they were closing down and no longer needed the services of their twenty van drivers. Every Christmas, they gave us twenty Players. This time they gave us an extra bonus. We not only got our wages and twenty Players, but a week's holiday pay and our cards on top. The governor certainly had the Christmas spirit that year, but not the sort I would have preferred.

I strolled back to the Labour Exchange yet again, and stayed there for the next two months. I fancied myself as a driving instructor at that time. I found a job myself. Those Exchange clerks were like a record: 'Sorry, nothing in today. Sorry, nothing in today. Click, click. Sorry, nothing in today . . . . .'

It would be a piece of cake to write a book about the driving instructor's job alone. If ever I attempted it, the title would be 'Absurdities in the Life of a Driving Instructor'. I got into this hazardous business at the time when driving schools had just started. They were nearly all little twopenny-halfpenny, one-man-bands then, working about twelve hours a day. My pay was five bob a day. There's a lot needs straightening out in that game, even today, but I will not go into all that.

I was never keen on being a driving instructor. To be off sick on this job was ten times worse than any other, for you might be letting down a pupil on their test day. Driving instructors were hard to come by then, though, and the school seemed to put up with my intermittent absenteeism better than earlier employers had done.

It suited most driving schools to take on their instructors on a self-employed basis. This saved them a nice sum in holiday pay and so on. At some schools, if the pupil didn't turn up the instructor wouldn't be paid, even though the pupil lost their fee. The bloke I worked for was more free-hearted. If the pupil didn't turn up, he was willing to pay you for the hour if you washed the car down. Yes at that time there was a lot wrong with the driving instructor's job. Things are not all that rosy, even today.

In March 1966, I decided to try the game that my father had been such a failure at in his young days. I had never really like the driving instructor's job. It was all yap, yap, yap; the same thing over and over again. What with our uneasy domestic life at the time, I just couldn't be bothered to put in all the jawing the job demanded. So I turned to the ice-cream game for security. Out in the evenings, out week-ends. Still, that didn't matter. This was how it had been nearly all our married life. If I hadn't been selling ice cream or teaching driving, I would have been at the pub, trying to earn a few bob.

The ice cream left me cold. I would never be a millionaire with that. Security? Yes, for five or six months in the summer. And in the winter? You've guessed back on my usual route to the Labour Exchange.

Why did I get through all these jobs? It was because I was seeking security, a thing I should have known I could never have had in my physical condition. If a firm put up with you having time off, you could not help feeling indebted to them. I didn't want to feel indebted to anyone. It made you feel that you owed them something, and at times their attitude made you feel that you were an inconvenience. I had the idea that if I could work for myself I would be indebted to no-one. Of course, I appreciated the few bosses who did put up with my absence, but I never felt happy being at the bosses' mercy.

I was thirty-eight now. I knew that there was no hope of regular employment for me unless I tried one more thing. It would take me eighteen months to two years to achieve, but if I did manage it I was sure of a job for life. I would have no fear of the sack and I wouldn't need to feel indebted to anyone. The thing I wanted to try was taxi driving. This entailed learning the streets of London, equipped with a moped, maps, notebook and pencil. Luckily, the licensing authorities decided that my asthma would not impair my work as a cab driver. I was accepted.

My mind was made up. I would work as hard as I could at this. I didn't care how long it took, for there was nothing else I could do. I certainly couldn't have been a driving instructor for the rest of my days. Some men liked the work, and wanted nothing else. Unfortunately, I was not one of them. I was now clear in my mind about what I wanted to do. I would try for this taxi cab licence. If I ended up by failing, I would give up. I would go back on the Labour and stay there till I died. That is how near I was to total apathy. I would make one almighty effort to save myself, like a drowning man grabbing at a small piece of wood. If I failed, then that would be it. I would be on the rubbish heap with all the other disabled and the rest of the unwanted. I accepted passively what was to come, whether good or bad.

If I had not passed my tests at the Hackney Carriage Office, I would not have got my licence on October 2nd, 1968, and my story would not have had quite such a happy ending.

For nineteen months I did the training, working part-time with a driving school. I saw Doll for about an hour a day. No wonder our marriage had run down. When I came home the night I passed, I was happier than I had been for years. I got home from the driving school as quick as I could to break the news to Doll. I had got my licence. From now on, things would be different. Life is peculiar, though. I got home and right away I told Doll about it. Well, I couldn't hold it back, it was so marvellous. But Doll had heard it all before, every time I started a new job.

It was like when I was going to become a credit salesman. When they saw how many jobs I had had, they didn't want to know. Thought I'd been inside. Then I was going to make my fortune selling ice cream. Every venture had ended the same. So Doll wasn't going to get all enthusiastic about any of my plans anymore. She had sat at home night after night for nineteen months now, and much as I hate to admit it, we were hardly husband and wife; hardly a real family; hardly the happy family we should have been for our daughter to grow up in.

Who was to blame? I have blamed the Government. I have blamed Fate, God, Providence and our society. I have blamed everybody and everything. I have even blamed my own luck. Who can you blame for an almost ruined life? At this moment

I can blame nobody and nothing.

Doll's lack of enthusiasm caused me to do my nut. Of course, another row ensued. We were on the eve of a better life; we would be able to get a bit of HP now, perhaps an old banger to get about in, perhaps even a holiday. Yet on the threshold of this new life, we rowed.

Now we do have some things that we never thought were possible. We never row now, though like all normal couples we have our little disagreements. If I have to take time off work it doesn't worry me as much as it did in the past. I know I have a job to go back to. I don't have to thank anyone for keeping my job open for me. With security like this, anyone's marriage, health and outlook on life must improve.

When I see down-and-outs and people in need, I cannot help being in full sympathy with them. The old saying is always at the back of my mind: 'There, but for the grace of God, go I'.

14. Afterword

When talking to some people about the past, they have told me that it is best forgotten, and better still, unwritten. How then do we measure how far we have come and how far we have to go before we can make this world a better place for all.

I feel that much has got to be changed. I want to see a time when people will become genuine. When a person is valued for what he or she is and not for what that person possesses. I want to see children treated on an equal footing with adults, when the myth, that is often wrong, is no longer quoted to children that 'you must respect your elders because they know from experience'. Experience teaches a good many people very little I am afraid. If we elders know what it's all about then why do we find our kids such a problem.

We could take more interest in children's education. Reading and writing is of course important, but why not make it more interesting. Not by reading stuff like 'the cat sat on the mat' but by letting kids make their own books. In this way books become more interesting. They learn how to work machines, how to book-bind and how to use figures. Why is it that education is only connected with schools, when one's whole life is education. An adult doing a job of work can teach a kid more in half an hour than he will ever learn sitting at a desk.

The kids on the estates are blamed for being a nuisance. Most estates have community halls, many of which, though, are for the sole purpose of adult entertainment. But why not have facilities for old and young alike. A place for kids to take their bikes to pieces, where they can learn an instrument, read, paint and so on. I don't think this would cost a lot of money. Most kids can become interested in anything − it is a natural thing with kids − all they need is encouragement. A place like this would also bring young and old together, and consequently they would understand each other more. Just think how long ago it was when you spoke seriously to a young person. I bet many of us could think back months or years.

I would like to see the media more open to ordinary people so that we could get the real essence of how people feel. So that they could put on plays, debate and discuss, while not having to rely on the so-called experts. Cameras and tape-recorders could be lent out to young and old, the same as library books are.

When I hear some of those middle class reactionaries talk they make me feel very superior indeed. To think they are supposed to have had the finest education money can buy and yet they talk such rubbish. They boast of being able to stand on their own two feet and declare we should all do the same. Cripples as well? 'I could never work for a boss,' they say, 'I like to be in authority'. Most of them never work anyway, boss or no boss. It makes my blood boil when skilled craftsmen, like carpenters, who can make a door frame that is able to hold up tons of concrete, or a metal worker who makes a whole staircase safe and sound for people to use, are criticised in some way. Most of their critics couldn't even knock a nail in. But that's understandable, for all these more menial tasks are done for them.

The Ritz wouldn't have suited me at all, nor any of those posh restaurants. If I ever did become rich, I would probably remain in Hackney, watching my telly in my living room.On Sunday evenings I would send out for some fish and chips, or jellied eels from Tubby Isaac's in Whitechapel, or (if I was a bit brassy) a portion of Chinese. I would be content with that sort of life.

I don't say I wouldn't travel. I probably would. But I would never uproot myself from the places and people I had grown to love over the years, the area where my parents had been brought up and their parents before them, for generations. No luxury home in the country could give me the same sense of security and belonging that Hackney could. The place and, (to some extent) the people have changed over the years, but this is where I belong and hope to remain in the future. It's noisy, smoky and grimy. Yet there is still something about this part of the East End that a native cannot do without.

As I have got older, I have come to realise just how neglected some disabled people are. For instance, it is next to impossible for someone with an ailment to get any sort of grant from the Government, unless their condition was a result of war service. If you have an illness that keeps you out of regular work, it's just hard cheese. There is plenty of sympathy, but little action for people in this situation.

I have discovered that although most large firms are required to take on a small percentage of disabled people, they are not compelled to do so. If a small firm accepts a registered disabled person, it is done as a favour, not as a duty. The disabled person must be grateful and think himself lucky that he has the opportunity to work at all. As far as I can see, the green card the

202

Labour Exchange issues to disabled people is about as advantageous as a car with no engine. In my experience, the card doesn't mean a thing to anyone. It is just for the records.

I have always thought that a scheme should be introduced so that people who are frequently off work could claim a certain amount of money from the DHSS, so as to bring their income up to a living wage. I realise that this is a big thing to ask, but where there's a will there's a way. Most disabled people need more nourishing food than healthy ones. Many have to live on a very restricted diet, unless they get something extra from the Social Security. The only trouble is, you have to be half dead before you can be considered for extra money for better food. The DHSS do give grants for those on a special diet; but thousands of disabled force themselves to work even when they feel really ill, rather than claim Social Security. I know. I have been one of them and I know what it is like on that money.

A person may be physically weak, but he forces himself to work when he should be at home resting. At the end of the week he has little to look forward to in the way of wages. He cannot claim anything from the DHSS because he has worked part of the week. If he is entitled to anything, it will probably be just enough to buy his cat a tin of food. He goes to his doctor (if he is able to get there) gets his certificate and sends it to the DHSS. The following week, if he is able to go to work, he will get his wages and maybe two or three days' pay from the Social Security — if he has been ill long enough, of course. Now he is fit again, he will be able to go on working for another few weeks until he is off sick again. Or until he gets the sack.

I am talking from the point of view of an asthmatic. People like me never know when an attack is going to come on. You can be as fit as a fiddle one day, and no-one would believe that you were an asthmatic unless you were a particularly severe case. People who are in and out of work like this become nervous and highly-strung. They are withdrawn and suffer bouts of deep depression. Cash is often short because of their erratic working life though there may be whole years when things are not too bad.

What can be the outcome but an unhappy home and a slow regression into even worse health? I sincerely believe that something should be done for people with genuine health problems, like asthmatics.

Everything in this day and age has got to be done at a certain time. You wake up at a certain time. You have to be at work at a certain time. You get your bus home at a certain time, and if you're not at home at a certain time the family starts to worry. And that is understandable since you have got home for the best part of your life at that time. It's no wonder that so few working class people go to evening classes and such places. A woman who goes to work, comes home and has a dinner to cook and the kids to see to doesn't have much time for herself. If she has any energy left, and it's not too late, she might go out to an evening class. That is, if the bus service has not become completely extinct. It is also very rare for good evening education centres to be just round the corner, and if you are particular about what subjects you would like to take up then a place nearby is unheard of.

If working people are criticised for not going to evening classes, it is not altogether their fault. To many people, it is just like school again and many of us didn't go on that very much when we were young. Learning was a binding, uninteresting, unenlightening task, not a joy which took up all one's interest and energy.

After my first book was published, a number of people told me about other people they knew who had bad experiences in their childhood. Whilst relating those experiences to me they have more or less suggested that I was not the only one to experience distress in childhood, so why was it necessary to write what I did? No, I was not the only one. There were in the past, and there will be in the future, and even now as you read this, children suffering from distress, children by the thousand. Physical beatings, terror, anxiety, humiliation, poverty and dirt, and if we take the whole world, even starvation. I wasn't the only one it's true, it's just that I happened to write about my experiences.

But there is more. There is a myth that childhood is the best time of a person's life. I personally don't think it's anything to go nuts about. Children are pushed around, bullied, ordered about, made servants of, kissed, caressed and shown off. And all this without being asked if they like it or not. And children have no voice, whatsoever. If a kid is clouted it is just taken for granted that he or she was wrong, even if mum or the teacher was in a bad mood at the time. Children have no one to put their case or plead their cause on these occasions. Is it any wonder that our kids are a nuisance. If they swear, if they are saucy, if they act tough and cocky we are annoyed. And so we should be. The thing is, where do the young learn their ways and attitudes? They also live in a society where the man has to act tough and the woman weak, stupid and helpless. The sort of fantasies that magazines put in our minds. I am sure most of us can recall the times when we have seen women act much tougher than men. Then there are men who are much better with children than women. But because we are brought up to these ideas we can easily accept them, and find it very difficult to accept any alternative way of life, which may well be to everyone's benefit.

15. Appendix: Cockney Speech

Cockney slang changes with the times, like standard English. It has its old slang terms, as well as its modern ones. For instance, the word for 'policeman' about forty years ago was 'rosser'. From there, it was 'copper', 'bogey', 'the law' and, in modern times, 'the fuzz' 'Trousers' were 'kicksies', then 'Rowton Houses', and so on. I am no authority on Cockney slang, but the following list contains words that I have heard, and in fact use myself quite naturally from time to time. I have also added some which were contributed by a number of my relatives, from whom I have learned that there is some Romany influence in Cockney slang.

Criminal slang

Beak	Magistrate, judge
Burner	Oxy-acetylene torch
Cane, stick	Jemmy
Case a gaff	Look over a house of factory
Cat man	One who climbs drain-pipes etc. to break into a building
Chubb	Lock
Click	Mob, gang
Creep	To make an entrance from the roof
Dicky	Clock
Eighteenpence	Fence (receiver of stolen goods)
Glimmer	Torch
Hoister, canon	Pickpocket
Info man	One who gives information (of layout of premises or police patrols)
Jacob's	Ladder
Kettle	Watch
Lobber	Till robber
Loid	Celluloid (used for opening window locks)
Overpull	Mask
Peter	Safe, cell
Sussed	Caught out
Turtle doves	Gloves
Wheeler	Driver

Money slang

Bike spanner, tanner	6d
Brown	1d
Cockerel	£10
Cows	10 shillings
Dadler	Farthing
Deana	Shilling
Handful	£5
Joey	Threepenny bit
Kasa	5 shillings
Kybosh	1/6 (one shilling and sixpence)
Monkey	£500
Pony	£25
Rouf	£4
Sheet	£1
Tosheroon	Half-crown (two shillings and sixpence)
Xis	£6

General slang terms

Almond rocks	Socks
Artful Dodger	Lodger
Ball of chalk	Walk
Barnet Fair	Hair
Battle cruiser	Pub (boozer)
Bees and honey	Money
Bins	Spectacles
Boracic lint	Skint, broke
Brussel sprout	Boy scout
Burnt cinder	Window
Burton	Broken, destroyed (eg 'gone for a Burton)
Bushel and peck	Neck
Butcher's hook	Look
Cain and Abel	Table
Cherry hog	Dog
Conan Doyle	Boil
Daisy roots	Boots
Dicky dirt	Shirt
Ding dong	Party
Doctor Crippen	Dripping
Dukes	Fists
Eightenpence	Sense
Frog and toad	Road
Greengages	Wages

Hampstead Heath	Teeth
Holy friar	Liar
Iron hoof	Pouf (male homosexual)
Jack Jones	Alone
Jack the Ripper	Kipper
Jam jar	Car
Jeremiah	Fire
Johnny Horner	Corner
Khyber Pass	Arse
Linen draper	Newspaper
Lob	Cash
Lord Lovell	Shovel
Lucifer	Match
Micky Rooney	Macaroni
Mince pies, mincers	Eyes
Mother's ruin	Gin
Nanny goat	Coat
Neptune's daughter	Water
North and south	Mouth
Peckham Rye	Necktie
Pen and ink	Stink
Plates of meat	Feet
Poke	Pocket
Rabbit and pork	Talk
Railings	Teeth
Rory O'More	Floor, door
Rosie Lee	Tea
Rowten houses	Trousers
Smash	Cash
Sweet and sours	Flowers
Tea leaf	Thief
Titfer tat	Hat
Toe rag	Fag
Tom tit	Shit
Top rod	Overcoat
Trouble and strife	Wife
Two and eight	In a state
Vera Lynn	Chin
Welcher	Non-payer
You and me	Flea